ELEMENTARY
PASCAL

THE ANALYTICAL ENGINE

ELEMENTARY PASCAL

AS CHRONICLED BY

John H. Watson

EDITED WITH COMMENTARIES BY

Henry Ledgard

AND

Andrew Singer

Vintage Books

A Division of Random House • New York

Library of Congess Cataloging in Publication Data
Ledgard, Henry F., 1943-
Elementary Pascal, as chronicled by Dr. John D. Watson.
Includes Index.
1.PASCAL(Computer program language)
I.Singer, Andrew, 1943-
II.Title
QA76.73.P2L395 1982   001.64'24   81-48288
ISBN 0-394-70800-8   AACR2

Manufactured in the United States of America

98765432   24689753   23456789

Contents

THE LAST BOW

Preface

Henry Ledgard and I were drinking tea and discussing a paper when the trunk arrived; or rather I should say when Edwina, Henry's wife, called to tell him that a trunk had come. Edwina is English and properly speaking the trunk is hers, but I'm getting ahead of the story. At the time, neither of us thought anything of it and we immediately returned to our tea and paper.

The following day I got in late. Thinking we might have lunch, I stopped at Henry's office. As I stepped in, I noticed a distinct change in the atmosphere from the day before. My friend was clearly preoccupied. He also looked a bit disheveled and rather tired. Now this is most unusual. Henry is a person of extremely regular habits. It is rare for him to retire later than nine, and he is usually up and about well before six. He nearly always appears well rested and neat. As we walked to the university cafeteria, he said little.

Finally, overcome with curiosity, I said, "Henry, is something wrong? You don't seem yourself this morning."

"It's the trunk," he replied, with an edge to his voice.

"Trunk?"

"The trunk that came for Edwina from England yesterday."

"Oh, that trunk. What about it?"

"It's a very strange trunk; that is, I mean its contents are strange. The trunk is full of manuscripts."

"What's so strange about that?"

"They all seem to have been written by a certain Dr. John Watson about a certain Mr. Sherlock Holmes."

"Now really, Henry, be serious."

"I am completely serious, but I haven't told you the best part of it yet. What do you suppose the manuscripts are about?"

"I refuse to have my leg pulled in this fashion, Henry!"

"Andrew, Holmes was an ace programmer. According to Watson, he used a successor to Babbage's Analytical Engine in his work. The manuscripts are Watson's chronicles of their experiences. Holmes's insights are brilliant. His deductive powers and methodical nature made him a natural programmer."

"Henry, how did Edwina come by this trunk?"

"It was a bequest from a great-aunt. She hardly knows the woman and can't imagine why it was willed to her at all."

"Henry, how many of Edwina's family know that you're a computer scientist?"

"Most of them, I suppose."

"Do you suppose this great-aunt might have known?"

"What are you getting at?"

"Just that it's a marvellous practical joke and you've been completely taken in."

The expression on Henry's face as I spoke struck me almost as funny as the situation itself, and I burst out laughing as we headed for the cafeteria door.

The laughter seemed a bit hollow a few days later when I saw the manuscripts themselves. Faded, brittle, and written in a somewhat cluttered hand, they certainly looked authentic. An actual sample of Watson's handwriting that Henry had obtained seemed to clinch it. No one would possibly go to this much trouble for a practical joke. Here was no hoax but a fascinating discovery.

Henry handed me a small bundle of copies.

"I thought you might find them interesting reading," he said with a smile. "Unless of course you still have some doubts?"

With a pained expression, I took the copies and retreated to the library. The manuscripts had been sorted into chronological order. A separate page on top was not part of a manuscript but a note addressed to the reader from Watson himself. I have reproduced it here.

To a Reader in the Future:

Although you may or may not be familiar with my numerous short sketches describing the exploits of Mr. Sherlock Holmes, you must know that my hope in publishing these has been to make the public aware of the Science of Deduction and my friend's remarkable skill as a practitioner of it.

Naturally, some of the cases in which Holmes had the kindness to invite my participation could not be openly discussed, and thus I have deliberately suppressed my notes wherever a matter of delicacy was involved. The records which follow, however, describe an extraordinary set of cases which fall into a wholly distinct class, and I have elected not to publish them for the most unusual reason that there does not exist as yet a suitable readership for them.

Therefore, I consign them to posterity and ask only that they not be published as a curiosity but rather at such time as they may find readers to whom they will seem contemporary.

John H. Watson, M.D., L.R.C.P., M.R.C.S.

Reading the manuscripts themselves, I realized that Watson had been most perceptive. Even today, computer literacy is rare, and it would be unlikely to suppose that a popular audience for these adventures exists. Except for their dependence on the peculiar programming language used by Babbage's Engine, they constituted a most lucid and enjoyable tutorial on problem solving with a computer.

I was still absorbed in my reading several hours later when I looked up to see Henry sitting across the table.

"Incredible, aren't they?" he said quietly.

"Amazing."

"Would you publish them?"

"Not the way they are."

"What then?"

"I would edit them and translate the programs into a contemporary programming language, perhaps produce several translations for different languages, Pascal, Basic, Ada, and so on. Then I'd add some commentary to address the more detailed issues of the individual languages. Do you think it would work?"

"Yes."

"I guess Edwina's aunt knew what she was doing."

And that is how we came to publish this book. With all due respect to Watson, we have endeavored to preserve his style altogether. Many of the manuscripts deal with problems of considerable complexity. We have selected only those that would be appropriate for a tutorial. Perhaps one day we will publish an edition of the more advanced cases.

The sole objective of this book is to teach you to program in Pascal, the language of this translation. We assume in this book, as Holmes assumed of Watson, that you, the reader, have probably never programmed before. Learning to program is not easy. Its essence lies in the ability to solve problems—by computer, of course.

Generally, each chapter of the book begins with one of the case studies of Sherlock Holmes. Here we see Holmes and Watson solving some problem. Following each case study, the commentary discusses in detail the issues arising from the problem presented by Holmes.

The first three chapters present Holmes's introduction to problem solving and programming. Like Watson, you are not expected to be able to duplicate the ideas presented, or even understand them fully. That will follow in due course. Hopefully, though, you will see the general effect of all that follows.

In Chapter IV, Holmes presents the first steps needed to write programs. By the end of Chapter VII, you should have completed the central issues in writing any computer program. At this point you will be well on your way.

The next five chapters should enlarge your skills considerably. In these cases, Holmes is dealing with somewhat larger problems and the programming tools needed to solve them effectively.

In the last chapter, Holmes and Watson confront a most difficult case from a computing standpoint. Holmes's solution brings into play almost all the ideas presented in this book.

In writing this text we have not found it necessary to cover all of the Pascal language, although several features omitted in the text are discussed in the problems at the end of each chapter. The portion of Pascal covered in the text is summarized in the Appendix, *Pascal at a Glance.* In any case, our version of Pascal closely follows that presented by Niklaus Wirth, its designer. Be careful—your local dialect may be ever-so-slightly different.

So come, dear reader, the game is afoot.

HENRY LEDGARD
ANDREW SINGER

Circumstantial Evidence

I

The Analytical Engine

N an incoherent and, as I deeply feel, an entirely inade-
quate fashion, I have endeavoured to give some account of
the remarkable career of Mr. Sherlock Holmes as a criminal investigator and consulting detective. As the reader is
undoubtedly well aware, my companion's interests were as
broad as Nature herself and he often spoke on an amazing variety of
subjects as though he had made a special study of each. In my modest
chronicles of the cases that I have had the privilege to share with Sherlock
Holmes, I have often alluded to his numerous publications, but I have said
nothing before of his unparalleled contributions to the development of the
Analytical Engine.

My first introduction to the Analytical Engine was in the late spring,
shortly after the conclusion of one of the most ghastly adventures we had
ever shared, which I have chronicled under the heading of "The Adventure
of the Speckled Band." The entire day Holmes was in a mood that some
would call taciturn. He was most unsettled, smoked incessantly, played
snatches on his violin, sank into reveries, and hardly answered the casual
questions that I put to him. We sat through a silent dinner together, after
which, pushing his plate aside, he revealed to me the problem with which
he was preoccupied.

"You can never foretell what one mind will come up with, Watson, but
you can say with precision what an average person will do. Individuals
vary, but percentages remain constant; and while we have not yet grasped
the results that the human mind alone can attain, it has its distinct
limitations. There are only particular individuals on whom we can rely to
produce the same chain of logical argument from one occasion to the
next."

"I certainly wouldn't argue with you, Holmes," I replied. "But as yet we haven't found a suitable replacement for human reasoning."

"Oh, on the contrary, Watson," he answered nonchalantly. "Have you ever heard of the Analytical Engine?"

"I know of no substitute for the mind of man."

Holmes chuckled. "Then you must learn of it. It is an ingenious mechanism, a machine that has displayed a considerable talent for deductive reasoning, far superior to the average logician. You recall my intervention in the matter of that notebook floating in the River Cam last month?"

"I am not likely soon to forget the sight of that bloated face staring up at me, Holmes," I replied grimly, considering the sorry state of mankind that such events should come to pass. "What connection has the late professor with this Engine?"

"HAVE YOU EVER HEARD OF THE ANALYTICAL ENGINE?"

"Well, as you may remember, my investigation led me to the Cavendish laboratories; and it was there that I had occasion to study the Engine, if only briefly. Since then I have been in correspondence with mathematicians at Cambridge who have been conducting experiments with it. Watson, I do not exaggerate when I say that the Analytical Engine is capable of solving, within minutes, complex numerical problems that would keep five of London's finest mathematicians working for hours. Furthermore, it is adept at logic and has a perfect memory for detail.

"The Engine also has its limits," he continued. "It can only undertake problems whose solutions are spelled out in minute detail and that are presented in its own peculiar language."

"Really, Holmes, sometimes you go too far with my patience!" I exclaimed. "You expect me to believe that this device is capable of solving problems, has a perfect memory, and actually speaks a language of its own?"

"No, no, my dear Watson, you take me too literally. The Analytical Engine does indeed have a language of its own, but communications must be written out."

"Now you tell me it can read?"

"In a sense, yes."

I threw up my arms in a desperate gesture and began to rise from the table.

"I fear I am going too fast for you, Watson. Bear with me for a moment and I shall do my utmost to explain all this to you. Everything I say is true, but let me assure you that the Analytical Engine hardly resembles a human being.

"Its 'language' is actually a highly logical code, designed by mathematicians in order to operate the Engine. This code is not difficult to master, but it does require considerable discipline. It has a very small vocabulary, which is nothing to compare with the English tongue. This vocabulary is arranged into statements according to a limited set of rules.

"The major problem in communicating with the Engine is that one must use the utmost care and precision in giving it instructions, for it has no imagination whatsoever and cannot correct even trivial errors in spelling or punctuation. It is, after all, like other machines in that it has no awareness of the tasks that it performs; therefore it will obey the most unreasonable of instructions. For example, if it is told to print the number zero *ad infinitum*, it will continue to do so for hours on end, until a human being finally causes it to stop."

"But Holmes, how does one give instructions to this Engine?" I asked, scarcely crediting my companion's remarks thus far and wondering whether perhaps his penchant for cocaine had finally betrayed his reason.

"By writing a set of instructions in code and supplying them mechanically to the Engine. Such a set of instructions is called a *programme*, because it is an orderly and precise procedure for solving a problem. The art of writing programmes is called, reasonably enough, *programming*."

"Of what relevance is this strange machine to you, Holmes?"

"I intend to employ the Engine whenever possible in my future criminal cases," he replied. "As you know, I have been rather overburdened with work in recent months, so the Engine's speed and potential accuracy are most attractive to me. It has a great capacity for dealing with large amounts of information as well."

"But, Holmes," I interrupted, "do you truly expect this device, if it is as unimaginative as you say, actually to solve crimes?"

"Not at all, my dear Watson," said Holmes with a laugh. "I daresay it is not clever enough to replace my brain; but it will be useful for storing information, as well as for performing certain repetitive tasks that absorb too much of my time. Of most interest to me is that it will provide a means of expressing my logical methods in a rigorous form, and perhaps be useful in communicating to others my modest attempts at formulating a Science of Deduction."

1.1 Commentary

Actually, Charles Babbage and his collaborator, Lady Augusta Ada Lovelace (Lord Byron's daughter), had between them worked out most of the fundamental principles upon which modern computing is based. The Analytical Engine was indeed the forerunner of today's computers.

Holmes's insight into the promises and pitfalls of the computer is striking. The ability to handle great amounts of data, to remember even the tiniest detail, to make extremely accurate calculations, and to obey instructions over and over again are all well recognized.

What are not so well recognized are the pitfalls: the often endless details, the intolerance to error, the annoying idiosyncrasies, and the need for unremitting rigor.

Your first attempt at programming is likely to be a frustrating experience. The demanding precision to which Holmes alludes is quite unfamiliar to most people. You must struggle to piece together a variety of computer instructions, making changes almost randomly and hoping somehow the program will work. You might desperately put a line into your program that says:

```
PRINT THE ANSWER
```

and expect the computer to print the correct result. This would be futile. To get a computer to do your

CHARLES BABBAGE

bidding, you must tell it precisely what you want it to do in exactly the proper way.

When you do this, you have at your command a kind of modern genie.

LADY LOVELACE

For example, this entire book has been typed using a specialized computer called a *word processor*. This computer has made it possible for us to modify the text in small and large ways and then print out revised versions quickly for study and further improvement. When we were finished revising the manuscript, this computer reproduced our text in a form that made it possible for another computer to typeset the book automatically. Babbage would be especially satisfied if he were alive today, for it was his desire to eliminate error from tide tables that led him to develop the Difference Engine from which the Analytical Engine evolved. In fact, this early computer was designed to set type to enable the printing of the tables.

In the chapters that follow, Holmes will introduce all that you need to know in order to write first-rate computer programs yourself. In the first adventure, "Murder at the Metropolitan Club," you will observe as Holmes writes an algorithm. The concept of an algorithm is the most fundamental idea you need to grasp in order to write programs. Having introduced the subject, Holmes then presents his algorithm coded in Pascal. It is there that we begin to discuss the subject of programming languages and how they are used to solve problems.

II

Murder at the Metropolitan Club

O Sherlock Holmes it was always *the* Engine. His precise and admirably balanced mind was eclipsed only by this mechanism of wood and metal—a series of gears, wheels, and levers, finely adjusted and exclusive of all human temperament. It came as no surprise, then, that he was deeply attracted to the potential of the Engine in his criminal investigations, and its development occupied his immense faculties and extraordinary powers for many of the years that I had the privilege of knowing him and following his cases.

It was only a short time after our first discussion of the Engine that he found a practical use for it. All of London was interested, and the fashionable world dismayed, by the murder of a renowned art dealer at the Metropolitan Club under most unusual and inexplicable circumstances. The crime was of interest in itself, but for Holmes it was also an opportunity to experiment with the Analytical Engine; and it was for this purpose only that he agreed to assist the official police in the matter.

The public were allowed to know certain particulars of the crime, but a good many of the facts, as they dealt with prominent members of society, were suppressed. It is not my task at this time to fill in the missing links, as I am under a specific prohibition from the lips of Sherlock Holmes, but rather to give some explanation of how the great detective was able to employ the extraordinary Engine. Let me say from the first that the case was solved without use of the device, as were so many of his cases. Following its conclusion, Holmes retraced his steps, outlining the circumstances attendant on the investigation to see whether the Engine would arrive at the same results as he himself had.

"You recall our visit last week to the Metropolitan Club in the Strand," he began, "and the renowned subject under investigation.

"An initial enquiry by Scotland Yard yielded four suspects," he said, recounting the case. "The four were registered in adjoining rooms above the club. One of them was Sir Raymond Jasper, a noted member of the bar, and another an accountant by the name of Robert Holman. The other two, a Colonel Reginald Woodley and a Mr. James Pope, were visitors from Northumberland, unconnected with each other, I should add. The police assembled a list of facts concerning the crime and these four gentlemen, but in their usual manner failed to recognise the singularities of these trifles and thus entirely overlooked their importance. I can never bring them to

"YOU RECALL OUR VISIT TO THE METROPOLITAN CLUB."

realize the importance of a man's sleeves or the great issues that may hang from a bootlace.

"Here, then, is a partial floor plan of the club's boarding rooms and the list of clues we assembled."

I have duplicated the floor plan here.

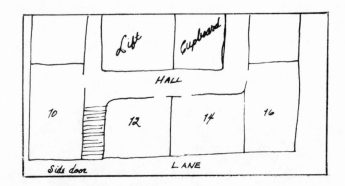

The clues were as follows :

1. Sir Raymond Jasper occupied Room 10.
2. The man occupying Room 14 had black hair.
3. Either Colonel Woodley or Sir Raymond wore a pince-nez.
4. Mr. Pope always carried a gold pocket watch.
5. One of the suspects was seen driving a four-wheel carriage.
6. The man with the pince-nez had brown hair.
7. Mr. Holman wore a ruby signet ring.
8. The man in Room 16 had tattered cuffs.
9. Mr. Holman occupied Room 12.
10. The man with tattered cuffs had red hair.
11. The man in Room 12 had grey hair.
12. The man with a gold pocket watch occupied Room 14.
13. Colonel Woodley occupied a corner room.
14. The murderer had brown hair.

"Well, my friend," I said, after examining the list, "these may be very good clues, but a glance at them does not tell me who the murderer was."

"Precisely why the police neglected them, and that is where the Analytical Engine comes into use. These clues are worthless unless we can determine the particular relationship of one to another and see how they fit into a larger scheme. To do so we need to devise an *algorithm* that both we and the Engine can follow."

"This all sounds very mathematical, Holmes," I suggested.

"It is, Watson," he replied. "But the mathematics themselves are childishly simple. Our algorithm may be compared to a recipe—a set of instructions to be carried out in a specific order. Our ingredients and how they are to be used, however, must be stated explicitly and rigorously if the Engine is to follow them correctly. There are a few items of importance concerning algorithms that I must relate to you. First and foremost, only one instruction is performed at a time; and secondly, after each instruction, the next step must be made absolutely clear. Finally, there must be a clearly defined stopping place, indicating that the problem has been solved and that the execution of the algorithm ends."

"But, Holmes," I asked, "since the clues themselves are steps by which one logically arrives at the solution, why do they not constitute an algorithm?"

"This is the key, Watson. The clues are *data*, not *instructions*. They have no orderly arrangement that shows their inter-relationship. It is just such an orderly arrangement that the algorithm confers. Now, Watson, if you wish to follow my future investigations, you would do well to learn the technique of creating algorithms yourself, for there is really no other way to understand the Analytical Engine's operation."

"Very well, Holmes," I replied. "But what must I do to start?"

"The first step," said Holmes, "is to try to imagine how you would tell someone else to solve the problem."

"Naturally I would keep track of all the relevant facts of the case," I ventured, "and then carefully examine all the clues that might relate to each of them."

"But think, Watson, to 'keep track of the facts' would mean to keep a table of the established facts; to 'examine the clues' would then mean to enter the facts in appropriate places in the table. Let us use this method in the first stage of developing an algorithm to solve the particular case with which we are concerned."

Holmes took a sheet of paper and began writing out what I had proposed. "Perhaps this is what you have in mind, Watson," he said, handing me the paper. It read :

1. Look at the next clue.
2. If the clue establishes a fact then
        record the fact
    else
        dismiss the clue.
3. Repeat this process until the murderer is found.

"Yes," I replied. "This seems to be a plausible method. Could we place these facts in some form of table to better illustrate this method?"

Beneath the algorithm I sketched the table that I have reproduced here.

SUSPECT.	COLONEL WOODLEY.	MR. HOLMAN.	MR. POPE.	SIR RAYMOND.
Hair Colour.				
Transport.				
Attire.				
Room.				

Holmes gave it a quick glance.

"Indeed, Watson, this approach is excellent; but there is a minor problem. We need a clearer, more rigorous attack. What does it mean, for instance, to say 'if the clue establishes a fact'? Some of the clues establish facts directly, whereas others do not; and exactly what does it mean to 'look at the next clue'? The Analytical Engine would certainly not be able to make any clear interpretation of these instructions, let alone follow them."

"Really, Holmes!" I cried. "One moment you are praising my efforts, the next I appear to be the fool."

"My apologies, Watson, I do not mean to try your patience, but it is essential that our approach to this problem be made without error. Bear with me and I will make it clear how we can put your efforts to good use. Let us consider two obvious clues. The first, 'Sir Raymond Jasper occupied Room 10,' means that we should set the room number of Sir Raymond to 10 in the table. This is an example of a known fact provided directly by a clue.

"Now, consider 'the man occupying Room 14 had black hair.' This means if the room of some suspect is 14, then set the hair colour of this same suspect to black in the table. This clue does not disclose a fact immediately, but only after some other fact has been established.

"Moreover," he continued, "we must assume initially that nothing in the table is known; to illustrate this we initially leave each space empty.

Gradually, as we examine our list of clues, we assign the proper item to each place in the table. Finally, we must state that the algorithm's result is to be the name of the murderer.

"I know all this seems rather fussy to you, but in designing an algorithm one must state the overall strategy carefully and in considerable detail. Here is a general sketch of how we require the algorithm to operate," he said, as he began writing again. When finished, he presented me with this summary :

1. Assume that nothing is known.
2. Establish the known clues.
3. As long as the murderer remains unknown, do the following: try the remaining clues.
4. Give the name of the murderer.

"An essential item in our algorithm, concerning which I have said nothing, is this third instruction. It is the command we give the Engine to try every clue repeatedly until one of them produces the solution. This is known among the mathematicians at Cambridge as a *loop*, and I shall provide you with a fuller account of its role at a later date. For now, let us return to our problem."

"But this version doesn't appear to be any more specific than the last, Holmes," I ventured.

"Absolutely correct, Watson. Even this version is too general for our purposes. As I have already told you, the Engine must be instructed as to exactly what to do at each step. We must, for example, specify which of the table entries can be set directly from our list of clues and how the remaining clues can be used to establish facts.

"Consider the clue 'Sir Raymond Jasper occupied Room 10.' This is a known clue and can be more precisely stated as:

Set ROOM of SIR_RAYMOND to 10

Likewise, 'The man occupying Room 14 had black hair,' one of the remaining clues, can be stated as:

If ROOM of some SUSPECT = 14 then
    set HAIR of SUSPECT to BLACK

Do you see the gist of it now, Watson?"

"Yes, Holmes," I said. "I am beginning to understand the phrasing of algorithms; but it still seems to be a laborious procedure."

"Laborious, yes—but after all, we want to state each clue *explicitly*, giving names to the persons and to the properties associated with each of them."

My companion's enthusiam for the task fired me and thus for the remainder of the evening I busied myself tediously pairing off the available facts. At last my results ran this way :

Assume all table entries are unknown

Set ROOM of SIR_RAYMOND to 10 . . . . clue 1

Set ATTIRE of MR_POPE to GOLD_WATCH . . . . clue 4

Set ATTIRE of MR_HOLMAN to RUBY_RING . . . . clue 7

Set ROOM of MR_HOLMAN to 12 . . . . clue 9

As long as the murderer is unknown, do the following:

    if ROOM of some SUSPECT = 14 then . . . . clue 2
        set HAIR of SUSPECT to BLACK

    if SUSPECT = COL_WOODLEY or SIR_RAYMOND then . . . . clue 3
        set ATTIRE of SUSPECT to PINCENEZ

    set TRANSPORT of some SUSPECT . . . . clue 5
        to FOURWHEEL_CARRIAGE

   . . .   .

    if HAIR of some SUSPECT is BROWN then . . . . clue 14
    set MURDERER to SUSPECT

Give the name of the MURDERER

Expectantly, I reviewed my deductions, but, alas, found that this algorithm did not, however I chose to look upon it, reveal the murderer's name. I retired with a heavy feeling of dissatisfaction.

The following morning, rising earlier than usual, I found Holmes already engaged in breakfast. He sat quietly munching his toast as I approached the table with a long foolscap document in my hand.

"Well, Watson," he said, pushing aside his plate, "what have you to report?"

"I fear my efforts have been wasted, Holmes. I can see nothing from this," I confessed.

"On the contrary, Watson, you can see everything. You, however, like Scotland Yard, fail to reason from what you see. You are too timid in drawing your inferences. Let's examine it further," he suggested, "for in this field errors often lead to improved understanding."

I presented the document to him and a revised table that I have duplicated below.

SUSPECT.	COLONEL WOODLEY.	MR. HOLMAN.	MR. POPE.	SIR RAYMOND.
Hair Colour.				
Attire.		RUBY RING	GOLD WATCH	
Room.		12		10

Heartened by his reaction, I ventured an observation that had troubled me when I had tried to fit the list of clues into an algorithm.

"This fifth clue, Holmes, I believe is irrelevant to the case," I suggested. "That one of the suspects is known to have driven a four-wheel carriage does not, in my estimation, have any bearing on the circumstances we are investigating."

"Splendid, Watson!" cried Holmes. "You have just discovered another important property of algorithms: they must contain *no superfluous instructions* and no loose ends."

He stood for a moment examining the document.

"Really, you have done very well indeed. You have correctly assumed that each suspect has a different attire characteristic. It is true, however, that you have made an error that could lead us entirely off the track."

I was deeply dismayed.

"Now think carefully, Watson," he continued. "Your statement,

If SUSPECT = COL_WOODLEY or SIR_RAYMOND then
    set ATTIRE of SUSPECT to PINCENEZ

does *not* embody the meaning of the third clue, which states that one of these two suspects wore just such an eyepiece. Your algorithm will give us the wrong answer. What we need here is a clearer translation of this clue. I would suggest,

If ATTIRE of SIR_RAYMOND ≠ PINCENEZ then
    set ATTIRE of COL_WOODLEY to PINCENEZ
If ATTIRE of COL_WOODLEY ≠ PINCENEZ then
    set ATTIRE of SIR_RAYMOND to PINCENEZ

You see, Watson, only when we know that one of these suspects does not wear a pince-nez can we establish that the other suspect has the eyepiece.

"The important point is that the algorithm must be absolutely *correct*, which means it must solve the problem you intend it to solve. The Analytical Engine will never know if your algorithm is correct or not. It will only obey your instructions.

"Now let us re-organize the clues, bearing in mind these last observations," said Holmes, sketching on a fresh sheet of paper the chart I have replicated here :

Clues establishing known facts:

    1. Sir Raymond Jasper occupied Room 10.
    2. Mr Pope always carried a gold pocket watch.
    3. Mr. Holman wore a ruby signet ring.
    4. Mr. Holman occupied Room 12.

The remaining clues:

    5. The man occupying Room 14 had black hair.
    6. Either Colonel Woodley or Sir Raymond wore a pince-nez.
    7. The man with the pince-nez had brown hair.
    8. The man with tattered cuffs had red hair.
    9. The man in Room 16 had tattered cuffs.
  10. The man in Room 12 had grey hair.
  11. The man with the gold pocket watch occupied Room 14.
  12. Colonel Woodley occupied a corner room.
  13. The murderer had brown hair.

We spent the remainder of the morning reconstructing the algorithm based on the arrangement of facts Holmes had outlined at our breakfast table. The result is reproduced here as Exhibit 2.1.

As he scanned the now complete algorithm, Holmes puffed at his pipe with satisfaction. "Excellent, Watson, I daresay that with a few days' study of the Engine's special language you'll be ready to test your algorithm on the Engine itself."

"Is it a difficult language?" I enquired.

"I should say that it will prove far less formidable to you than did Latin or Greek at Wellington. The important thing is that you now understand the key principle on which the Engine's operation rests."

"And I now know the murderer's true identity!" I exclaimed.

"Indeed," replied Holmes dryly.

Definitions:

    HAIR   : row of hair colours for the suspects
    ATTIRE : row of attire characteristics for the suspects
    ROOM   : row of room numbers for the suspects
    SUSPECT, MURDERER: one of the suspects

Algorithm:

    Set all table entries and **MURDERER** to unknown

    Set **ROOM** of SIR_RAYMOND to 10
    Set **ATTIRE** of MR_POPE to GOLD_WATCH
    Set **ATTIRE** of MR_HOLMAN to RUBY_RING
    Set **ROOM** of MR_HOLMAN to 12

    As long as **MURDERER** is unknown, do the following:
      if **ROOM** of some SUSPECT = 14 then
        set **HAIR** of SUSPECT to BLACK
      if **ATTIRE** of SIR_RAYMOND ≠ PINCENEZ then
        set **ATTIRE** of COL_WOODLEY to PINCENEZ
      if **ATTIRE** of COL_WOODLEY ≠ PINCENEZ then
        set **ATTIRE** of SIR_RAYMOND to PINCENEZ
      if **ATTIRE** of some SUSPECT = PINCENEZ then
        set **HAIR** of SUSPECT to BROWN
      if **ATTIRE** of some SUSPECT = TATTERED_CUFFS then
        set **HAIR** of SUSPECT to RED
      if **ROOM** of some SUSPECT = 16 then
        set **ATTIRE** of SUSPECT to TATTERED_CUFFS
      if **ROOM** of some SUSPECT = 12 then
        set **HAIR** of SUSPECT to GREY
      if **ATTIRE** of some SUSPECT = GOLD_WATCH then
        set **ROOM** of SUSPECT to 14

      if **ROOM** of some SUSPECT = 10
    and SUSPECT ≠ COL_WOODLEY then
        set **ROOM** of COL_WOODLEY to 16
      if **ROOM** of some SUSPECT = 16
    and SUSPECT ≠ COL_WOODLEY then
        set **ROOM** of COL_WOODLEY to 10

      if **HAIR** of some SUSPECT = BROWN then
        set **MURDERER** to SUSPECT

    Write the name of the **MURDERER**

Exhibit 2.1   *Final Algorithm for the Metropolitan Club Murder*

2.1   Algorithms Reviewed

Of all the topics we will discuss in this book, the most fundamental is the concept of an *algorithm*. Over a century ago Holmes realized that people are accustomed to taking many things for granted when they deliver instructions to others, and he warned against making the same error when designing an algorithm for the Engine.

The rigor demanded by a computer algorithm is the essence of programming, no matter which special language you are working in. Let's quickly review the properties of an algorithm discussed by Holmes, for his treatment of the subject in this chapter gives us the key to all that we will take up in later pages.

Generally, an algorithm is a sequence of instructions given to solve some problem. Any algorithm must have the following characteristics:

1. *It must be organized properly.*   An algorithm reflects some sequence of instructions carried out in the real world. Accordingly, the instructions must be arranged in some meaningful way in order to solve the problem at hand.

2. *It must go step by step.* Each instruction in the algorithm must be some form of imperative statement to carry out a given step in the problem solution. After each step, the next step in the solution must be unambiguous.

3. *It must be precise.* The instructions given in an algorithm can leave no room for ambiguity. Thus it must be possible to interpret the instructions in only one way.

4. *It must make the data explicit.* Each item we choose to include in our algorithm must be clearly identified. For example, if an algorithm has something to do with suspects and room numbers, and these are calculated during the course of the algorithm, then these items need to be described explicitly.

5. *It must contain no irrelevant information.* There can be no loose ends, no extraneous instructions, no frills. The algorithm must state only the relevant instructions needed to be carried out.

6. *It must be correct.* An algorithm is always directed toward its single goal—to establish results that will be known upon its completion. The results must be exactly what you want.

All of these features are things that we often take for granted. In an algorithm, we must be rigorous to the last detail.

Before going on to the next chapter and discussing how we express algorithms in Pascal, let's review a few last steps in the algorithm to solve the murder at the Metropolitan Club.

As you recall, Watson prepared a table containing facts established by the known clues. In Table 2.1 we show the effects of executing the algorithm further.

In particular, Table 2.1 shows the entries established after two successive executions of the repeated instructions given in Holmes and Watson's algorithm. After executing the instructions once, the facts given in Table 2.1a are established; after another execution, the facts given in Table 2.1b are established. Thus the algorithm slowly fills the table with newly established facts. We leave it to you to execute the instructions again in order to establish the identity of the murderer.

TABLE 2.1 *Facts Established after Two Executions of the Loop*

(* denotes a fact obtained during the given execution of the loop.)

a. Facts established after first execution:

Suspect	Colonel Woodley	Mr. Holman	Mr. Pope	Sir Raymond
Hair Color		GREY*		
Attire		RUBY RING	GOLD WATCH	
Room	16*	12	14*	10

b. Facts established after second execution:

Suspect	Colonel Woodley	Mr. Holman	Mr. Pope	Sir Raymond
Hair Color		GREY	BLACK*	
Attire	TATTERED CUFFS*	RUBY RING	GOLD WATCH	
Room	16	12	14	10

III

Holmes Gives a
Demonstration

HERLOCK Holmes had spent several days in bed, as was his habit from time to time, and emerged one morning with several documents in his hands. He had a horror of destroying papers, especially those connected with his past cases, and I thought at first sight that he had been sifting through some old notes; but he announced as he entered the room that what he held was a new version of the algorithm we had worked out concerning the dreadful business at the Metropolitan Club. This rendering, he informed me, was composed entirely in the Engine's special language, Pascal.

Holmes seemed quite pleased with his work and offered the documents for my study. I have duplicated them here as Exhibit 3.1.

"You expect me to make sense of this ineffable twaddle, Holmes?" I exclaimed, for this new version appeared to be written with the oddest assortment of English terms, numbers, and punctuation marks tossed about at random.

Holmes walked to the mantelpiece and began filling his pipe with that abhorrent shag he kept in the toe of a Persian slipper.

"These five lines, for instance," I said, tapping the papers, "the ones following the first line of the programme, hardly appear to be written in code at all and do not have the cryptic appearance of the rest of this document."

"Those are *comments*, Watson," replied Holmes, as he lit his pipe. "In Pascal, all comments begin with a left brace and end with a right brace. Here they are used to make observations on the programme's content, entirely for the human reader's enlightenment. They do not contain instructions to the machine and have no effect on the programme's operation. You might consider them as asides to communicate in ordinary English any information the programmer wishes to include concerning the programme.

"I can hardly imagine how the deuce you arrived at these results," said I, still amazed at the complexity of this latest document.

"I reached this one," said Holmes, pointing to the papers with the stem of his briar, "by sitting upon five pillows and consuming an ounce of shag. You have not, I hope, learned to despise my pipe and my lamentable tobacco? It must take the place of food these days if I am to master this Engine.

"Now let me continue, Watson, and explain some other points that are not self-evident from a glance at the programme. Immediately after the five lines of comments we come to the section of *constant declarations*. Here we state that the colours RED, BLACK, GREY, and BROWN are to be represented throughout the programme by the integer numbers 1, 2, 3, and 4, respectively. Likewise, the four attire characteristics, PINCENEZ through TATTEREDCUFFS, as well as the names of the four suspects, are denoted by the numbers 1 through 4. Lastly, the state of being UNKNOWN is represented by 0."

"But Holmes," I asked, "how does this make a pennyworth of difference to us?"

"For reasons you will understand better as we proceed, Watson. In writing a programme one must choose names for all the entities of the algorithm. Here all the entities are represented by numbers. The declarations simply tell the Engine these facts. Constant declarations define entities that are to remain as fixed values throughout the programme, and this is the reason for their name.

"The next part of the programme consists of *variable declarations*. Here we specify that SUSPECT and MURDERER are to be assigned whole-number values during the programme's execution. These numerical values may vary at different points in the programme.

"Notice that HAIR, ATTIRE, and ROOM represent the three rows of our rudimentary table of data. Now, each of these rows is represented by an *array*; the four entries in each row represent the names of the suspects."

"This seems a bit much to digest at once, Holmes," I protested.

"It will all become quite clear to you, Watson, as we work further with the Engine. For the moment let us study the structure of a programme, using our work on the affair at the Metropolitan Club as a guide.

```
program METROPOLITANCLUB (OUTPUT);

{ -- This programme examines the clues given for the murder
  -- at the Metropolitan Club. The three arrays HAIR, ATTIRE, and
  -- ROOM are used to establish the facts as they are determined.
  -- The programme outputs the name of the murderer. }

  const
     UNKNOWN = 0;
     RED = 1;          BLACK = 2;        GREY = 3;       BROWN = 4;
     PINCENEZ = 1;     GOLDWATCH = 2;    RUBYRING = 3;   TATTEREDCUFFS = 4;
     COLWOODLEY = 1;  MRHOLMAN = 2;     MRPOPE = 3;     SIRRAYMOND = 4;

  var
     SUSPECT, MURDERER:  INTEGER;

     HAIR  : array [COLWOODLEY .. SIRRAYMOND] of INTEGER;
     ATTIRE: array [COLWOODLEY .. SIRRAYMOND] of INTEGER;
     ROOM  : array [COLWOODLEY .. SIRRAYMOND] of INTEGER;

begin
     { -- Assume nothing is known }
     MURDERER := UNKNOWN;
     for SUSPECT := COLWOODLEY to SIRRAYMOND do begin
        HAIR[SUSPECT]    := UNKNOWN;
        ATTIRE[SUSPECT]  := UNKNOWN;
        ROOM[SUSPECT]    := UNKNOWN
     end;

     { -- Establish known clues }
     ROOM[SIRRAYMOND] := 10;
     ATTIRE[MRPOPE]    := GOLDWATCH;
     ATTIRE[MRHOLMAN] := RUBYRING;
     ROOM[MRHOLMAN]    := 12;

     { -- Repeatedly try the remaining clues }
     SUSPECT := COLWOODLEY;
     while MURDERER = UNKNOWN do begin
        if (ROOM[SUSPECT] = 14) then
           HAIR[SUSPECT] := BLACK;
```

Exhibit 3.1   *Holmes's Programme for the Metropolitan Club Murder*

```
      if (ATTIRE[SIRRAYMOND]<>UNKNOWN) and (ATTIRE[SIRRAYMOND]<>PINCENEZ) then
         ATTIRE[COLWOODLEY] := PINCENEZ;
      if (ATTIRE[COLWOODLEY]<>UNKNOWN) and (ATTIRE[COLWOODLEY]<>PINCENEZ) then
         ATTIRE[SIRRAYMOND] := PINCENEZ;
      if (ATTIRE[SUSPECT] = PINCENEZ) then
         HAIR[SUSPECT] := BROWN;
      if (ATTIRE[SUSPECT] = TATTEREDCUFFS) then
         HAIR[SUSPECT] := RED;
      if (ROOM[SUSPECT] = 16) then
         ATTIRE[SUSPECT] := TATTEREDCUFFS;
      if (ROOM[SUSPECT] = 12) then
         HAIR[SUSPECT] := GREY;
      if (ATTIRE[SUSPECT] = GOLDWATCH) then
         ROOM[SUSPECT] := 14;

      if (ROOM[SUSPECT] = 10) and (SUSPECT <> COLWOODLEY) then
         ROOM[COLWOODLEY] := 16;
      if (ROOM[SUSPECT] = 16) and (SUSPECT <> COLWOODLEY) then
         ROOM[COLWOODLEY] := 10;

      if (HAIR[SUSPECT] = BROWN) then
         MURDERER := SUSPECT;

      if (SUSPECT = SIRRAYMOND) then
         SUSPECT := COLWOODLEY
      else
         SUSPECT := SUSPECT + 1
   end; { -- remaining clues }

   { -- Print the name of the murderer }
   if MURDERER = COLWOODLEY then
        WRITE ('THE MURDERER IS COLONEL WOODLEY.')
   else if MURDERER = MRHOLMAN then
        WRITE ('THE MURDERER IS MR. HOLMAN.')
   else if MURDERER = MRPOPE then
        WRITE ('THE MURDERER IS MR. POPE.')
   else
        WRITE ('THE MURDERER IS SIR RAYMOND.')
end.
```

Exhibit 3.1 *Continued*

"Allow me to summarize for you exactly what the main body of the programme accomplishes. In the section immediately following the declarations, we explicitly state that the **MURDERER** and all table entries are **UNKNOWN**. Then in the next segment we make a note of our known clues. For instance, the statement,

```
ROOM[SIRRAYMOND] := 10
```

explicitly sets the **SIRRAYMOND** entry of our **ROOM** row to 10.

"As for the remaining clues, the **SUSPECT** is initially set to COL-WOODLEY; notice that this departs slightly from our original algorithm. So long as the **MURDERER** remains **UNKNOWN**, the programme tests the remaining clues. The ensuing *loop*, which is signalled by the special word while, tests all the clues against the given **SUSPECT**. At the end of this loop, **SUSPECT** is set to the next name on our list, and the clues are tried again.

"LET US TALK OF LIGHTER MATTERS."

"Finally, when the programme arrives at a value for **MURDERER** different from **UNKNOWN**, it prints the name of our man.

"Have I not always said that when you have eliminated the impossible, whatever remains, however improbable, must be the truth? This process of elimination is exactly what our programme will do for us, Watson."

Although this exposition of the programme seemed to follow readily from our algorithm, I remained confused by some of the odd grammar and vocabulary of this programme. Ordinary words like "while" or "if" seemed to take on entirely new meanings in Pascal, and I questioned Holmes on this point.

"The words that baffle you, Watson," he explained, "are known as *keywords*, and are the framework for constructing logical operations within the language itself. Once you have learned more of the grammar of Pascal you will be able to write simple programmes of your own with little difficulty."

"Very well, Holmes, but what of the names such as **SUSPECT**, **ROOM**, and **RED**? As you chose these names yourself, I surmise they are not part of the special Pascal lexicon. Yet are there not some restrictions as to how such names may be conceived?"

"Certainly," said Holmes, replacing his pipe upon the mantelpiece. "There are specific rules governing the formation of constant and variable names. For example, compound names such as **GOLDWATCH** and **SIRRAYMOND** must be run together, contrary to our ordinary spelling conventions. We shall examine this matter in greater detail later. You should be aware even now, however, that Pascal does not require that such names be meaningful. We could just as well have selected the word **TOBACCO** or **GMXZYP** instead of **SUSPECT** to denote the variable, but then the intent of this name, and of the programme as a whole, would be unclear to anyone examining it."

"The punctuation makes little sense to me," I protested. "It looks like ordinary punctuation but used in an utterly illogical manner. Why do some lines end with semicolons whereas others do not?"

Holmes seemed a trifle disconcerted at this remark and returned the programme to the pile of earlier versions on the table.

"Oddly enough, Watson, the usage of semicolons *is* somewhat illogical and difficult to encapsulate briefly. Come now, let us talk of lighter matters, for Pascal is a subject that is best absorbed in moderate doses at the outset."

3.1   General Program Structure

We now have a working model of a typical Pascal program. We have seen a problem—in this case, a search for the identity of a criminal—presented as an algorithm and translated into Pascal. If you find this program a bit overwhelming, hang in there. Our intent here is only to give you a taste of what we'll be getting into later.

As you have probably already observed, the writing of programs requires that you know a number of sometimes odd conventions. Watson's mystification at some of the things mentioned by Holmes is true of us all. For starters, let's examine some of the major components of Holmes's program.

Let's first look at the overall structure of the program for the murder at the Metropolitan Club:

```
program METROPOLITANCLUB (OUTPUT);
    -- declarations
begin
    -- statements
end.
```

All programs begin with the word program followed by the name of the program. In Holmes's case, the program is named METROPOLITAN-CLUB. Following the name of the program, you see the name OUTPUT. This means that the program prints some results, in this case, the name of the murderer. If your program also reads in some data to be used in the calculation of the results, you must include the name INPUT in the first line of the program. For example, you might have the following heading:

```
program TIMEOFDEATH (INPUT, OUTPUT);
```

This convention may not seem very reasonable to you, but the general rule is that if your program reads in data, you must write INPUT in the program heading; and if your program prints some data, you must write OUTPUT in the program heading. We will have some more to say on this subject when we get to our chapter on input and output, but that should suffice for now.

Following the program heading are definitions for all of the objects in a program. Each definition is called a *declaration*. In Pascal, this rule must be followed strictly. Every name used by the programmer must be defined in a declaration. For example, in Holmes's case, SUSPECT is the name that stands for one of the suspects. This name must be declared, as in:

```
SUSPECT: INTEGER;
```

This declaration means that the name SUSPECT will hold integer values during the course of the algorithm portion of the program. As we know, the integer values 1 through 4 stand for each of the four suspects.

Similarly, the row of hair colors for each suspect in Watson's table must also be defined:

```
HAIR: array[COLWOODLEY..SIRRAYMOND] of INTEGER;
```

The row of the table is named HAIR. The value of each row entry is indexed by one of the names COLWOODLEY through SIRRAYMOND, corresponding to the four suspects; the values themselves are defined as integers. Notice here that even the names COLWOODLEY through SIR-RAYMOND must also be defined in a declaration, in this case, declared as having the integer values 1 through 4. All of this gets back to our original point—all names used in the program must be declared by the programmer.

Next we come to the algorithm portion of the program. An algorithm is written as a sequence of *statements*. There are several kinds of statements in Pascal. Each of them specifies some action to be carried out by the computer. For example, the statement,

```
MURDERER := UNKNOWN
```

sets the value of MURDERER to the value of the constant named UN-KNOWN. As we see in the declarations, the value of the constant UN-KNOWN is 0.

Other statements in Pascal allow complex actions to be specified. For example, a statement of the form,

```
for SUSPECT := COLWOODLEY to SIRRAYMOND do begin
   -- actions to be taken for each suspect
end
```

specifies a series of actions to be taken for each of the four suspects. The statement having the form,

```
while MURDERER = UNKNOWN do begin
   -- actions to be taken for each clue
end
```

specifies a series of actions to be executed as long as MURDERER remains UNKNOWN.

This is enough for digestion now. All of these points will be taken up in greater detail in later chapters by Holmes; and we, too, shall give them greater attention. For the remainder of this chapter, however, let's take a closer look at the individual components of a program.

3.2   The Units of a Pascal Program

At the most elementary level, a Pascal program consists of a sequence of symbols. The possible symbols are given in Table 3.1. The arrangement of symbols is subject to numerous and sometimes complex conventions that you will have to learn as you go along. Here we pin down a few of the more primitive conventions, including the rules for writing names, numbers, character strings, and comments.

TABLE 3.1   *Pascal Symbols*

Digits

```
0  1  2  3  4  5  6  7  8  9
```

Letters

```
a  b  c  d  e  f  g  h  i  j  k  l  m
n  o  p  q  r  s  t  u  v  w  x  y  z

A  B  C  D  E  F  G  H  I  J  K  L  M
N  O  P  Q  R  S  T  U  V  W  X  Y  Z
```

Special Symbols

```
+  -  *  /  =  <  >  [  ]  '  (  )
.  ,  :  ;  ^  >=  <=  <>  :=  ..  {  }
```

Keywords

and	else	label	packed	until
array	end		procedure	
			program	
		mod		var
begin	file		record	
	for	nil	repeat	while
case	function	not		with
const			set	
	goto	of		
div		or	then	
do	if		to	
downto	in		type	

Identifiers

An *identifier* is a name created by the programmer. It consists of one or more letters or digits, but the first character must always be a letter. An identifier can be as long as you wish but must fit on a line. Some examples are:

```
RED                 ROOM10
MURDERER            ROOM12
SIRRAYMOND
METROPOLITANCLUB
```

In identifiers, uppercase and lowercase letters are treated as being equivalent, which means that the identifier,

```
SUSPECT
```

is the same as:

```
Suspect
```

If your computer doesn't handle lowercase letters, this rule need not concern you.

Watch out, though, for the following restriction, which is common to many implementations of Pascal. Although you can write very long identifiers, two identifiers are considered as different only if the *first eight* characters differentiate them. Suppose, for example, you write a program involving two murderers. It may be tempting to call them MURDERER1 and MURDERER2. Here however the first eight characters of each identifier are the same, so the computer will think that they are actually the same murderer. Tricky. You will have to think of other names, for example, FIRSTMURDERER and SECONDMURDERER.

Keywords

There are 35 keywords in Pascal. A *keyword* is a special identifier that tells the computer what to do. For example, the keyword program introduces a program. Other keywords have more ubiquitous meanings. For example, the keyword end marks the end of something—the end of a sequence of statements, for instance, or the end of the program.

You don't have to memorize all the keywords. The important point is that each has a specific role. Furthermore, the keywords in Pascal are said to be "reserved," meaning that you may not use them as identifiers in your program. For example, if Holmes wished, he could change the name SUSPECT to TOBACCO, although it would be quite senseless; but he could not change it to PROGRAM or ARRAY because these are reserved.

Numbers

Suppose you wish to compute the number of feet to the scene of a crime, or an amount of money embezzled in a series of bank transactions. Pascal, like any other programming language, has a rather fixed set of conventions for writing numbers.

The first kind of number you can write is an *integer*, which means a whole number. An integer is represented by a sequence of digits, possibly preceded by a plus or a minus sign:

```
      0        10
   1776       +10
 100000       -10
```

Negative numbers can be used to represent things like a temperature of minus 10 degrees or a bank balance that is "in the red."

The second kind of number you can write in Pascal is a *real number*. A real number must have either a decimal point, a letter E followed by a scale factor (which means "times ten to the power of"), or both. For example, you may write the numbers,

```
12.34
1234E-2
0.1234E2
0.1234E+2
```

all of which stand for the same real number.

The E notation (often called scientific notation or floating point notation) is especially useful for very large or very small numbers, which might arise if you are trying to calculate the distance between two planets or the weight of a molecule. Instead of writing,

```
123000000000000
0.0000000000000456
```

you can write:

```
1.23E+14
4.56E-14
```

This saves you from counting zeros to find how large or small a number is.

These are the only conventions you can use for writing numbers. Be careful, for as much as you would like, you cannot write numbers like:

```
2.        { you must write 2.0 }
 .3       { you must write 0.3 }
1,000     { you must write 1000 }
$123      { you must write 123 }
```

So whatever number you have in mind, you must represent it as either an integer or as a real number. Normally you use integers to represent things you can count (the number of suspects or the scheduled time of a train arrival, for example) and real numbers to represent things you measure cannot be determined exactly (the number of feet to the scene of a crime or the weight of a molecule, for example).

Character Strings

Often when you use a computer program, you want your program to print messages telling you what is going on. You can do this with *character strings*, such as:

```
'ENTER YOUR PASSWORD'
'THE MURDERER IS MR. POPE.'
```

To print a character string, you simply include it in a WRITE statement, just like

```
WRITE ('THE MURDERER IS MR. POPE.');
```

in Holmes's program.

A character string consists of a sequence of characters enclosed by single quotes. You might have expected that a character string would be enclosed by double quotation marks ("); so be careful, as a single quotation mark, an apostrophe ('), must be used.

The characters that you can put in a character string can be any character that your computer recognizes, even such characters as $ and %. What if you would like to have an apostrophe itself as part of a character string? It's simple. Just type two apostrophes in a row, and it will come out as a single apostrophe. Thus we may have:

```
'THE MURDERER''S HAIR IS BROWN'
'NOTE THE PAIR OF SINGLE QUOTES ABOVE'

'STRINGS MAY CONTAIN SPECIAL CHARACTERS'
'LIKE $ AND %'
'as well as lower case letters'
```

Note that each string must fit on a line.

Comments

One of the most useful features of programming languages is the ability to annotate your program with *comments*. Completely ignored by the computer, comments are there entirely for the enlightenment of a human reader.

For example, in the sequence

```
{ -- Establish known clues }
ROOM[SIRRAYMOND] := 10;
ATTIRE[MRPOPE]   := GOLDWATCH;
ATTIRE[MRHOLMAN] := RUBYRING;
ROOM[MRHOLMAN]   := 12;
```

the first line is a comment.

A comment consists of any sequence of characters enclosed by curly braces. The text of your comment may include anything you like except a right brace (}).

```
{ -- Long comments can be written and
  -- extend over two or more lines. }
```

As far as running your program is concerned, the comment will have no effect and will be treated just as if it were a blank space.

One not-so-minor point. If the brace characters { and } are not available on your computer, you can enclose comments with the symbols (* and *) instead. For example:

```
(* -- Establish known clues *)
```

No matter which symbols you use, be sure to close off each comment with its terminating *) or }. If you don't, all the program text following the comment will be treated as part of the comment itself.

3.3   Spacing and Punctuation

It is much easier to read,

```
for SUSPECT := COLWOODLEY to SIRRAYMOND do begin
    HAIR[SUSPECT]   := UNKNOWN;
    ATTIRE[SUSPECT] := UNKNOWN;
    ROOM[SUSPECT]   := UNKNOWN
end;
```

than

```
for SUSPECT := COLWOODLEY to SIRRAYMOND do begin HAIR
[SUSPECT]:=UNKNOWN;ATTIRE[SUSPECT]:=UNKNOWN;ROOM
SUSPECT]:=UNKNOWN end;
```

The only difference between the two examples is simply the use of spacing. The computer will ignore blank spaces and blank lines, but the human reader will not. In fact, the proper spacing of programs can go a long way in making your intent clear.

There are a few restrictions on the placing of blank spaces and blank lines. These restrictions need not concern you very much, as they are reasonably obvious. For example, you may not put blank spaces between the characters of an identifier or between the : and the = of a :=. And, of course, at least one blank must be inserted between adjacent keywords, such as between the do and begin above.

Finally, the end of a line is treated as if it were a blank space, at least as far as the computer is concerned. All of these rules follow common intuition, and generally speaking, you may insert blank spaces and blank lines wherever convenient.

Now we come to the treacherous rules for the placement of semicolons. The first rule is simple. A semicolon is required at the end of a program heading, as in:

```
program METROPOLITANCLUB (OUTPUT);
```

As we shall see later, the same rule applies to procedure and function headings.

The second rule is just as simple, but a bit more embracing: a semicolon is required after each declaration. For example, a semicolon is required after the constant declaration,

```
UNKNOWN = 0;
```

and after each declaration of a list of variables, as in:

```
SUSPECT, MURDERER: INTEGER;
```

Things begin to get a bit more sticky when we come to the algorithm part of a program. A semicolon must be placed after each statement in a sequence of statements *except* the last. For example, consider the following:

```
for SUSPECT := COLWOODLEY to SIRRAYMOND do begin
    HAIR[SUSPECT]    := UNKNOWN;
    ATTIRE[SUSPECT]  := UNKNOWN;
    ROOM[SUSPECT]    := UNKNOWN    { -- no semicolon }
end; { -- semicolon required }

{ -- Establish known clues }
```

Here we see three statements in a sequence bracketed by the keywords begin and end. A semicolon is thus required after each of the first two statements. The entire sequence between the symbols for and end is also a statement that is part of a longer sequence of statements, hence a semicolon is required after the closing keyword end.

But watch out, there is more. Pascal allows you to write invisible statements called "empty" statements. Imagine, an invisible statement! Accordingly, you can place an empty statement after the statement

```
ROOM[SUSPECT] := UNKNOWN
```

above; and thus you can if you wish, place a semicolon after this third statement. If it puzzles you, you are right! It would be better not to get involved with empty statements. Suffice it to say, the rules given above will serve you in good stead. If you have any doubts about the placement of semicolons, you can always refer to the Appendix, which summarizes the formation rules for writing programs in Pascal.

The Game Afoot

IV

The Adventure
of the Bathing Machine

HE summer following the little matter of the Vatican cameos was made memorable by three cases of interest, in which I had the privilege of being associated with Mr. Sherlock Holmes and of studying his methods in the use of the Analytical Engine. In glancing over my somewhat jumbled notes of these cases, I find they brought him the fewest personal opportunities in his long and admirable career. Each, however, did provide him with a chance for testing out the Engine's varied capabilities, including a telegraphic arrangement he made at considerable expense for communicating with the Engine over great distances. To Holmes the cases were of themselves of only secondary interest; and although he saved Scotland Yard a good deal of embarrassment in the first of these, the official police took full credit for concluding the affair.

Upon attending one of my new patients one fine June morning, I returned to Baker Street to find Holmes packing his valise in those high spirits that told me he was off on some new adventure.

"You are preparing for a trip," I remarked, eager to display my own deductive faculties.

"Yes, Watson," replied Holmes. "And perhaps your native shrewdness can deduce my destination?"

I studied his packages for a moment. "Off on some scholarly pursuits, I see. Perhaps to Cambridge and the Analytical Engine."

"There is such a delightful freshness about you, my dear Watson. You've really done very well indeed."

I was immensely pleased.

"It is true, however," he continued, "that you have missed everything of importance. As it happens, I leave this afternoon for the Yorkshire coast. Now, Watson, would you care to join me?"

I hesitated for a moment, and then replied. "Indeed I would, Holmes. There is a lull in my practice just now and I could benefit from a change of scene. You have a case, then?"

"A small matter, but not without points of interest," replied Holmes. "We can consider it on the train. Can you meet me at King's Cross at noon?"

"Yes of course, Holmes."

Holmes departed, and I hurried away to pack my bags for a few days by the sea.

As our train lurched northwards, Holmes was deep in thought. Framed in his ear-flapped travelling cap, he hardly spoke until we had passed well out of London. As the grey of the city turned to the green of the countryside, he proceeded to sketch for me the events in an extraordinary matter which had become a topic of conversation the length and breadth of England.

"HE PROCEEDED TO SKETCH FOR ME THE EVENTS."

"I take it you are familiar, Watson, with this matter of the disappearance of the Baroness of Whitelsey?" asked Holmes.

"Only what I have learned from what the *Telegraph* and the *Chronicle* have had to say."

"Well then," he began, "let us review what the papers have reported thus far. It seems that the Baroness was spending a few days at the seaside resort of Scarborough and was daily taking the healthful waters of the North Sea. On each occasion she was taken down to the water's edge in a hired bathing machine, and on each occasion she was accompanied by the same attendants. At her request they would retire to the beach side of the machine while the Baroness dipped into the waters. Now, on the morning of the third

"SHE WAS TAKEN DOWN IN A HIRED BATHING MACHINE."

of July, the attendants, at the conclusion of this minor ritual, hauled the machine back over the beach only to find it empty. A quick search of the shore revealed nothing, and the matter was placed in the hands of the local police. Needless to say, the Baroness has not been seen since."

After a brief pause, I casually remarked that the accusing finger of the law would certainly point in the direction of these attendants.

"Yes, Watson," he answered. "Our dear Inspector Lestrade has been called in by the local police and he naturally suspects foul play on the part of these fellows, all of whom were detained. Of course he does not have a shred of evidence, but remains adamant about a conviction. The family of one of these unfortunate attendants has asked me to look into the matter."

"Isn't it possible," I suggested, "that the Baroness met with an accidental end and that the attendants tried to conceal her drowning?"

"Possible, yes, and highly probable," replied Holmes. "But it is a capital error to theorize before one has collected one's data. However, as Lestrade has already settled upon this theory, it is up to me to look for an alternative."

With that Holmes lapsed into silence for much of the remainder of our journey, sinking into that deep concentration that some might think morose but that I knew to be a sign that he was pondering a most difficult case.

We arrived without incident and took furnished rooms in the hotel at which the Baroness had been staying. I found the trip fatiguing, but Holmes left immediately to pursue his investigations without so much as unpacking his bag. I dined alone and retired early. Lulled by the seaside air and a single glass of port, I slept late into the next morning.

I awoke to find that Holmes had already breakfasted and gone out again, leaving behind this note :

> *Watson — I've gone to Whitby, some 20 miles up*
> *the coast. Kindly establish a connection with the*
> *Analytical Engine through the local telegraph office.*
> *Holmes*

The director of the local telegraph office was most helpful, but in spite of this, I was occupied with filling this request for most of the morning.

When Holmes returned, he appeared elated. "A most profitable morning, Watson. The mystery of the Baroness of Whitelsey is solved to my satisfaction, but we need to resolve one final point. This provides us with an admirable opportunity for testing our new telegraph arrangements for communicating with the Engine.

"Now, the one bit of information we need to determine is the state of the tide at the time that the Baroness vanished. Let us establish this as a problem for the Engine.

"As you know, Watson, tides vary according to a 12 hour and 25 minute cycle. Since high tide today is at 11.00 A.M., tonight it will occur at 11.25 P.M. Let us define the problem in terms of what we know, what is given, and what we wish to determine :

The knowns:	Tides recur every 12 hours and 25 minutes.
The givens:	It is now July 28, and high tide is at 11.00 A.M. The Baroness disappeared on July 3, at 9.00 A.M.
To find:	The state of the tide at the time of the mysterious disappearance.

"Well, Watson, this begins to define the problem. Let me present my algorithm for solving it. First I will explain generally how the algorithm works and then explain some key ideas illustrated by it."

Holmes then presented his simple algorithm, which I have reproduced in Exhibit 4.1.

"First, we express the time for a complete tide cycle in minutes."

"But why in minutes, Holmes?" I asked.

"That is due to a limitation of the Engine, Watson. It cannot work directly with dates and times the way we can. For example, it is inconvenient to read in a date and time such as July 28th, 11.00 A.M.; thus in my algorithm all dates and times are converted to minutes. As you will see, in dealing with dates we can readily express them in terms of the total number of minutes that have elapsed since the beginning of the month.

"We read in TODAYS_DATE as the number 28, representing the 28th of the month. The TIDE_HR is read as 11, for 11.00 A.M. Similarly, the EVENT_DATE and EVENT_HR are read in as 3 and 9, respectively, representing July 3rd and 9.00 A.M., the last time the Baroness was seen. In order to do our computations, we must first convert our dates and times to minutes that have elapsed since the beginning of the month. Thus our first calculation is:

Set MINS_TO_HIGH_TIDE to (TODAYS_DATE - 1) * MINS_PER_DAY

Today's date is 28, but only 27 full days have gone by this month. Thus we subtract 1 and multiply by the number of minutes in a day. This gives the number of minutes in the 27 complete days that have elapsed since the beginning of the month.

"We must also consider the 11 hours between midnight and high tide today. So we use a second calculation,

Set MINS_TO_HIGH_TIDE to MINS_TO_HIGH_TIDE +
                        TIDE_HR * MINS_PER_HR

to add the number of minutes that have gone by today to our previous total. We now have the total number of minutes from the beginning of the month until high tide today.

"Next, we follow an identical procedure to arrive at a figure in minutes for the time of the swim and subsequent disappearance."

"But Holmes, why do you calculate from the beginning of the month?"

"That is arbitrary, Watson. I need some date as a reference, and the first of the month is convenient since it allows us to express our input in terms of days of the month.

"We now have the time of today's high tide and also the time of the disappearance, expressed in minutes. We subtract one from the other,

Definitions:

— Express the knowns:
MINS_PER_HR is 60 minutes
MINS_PER_DAY is 1440 minutes
MINS_PER_TIDE_CYCLE is 745 minutes

Algorithm:

— Obtain the givens:
Read TODAYS_DATE, TIDE_HR, EVENT_DATE, EVENT_HR

— Convert times to minutes since the beginning of the month:
Set MINS_TO_HIGH_TIDE to (TODAYS_DATE - 1) * MINS_PER_DAY
Set MINS_TO_HIGH_TIDE to MINS_TO_HIGH_TIDE +
                              TIDE_HR * MINS_PER_HR

Set MINS_TO_EVENT to (EVENT_DATE - 1) * MINS_PER_DAY
Set MINS_TO_EVENT to MINS_TO_EVENT + EVENT_HR*MINS_PER_HR

— Find elapsed time:
Set ELAPSED_TIME to MINS_TO_HIGH_TIDE - MINS_TO_EVENT

— Find the number of elapsed tide cycles:
Set TIDE_CYCLES to ELAPSED_TIME / MINS_PER_TIDE_CYCLE

— Output the result:
Write TIDE_CYCLES

Exhibit 4.1 *Holmes's Algorithm for Calculating Tides*

Set ELAPSED_TIME to MINS_TO_HIGH_TIDE - MINS_TO_EVENT

to find the elapsed time in minutes.

"The rest is simple. We divide the elapsed time by the number of minutes in a complete tide cycle, thus giving the number of tide cycles that have taken place in the interim. In this way, our final answer will be expressed in terms of high tide as a reference point.

"Watson, this algorithm demonstrates several key ideas about programming that I would like to explain to you, if you will hear them."

"Of course."

"Very well," Holmes continued. "The first thing to understand is the idea of a *variable*. Each variable we use in the program will have a name that we give to it. Think of a variable as a piece of information that can vary as the program progresses, such as the depth to which the parsley had sunk into the butter that hot day when the dreadful business of the Abernetty family was first brought to my attention."

"But what will cause the variables to change in value?" I asked.

"We will set and change the values of all the variables by the way we write the program," Holmes replied. "They will be completely under our control. Look again at the algorithm for our problem. Here you see several variables, for example, the variables named TODAYS_DATE and TIDE_CYCLES.

"Next, we have the idea of an *expression*. An expression is a formula for computing a value. You can see some examples in my algorithm. Consider the statement:

Set MINS_TO_HIGH_TIDE to (TODAYS_DATE - 1) * MINS_PER_DAY

Here MINS_TO_HIGH_TIDE is a variable whose value we are trying to establish. We use the expression

(TODAYS_DATE - 1) * MINS_PER_DAY

to express the fact that we want the Engine to subtract 1 from TODAYS_DATE and multiply the result by the number of minutes in a day."

"Does it not strike you as curious, Holmes, that the asterisk should represent multiplication?"

"Not at all, Watson. The Engine would have difficulty in sorting out the letter 'x' from the usual multiplication symbol."

"A statement used to set a variable based on an expression is termed an *assignment*, because it assigns a value to a variable. You can think of an assignment as establishing a fact about a variable. In the algorithm, all assignments have the form:

Set *variable* to *expression*

That is, an assignment consists of an expression to be computed and a variable that is to take on the value of the expression.

"It is very important to notice, Watson, that the values of variables may change as the program progresses. We use assignments to elaborate progressive states of knowledge about the data. Consider, for example, the two statements from my algorithm:

Set MINS_TO_HIGH_TIDE to (TODAYS_DATE - 1) * MINS_PER_DAY
Set MINS_TO_HIGH_TIDE to MINS_TO_HIGH_TIDE +
                          TIDE_HR * MINS_PER_HR

The first we have already discussed. When it is evaluated, the variable MINS_TO_HIGH_TIDE will be given a value consisting of the number of minutes from the beginning of the month until midnight last night. In the second assignment, the variable is revised to include also the number of minutes that have elapsed today. Notice especially that the expression in the second assignment contains the variable MINS_TO_HIGH_TIDE, the same variable whose value is to be changed.

"Here," he said, pushing a sheet of paper my way, "I have already written out my algorithm in the language of a Pascal programme. You shouldn't find it at all difficult to decipher."

I studied it for a moment. It was quite a short programme, and I have replicated it here as Exhibit 4.2.

"I take it that this curious symbol that resembles a colon followed by an equal sign denotes assignment in the Pascal language?"

"Precisely," replied my companion. "In Pascal we need only say:

```
MINSTOHIGHTIDE := (TODAYSDATE - 1) * MINSPERDAY
```

"I must admit, however, that the elements of originality and enterprise are not too common to the scientific world. The symbol is, indeed, distinctly unimaginative."

"Now, Watson, let us enter the data to the programme by using this telegraph arrangement. We shall soon have our answer."

It was a brisk walk in the bracing sea air to the telegraph office. In a matter of minutes our connections were established. Holmes then carefully telegraphed the numbers

28   11   3   9

representing

July 2̲8̲   1̲1̲.00 am   July 3̲   9̲.00 am

After a few minutes the results of his programme came clacking back at us over the telegraph. He began scribbling down numbers on a small pad of paper and finally tore the sheet loose.

"Precisely what I had expected," he exclaimed. "There have been nearly forty-eight and a half tide cycles between today's high tide and that fateful episode. This means, Watson, that the tide then differed by roughly half a cycle, which places the mysterious bathing machine well out of reach of the sea. Low tide, Watson! We can turn this little bit of information over to Lestrade and save these poor attendants from any further humiliation."

"But how does this possibly remove them from suspicion?" I asked.

"Elementary, Watson. If the attendants had drowned her, the incoming tide would have washed her body onto the shore to be discovered later. But it was not discovered. No, Watson, there is more to it, as her family has suggested privately. The Baron Whitelsey is known as a cruel man who abused his wife; I venture to say that the Baroness swam out to sea and made good an escape with the help of a confederate. Let us wish her well in her new life. I doubt that she will be seen on these shores again."

```
program TIDES (INPUT, OUTPUT);

{  -- This programme reads in the day of the month and the hour of
   -- high tide, as well as the day and hour of some earlier event.
   -- Times must be given in 24-hour form; for instance
   -- 3 p.m. is given as 18.
   -- The programme computes the number of tide cycles during the
   -- elapsed time. }

   const
      MINSPERHR        =   60;
      MINSPERDAY       = 1440;
      MINSPERTIDECYCLE =  745;
   var
      TODAYSDATE,     TIDEHR,
      EVENTDATE,      EVENTHR,
      MINSTOHIGHTIDE, MINSTOEVENT, ELAPSEDTIME: INTEGER;

      TIDECYCLES: REAL;

begin
   READ (TODAYSDATE, TIDEHR, EVENTDATE, EVENTHR);

   MINSTOHIGHTIDE := (TODAYSDATE - 1) * MINSPERDAY;
   MINSTOHIGHTIDE := MINSTOHIGHTIDE + TIDEHR * MINSPERHR;

   MINSTOEVENT    := (EVENTDATE - 1) * MINSPERDAY;
   MINSTOEVENT    := MINSTOEVENT + EVENTHR * MINSPERHR;

   ELAPSEDTIME    := MINSTOHIGHTIDE - MINSTOEVENT;
   TIDECYCLES     := ELAPSEDTIME / MINSPERTIDECYCLE;

   WRITE ('THE NUMBER OF TIDE CYCLES IS', TIDECYCLES)
end.
```

Exhibit 4.2 *Holmes's Programme for Calculating Tides*

4.1   Variables and Assignment

Central to all programs is the notion of a variable and the related concept of assignment. A variable is a name for a piece of information that varies as the program progresses. An assignment is an action that changes this information.

The dominant feature of Holmes's program for calculating tides is the use of names to refer to values needed in the course of the computations. This is a characteristic of all computer programs. For example, we may have:

```
TODAYSDATE - 1     { the value of TODAYSDATE minus 1 }
2 * VELOCITY       { 2 times the value of VELOCITY }
SIN(PI/4)          { the sine of the value of pi divided by 4 }
```

In each of these forms a piece of information (for example, some number of days) is associated with a name (for example, TODAYSDATE). This piece of information is called a *value*. This value is not given directly (for example, the value may be 28), but instead is referred to by a name (for example, TODAYSDATE). This name is called a *variable*, since the value associated with the name will be established or changed during the course of the program.

An *assignment* is the means by which we establish or change the value of a variable. For example, we may have:

```
NUMSUSPECTS := 0
NUMSUSPECTS := NUMSUSPECTS + 2
MINSTOHIGHTIDE := (TODAYSDATE - 1) * MINSPERDAY
```

In the first case, the value of NUMSUSPECTS is set to zero. In the second case, the value of NUMSUSPECTS is incremented by two. In the third case, the value of MINSTOHIGHTIDE is set to the value computed by the given formula.

The point of all of these assignments is identical. At each step in our program we have established certain facts about the state of our knowledge. An assignment reflects the fact that we have established a new state of knowledge.

The general form for writing all assignment statements is simple:

variable := expression

When this statement is acted upon by the computer, it means the following:

1.   Compute the value of the expression
2.   Then associate this value with the variable

While the rules are simple, you must be careful to obey them precisely.

Consider the following sequence of assignment statements, where the variables MYSCORE and YOURSCORE have initially unspecified values.

```
MYSCORE    := 0;
    { value of MYSCORE is 0, YOURSCORE is unspecified }
YOURSCORE := 1;
    { value of MYSCORE is 0, YOURSCORE is 1 }
MYSCORE    := 2;
    { value of MYSCORE is 2, YOURSCORE is 1 }
YOURSCORE := MYSCORE;
    { value of MYSCORE is 2, YOURSCORE is 2 }
YOURSCORE := 2 * MYSCORE
    { value of MYSCORE is 2, YOURSCORE is 4 }
```

We see here that each statement in the sequence is executed step by step. Furthermore, each assignment establishes a new value for only one variable.

The assignment

```
NUMSUSPECTS := NUMSUSPECTS + 2
```

given above perhaps deserves a little special attention. Here the variable whose value is being set also occurs in the expression given on the right side of the statement. This causes no problems. First, the value of the expression is obtained; then this value is assigned to the variable, just as before. This statement has exactly the same effect as the following sequence:

```
VALUE       := NUMSUSPECTS + 2;
NUMSUSPECTS := VALUE
```

In both cases, the value of NUMSUSPECTS has been incremented by two.

4.2   Declaring Variables

Pascal, like all programming languages, has a number of strictly applied rules regarding the use of variables. One such rule is that all variables used in the program must be stated in a *declaration.* A declaration is a statement of some fact that will be true throughout your program. For variables, the declaration states the name of the variable and the type of information it represents.

For example, consider the following declaration:

```
NUMSUSPECTS: INTEGER;
```

This declaration introduces a variable named NUMSUSPECTS, and specifies that the information it represents will be an integer number. This last fact is particularly important. It means that whenever you attempt to give the variable a value, the computer will check that the value is indeed an integer number. If you try to assign the variable some other type of value, the computer will complain. Do not be alarmed by this fact—it should be precisely what you want. If the computer does not complain, you can be assured that whenever you refer to this variable, it will stand for an integer number.

Consider next the following declaration:

```
TIDECYCLES: REAL;
```

This declaration is just like the declaration above except that here the variable TIDECYCLES is specified as REAL. This means that the value of the variable will always be a real number. The variables NUMSUSPECTS and TIDECYCLES are said to have different *types*. We will have more to say about types later on, but for now we make the following points. A type tells the computer what kind of value a variable can hold. Once the type of a variable has been specified, it is only possible to assign values of the same type. Thus you cannot assign a real number to an integer variable; that is, you cannot say:

```
NUMSUSPECTS := 12.6    { erroneous assignment }
```

This is quite reasonable, since 12.6 is a rather unusual number of suspects. When we get to other types of data, we will see that this rule is rigidly enforced.

Pascal, however, allows you one exception. You can write

```
TIDECYCLES := 10
```

and Pascal takes this to mean the following: the integer 10 is converted to an equivalent real number, and this real value is assigned to the variable TIDECYCLES. Note that this is the same as saying:

```
TIDECYCLES := 10.0
```

As good practice, it is best to assign explicit real values to real variables, just as you must assign explicit integer values to integer variables.

In most programs you will have many variables, and many of these will be of the same type. Pascal lets you declare several variables at one go by simply giving the list of variables followed by their common type. For example, we may write

```
TODAYSDATE, HIGHTIDEHR, ELAPSEDTIME:  INTEGER;
```

which declares three variables of type INTEGER.

One last little rule. In Pascal, all of the declarations for variables must be grouped together before the statement part of the program. Further, all of the variable declarations must be preceded by the keyword var. Thus, a complete list of variable declarations for a program might look like:

```
var
    TODAYSDATE,     TIDEHR,
    EVENTDATE,      EVENTHR,
    MINSTOHIGHTIDE, MINSTOEVENT, ELAPSEDTIME:  INTEGER;

    TIDECYCLES:  REAL;
```

4.3   Declaring Constants

While a variable is a piece of information that varies as a program progresses, we often have pieces of information that are known before the program is started and that do not change as the program progresses. Such known facts can be stated with a *constant declaration*.

Consider the following constant declaration:

```
MINSPERHR = 60;
```

This declaration specifies a constant named MINSPERHR, whose value is fixed at 60. The constant declaration establishes the association between the name MINSPERHR and its value. Obviously we will not be wanting to change the number of mintues per hour during execution of the program.

More generally, a constant declaration can be used to name any value that is known when the program is written. Just as for variable declarations, all constant declarations must be preceded by a keyword, in this case, the keyword const. For example, we may have the constant declarations:

```
const
    MINSPERHR = 60;     { the number of minutes per hour }
    UNKNOWN   = 0;      { standard value for unknown items }
    PI = 3.14159;       { the value of pi }
    MAXTAXRATE = 70.0;  { the maximum rate of tax }
```

In all of these constant declarations, a name is associated with a simple integer or real number. Throughout the program the name and the number can be used interchangeably.

Just as for declared variables, the name of a constant has a defined type. A constant's type is simply that of the value given in the constant declaration. For example, MINSPERHR is of type INTEGER and PI is of type REAL. The group of constant declarations for a given program must precede the group of variable declarations.

Before going on, one other point. Character strings can also be given a name using a constant declaration, as in:

```
const
   BLANK   = ' ';
   HISNAME = 'MYCROFT';
```

These names can be used in WRITE statements, such as

```
WRITE ('HIS NAME IS', BLANK, HISNAME)
```

which prints

```
HIS NAME IS MYCROFT
```

just as you would expect.

4.4 Expressions

In every program we want to compute some results. To do this we need to write expressions. An *expression* is a formula for computing a value.

Consider the very simple expression:

```
TODAYSDATE - 1
```

This expression subtracts one from the existing value of the variable TODAYSDATE. In this expression, we have a subtraction *operator* and two *operands*, TODAYSDATE and 1. Next, consider the expression:

```
ELAPSEDTIME / MINSPERTIDECYCLE
```

Here we have a division operator and two operands, ELAPSEDTIME and MINSPERTIDECYCLE. The value of the expression is the real number that is the quotient of the two values.

Both of these expressions illustrate properties that are common to all expressions. First, an expression contains some special symbols like + and / called *operators*. Second, the operators are applied to the values of the *operands*. The operands may be numbers, variables, constants, or other parenthesized expressions. Third, when an operator is applied to operands, a result is computed and this result has a given type. In the first expression above, an integer result is computed; in the second, a real result is computed.

Table 4.1 lists all of the arithmetic operators in Pascal, along with the types of their operands and the type of the result. With

```
+  -  *
```

you may combine integer values with real values. The type of the result will be a real number if either of the operands is a real number, and an integer number otherwise. For example,

```
PI + 2
```

is the same as:

```
PI + 2.0
```

In both cases, the result is a real number.

TABLE 4.1   *Arithmetic Operations in Pascal*

Operations with Two Operands

Operator	Operation	Type of Operands	Type of Result
+	addition	INTEGER or REAL	INTEGER or REAL
–	subtraction	INTEGER or REAL	INTEGER or REAL
*	multiplication	INTEGER or REAL	INTEGER or REAL
/	real division	INTEGER or REAL	REAL
div	integer division with truncation	INTEGER	INTEGER
mod	remainder after integer division	INTEGER	INTEGER

Operations with One Operand

Operator	Operation	Type of Operand	Type of Result
+	identity	INTEGER or REAL	INTEGER or REAL
–	sign inversion	INTEGER or REAL	INTEGER or REAL

The operators div and mod deserve a special note. The operator div gives the integer part of the result when one integer is divided by another. The operator mod (for modulo) gives the corresponding remainder. For example, we may have:

```
7 div 2    { value is 3 }
7 mod 2    { value is 1 }
```

These little operators are quite handy. For example, suppose you are standing in a train station and the time on the clock is 1432. In more familiar notation, you take this as 2 hours and 32 minutes p.m. How would you get this in Pascal? You would write something like:

```
HOURS := TRAINTIME div 100;
MINS  := TRAINTIME mod 100
```

This determines the number of hours and the number of minutes in the given train time. Furthermore, if you know that the number of hours is greater than 12 (for example, 14), you can write

```
PMHOURS := HOURS mod 12
```

to compute the corresponding p.m. hours.

As indicated in Table 4.1, plus and minus may be used with a single operand. This is allowed only at the beginning of an expression, as in:

```
XCOORDINATE := -10.0;
YCOORDINATE := +10.0
```

Of course, you will often want to write expressions with several operands and operators, just as you do in conventional arithmetic. For example, you may wish to write

```
(TODAYSDATE - 1) * MINSPERDAY
```

or:

```
TOTALCASH + DEPOSITS - WITHDRAWALS - EMBEZZLEMENT
```

To do things like this you have to remember a few rules. The rules are:

■ Parenthesized operands are evaluated before unparenthesized operands.

■ The operators *, / , div, and mod are applied before - and +.

■ Otherwise, evaluation proceeds in textual order from left to right.

These rules are intended to make the writing of expressions easier. Thus if you write,

```
1 + NUMWIDGETS*2
```

and NUMWIDGETS is 3, the result is 7 (which is what you want) and not 8.

To make sure that you have these rules straight, consider the following pairs of expressions. The expression on the left will give the same value as the expression on the right.

```
1 + 2 + 3      (1 + 2) + 3       { value is 6 }
1 - 2 - 3      (1 - 2) - 3       { value is -4 }
1 + 2 * 3      1 + (2 * 3)       { value is 7 }
1 * 2 + 3      (1 * 2) + 3       { value is 5 }
- 1 - 2 - 3    ((-1) - 2) - 3    { value is -6 }
```

This may look a bit tricky, but in normal practice you should have no problem. With proper spacing you can write your expressions like

```
1 + NUMWIDGETS*2
```

rather than

```
1+NUMWIDGETS * 2
```

so that you and the reader will have no doubt as to what you mean.

Furthermore, whenever there is a problem, just put parentheses in your expressions to make your intent exactly clear. For example, it is probably not a good idea to write something like:

```
- A - B - C
```

You can make things look a lot better simply by writing

```
- (A + B + C)
```

which leaves no mystery for the reader.

Using Predefined Functions as Operands

Consider the expression:

```
SQRT(5.0) + 1.0
```

This expression adds 1.0 to the square root of 5.0. Our interest here centers on the SQRT in:

```
SQRT(5.0)
```

In mathematical parlance, SQRT is called a *function*, in this case a function to compute the square root of its argument. In Pascal there are a number of such functions that are predefined in the language. For example, you can compute the absolute value of a number or its mathematical sine. A list of all of these functions is given in Table 4.2. To use these functions, you simply write the name of the function followed by its argument enclosed in parentheses, as shown above. All of this works just as you would expect and should cause no problems.

TABLE 4.2 *Predefined Arithmetic Functions in Pascal*

(x denotes an expression whose value is either integer or real, unless stated otherwise.)

ODD(x)	True if the value of x is an odd number, and false otherwise. The value of x must be an integer.
ABS(x)	The absolute value of x. If the value of x is an integer, the result is an integer; otherwise, the result is a real number.
SQR(x)	The square of x. If the value of x is an integer, the result is an integer; otherwise, the result is a real number.
SQRT(x)	The positive square root of x, where x must be non-negative. Result is a real number.
SIN(x)	The sine of x, where x is expressed in radians. Result is a real number.
COS(x)	The cosine of x, where x is expressed in radians. Result is a real number.
LN(x)	The natural logarithm of x, where the value of x must be greater than zero. Result is a real number.
EXP(x)	The value of the base of natural logarithm raised to the power of x. Result is a real number.
ARCTAN(x)	The principal value (in radians) of the arctangent of x.
TRUNC(x)	The value of x (which must be a real number) truncated to its integer part. For example, TRUNC(4.6) is 4 and TRUNC(-4.6) is -4.
ROUND(x)	The value of x (which must be a real number) rounded to the nearest integer. For example, ROUND(4.62) is 5 and ROUND(-4.6) is -5. If x is zero or positive, ROUND(x) is equal to TRUNC(x + 0.5); for negative x, ROUND(x) is equal to TRUNC(x - 0.5).

Before going on, we must mention two important rules that you have to remember when you write an expression. The first is that if you use a variable in an expression it must already have been assigned a value. If it hasn't, the computer will not know what to do; and, most likely, your program will come to a stop or given bizarre results. For example, if you write

```
NUMSUSPECTS + 1
```

and you have not already given a value to NUMSUSPECTS, the result will be trouble.

Second, you must be careful when writing expressions containing both integer and real number values. For example, if INTVALUE is an integer variable and REALVALUE is a real variable, then

```
INTVALUE + REALVALUE
```

will give a real result. Watch out for this, for you cannot say:

```
INTVALUE := INTVALUE + REALVALUE  { -- erroneous }
```

If you want to assign a real value to an integer variable, you have to use one of the functions TRUNC or ROUND given in Table 4.2. Thus you can say something like

```
INTVALUE := TRUNC(INTVALUE + REALVALUE)
```

to truncate the real result computed by the addition of INTVALUE and REALVALUE.

4.5 Reading and Writing Information

In almost every program you write, you are going to want to read in some data and print some results. Doing this is easy. Consider the statement:

```
READ (TODAYSDATE, TIDEHR, EVENTDATE, EVENTHR)
```

When the computer executes this statement, it will ask you for four values. You may give it something like

```
28   11   3   9
```

or something like:

```
28    11
 3     9
```

When you give it these values, the four variables will be assigned the values that you typed in. This is exactly the same as writing

```
TODAYSDATE  :=  28;
TIDEHR  :=  11;
EVENTDATE   :=  3;
EVENTHR     :=  9
```

in your program. That is, reading data is exactly the same as assigning values to variables.

The general rule for reading data is thus quite simple. You simply use the name READ followed by the parenthesized list of variables whose values you want to read.

For printing your results, the process is just the opposite. For example, consider the statement:

```
WRITE (TIDECYCLES)
```

When the computer processes this statement, it will simply print the value of TIDECYCLES. If you want, you can say:

```
WRITE ('THE NUMBER OF TIDE CYCLES IS', TIDECYCLES)
```

In this case, your program will write the characters THE NUMBER OF TIDE CYCLES IS followed by the value of the variable of TIDECYCLES.

More generally, you may print out any character string or the value of any expression, provided that each of these items is separated by commas. Thus all of the following statements are acceptable:

```
WRITE ('SOME INTRODUCTORY MESSAGE')
WRITE ('YOU CAN PRINT CHARACTERS LIKE $ AND +')
WRITE (ONEVARIABLE, ANOTHER, ANDANOTHER)
WRITE ('PI divided by 4 is ', PI/4)
```

There is an old computer adage: you read variables and write expressions. It really is just about that simple.

Some closing details. When you use READ, the computer will ignore any line boundaries and keep reading until it gets the input values it wants. When you use WRITE, the computer will print the output values so as to put several values on a line. The computer has its own way of printing your data, and the results may not always be nice to look at.

If you want to control the situation a bit more, you can also use READLN and WRITELN. With

```
READLN (TODAYSDATE, TIDEHR);
READLN (EVENTDATE, EVENTHR)
```

the computer will expect EVENTDATE and EVENTHR on a new line, and then advance to the next line before reading any more data. With

```
WRITELN ('THE NUMBER OF TIDE CYCLES IS', TIDECYCLES)
```

the computer will print the message and value on a single line, and then advance to the next line before writing any more results.

One handy little detail. If you say

```
WRITE ('NUMBER OF SUSPECTS IS', NUMSUSPECTS)
```

the computer will normally use eight or ten spaces for printing the value of NUMSUSPECTS. Thus your output may look like:

```
NUMBER OF SUSPECTS IS          4
```

To make things nicer, you can say:

```
WRITE('THE NUMBER OF SUSPECTS IS', NUMSUSPECTS:2)
```

The 2 in

```
NUMSUSPECTS:2
```

tells the computer that two spaces are to be used for printing the value of NUMSUSPECTS. Thus your output will be:

```
THE NUMBER OF SUSPECTS IS 4
```

For printing real numbers, if you say

```
WRITE ('THE NUMBER OF TIDE CYCLES IS', TIDECYCLES)
```

the computer will print something like:

```
THE NUMBER OF TIDE CYCLES IS 1.463100000000E+01
```

However, if you say

```
WRITE ('THE NUMBER OF TIDE CYCLES IS', TIDECYCLES:9)
```

the computer will print

```
THE NUMBER OF TIDE CYCLES IS 1.46E+01
```

and if you say

```
WRITE ('THE NUMBER OF TIDE CYCLES IS', TIDECYCLES:6:2)
```

the computer will print:

```
THE NUMBER OF TIDE CYCLES IS 14.61
```

In this last case, conventional decimal notation is used. The 6 in 6:2 means the value will occupy six character positions. The 2 in 6:2 means two digits will be given to the right of the decimal point.

We will take this up in much greater detail in Chapter 11, but this should suffice for most cases. The exact behavior of input and output depends upon the Pascal system you are using, and no doubt you will have to check your manual.

Many of the ideas we have talked about in this chapter are illustrated in the program of Example 4.1. This program reads in six integer values, representing the number of pennies, nickels, and so forth and prints the value of the coins in dollars and cents. The program, like all of the others in this book, was written with a great concern for you, the reader. You see that when programs are well written, the need for remembering the many detailed conventions of Pascal is greatly diminished.

```
program COUNTCHANGE (INPUT, OUTPUT);

{   -- This program reads in six integer values, respectively
    -- representing the number of pennies, nickels, dimes, quarters,
    -- half-dollars, and silver dollars in coinage.
    -- The program outputs the total value of the coins in dollars
    -- and cents. }

    var
        NUMPENNIES,  NUMNICKELS,  NUMDIMES,
        NUMQUARTERS, NUMHALVES,   NUMDOLLARS,
        TOTALCHANGE, DOLLARS,     CENTS:    INTEGER;

begin
    TOTALCHANGE := 0;

    READ (NUMPENNIES);
    TOTALCHANGE := TOTALCHANGE + 01*NUMPENNIES;

    READ (NUMNICKELS);
    TOTALCHANGE := TOTALCHANGE + 05*NUMNICKELS;

    READ (NUMDIMES);
    TOTALCHANGE := TOTALCHANGE + 10*NUMDIMES;

    READ (NUMQUARTERS);
    TOTALCHANGE := TOTALCHANGE + 25*NUMQUARTERS;

    READ (NUMHALVES);
    TOTALCHANGE := TOTALCHANGE + 50*NUMHALVES;

    READ (NUMDOLLARS);
    TOTALCHANGE := TOTALCHANGE + 100*NUMDOLLARS;

    DOLLARS := TOTALCHANGE div 100;
    CENTS   := TOTALCHANGE mod 100;
    WRITE ('CHANGE IS ', DOLLARS:2, ' DOLLARS AND ', CENTS:2, ' CENTS.')
end.
```

Example 4.1   *Counting Change*

V

A Study In Cigar Ash

OU see, Watson," remarked Sherlock Holmes, as we sat together one frosty evening considering a recent report that the missing Baroness of Whitelsey had been seen in Vienna, "I attribute much of my professional success to the fact that I regard detection as a science as well as an art; and unlike most of my colleagues, I have never regarded it as drudgery. Detection takes its purest form as deductive reasoning and is comparable only to mathematics in its elegance and intellectual challenge. For this reason, the Analytical Engine, based as it is upon mathematical principles, has seemed a most attractive tool for my labours."

"What is your next plan for using the Engine?" I asked, sensing that my friend was ready to launch some new idea.

"My plan, Watson, is to use this remarkable Engine as a storehouse for some of the minutiae that clutter my mind. Take for instance my monograph, 'Upon the Distinction Between the Ashes of the Various Tobaccos,' " he said, gesturing to a dusty volume that lay before us on the table.

"In this treatise I have described and classified a hundred and forty types of cigarette, cigar, and pipe tobaccos, with coloured plates illustrating the various sorts of ashes. Although I took a special interest in retaining such details as, say, the exact appearance of MacDuffy versus Lunkah cigar ash, most investigators would lack the patience to do so; and I cannot say I blame them.

"The brain is after all like an attic of vast but limited capacity that we fill with whatever matter we deem important for the future. Since the walls of this attic cannot be stretched like India rubber, as we amass more and more information some of the old is jostled out to make room for the new. It would be helpful if we had a device to remember vast quantities of data for us and to supply us with information pertaining to these data whenever we so request. I claim, Watson, that the Analytical Engine is wonderfully suited to this task.

"As an exercise to test my idea, I have prepared a table listing the properties of the ten most commonly smoked cigars in London."

Holmes's table of ash properties is given here.

CIGAR TYPE.	TEXTURE.	COLOUR.	PARTICLES.	NICOTINE.
Espanada	Caked	Dark	No	++
Heritage	Flaky	Light Grey	No	++
Latino	Varied	Dark	Yes	+
Londoner	Caked	Brown Tint	No	++
Lunkah	Granular	Dark Grey	No	++
MacDuffy	Flaky	Dark Grey	No	++
Old Wood	Varied	Brown Tint	Varied	+++
Top Hat	Caked	Dark Grey	No	++
Trichinopoly	Flaky	Dark	No	++
West Country	Fluffy	Light Grey	No	++

While I studied his document, Holmes walked over to the fire and took down a small brass box from the mantlepiece. This he opened, and quietly he smelled the single cigar which it contained.

"I should like to design a programme that would identify the cigars bearing certain specified ash characteristics. Moreover, if the specified characteristics did not match any of these ten cigars, the Engine should indicate this so that I could then research the matter myself."

"I take it, then, that there are particular characteristics of this programme that are of interest?" I queried, for I still had little experience in constructing programmes.

"Precisely, Watson," replied my friend. "The central issue is the need to make decisions and take appropriate actions as the consequence of a given condition. Of course, this is a very common problem in the work of detection.

"There are any number of combinations we can make of the various conditions. We may specify that a certain action be taken under a certain set of circumstances, such as:

if texture is caked then
  — *perform action A*

Another situation that arises is that of two possible actions, with the choice between them depending upon a single condition. For instance,

if texture is caked then
  — *perform action A*
else
  — *perform action B*

Finally, we may be faced with a number of possible courses of action, with our choice depending upon one of several conditions:

if texture is caked then
  — *perform action A*
else if texture is flaky then
  — *perform action B*
else if texture is granular then
  — *perform action C*
else (if none of the conditions above are met)
  — *perform action D*

"I understand, Holmes, but how do you solve this problem in terms comprehensible to the Analytical Engine?"

"Simple, Watson," said Holmes. "All we do is organize the decisions in the form of a consistent algorithm and then translate the algorithm into the machine's language. Here I have listed all the choices of properties for a cigar. Notice that the normal cigar has no

"HE SMELLED THE SINGLE CIGAR WHICH IT CONTAINED."

particles and has a nicotine content marked with two plus signs. Furthermore, there are two basic kinds of cigar ash. There is Stock 1, which is flaky or caked, and Stock 2, whose characteristics are fluffy or granular."

Holmes's ash classification is reproduced here as follows :—

Colour . . . . Dark, Dark Grey, Light Grey, Brown Tint
Texture . . . . Flaky, Caked, Granular, Fluffy
Particles . . . . No, Yes
Nicotine . . . . +, ++, +++

```
Normal Strength . . . . . ++, no particles
Stock 1 Cigar     . . . . . Flaky or Caked
Stock 2 Cigar     . . . . . Granular or Fluffy
```

"My strategy," Holmes continued, "is to command the Engine to read a list of properties pertaining to cigar ash. The programme will then determine whether the cigar is of normal strength and whether it is of Stock 1 or Stock 2. With these questions settled, it will then be able to determine whether the cigar is one of the ten types listed in the table. If so, it will name the cigar; if not, it will report this and merely indicate the cigar's strength or class."

Holmes then produced his algorithm, which is given in Exhibit 5.1. It seemed entirely clear, and I followed his logic almost instantly.

"But surely, Holmes, the Engine does not recognise the properties of cigar ash. How could the Engine distinguish between those with flaky and those with granular texture?"

"Very true, Watson. It is up to the programmer to distinguish the properties of cigar ash and then interpret this information for the Engine in terms it will understand. The distinctive properties will be ciphered as numbers and read by the device in this form. Thus, for example, I shall use 1 for flaky, 2 for caked, 3 for granular, and 4 for fluffy. The Engine will read numbers corresponding to each of the properties TEXTURE, COLOUR, PARTICLES, and NICOTINE, respectively, as I shall show you."

Holmes thereupon produced a sheet of paper and sketched the following example:

```
Sample Input:  1  1  1  2
Sample Output: CIGAR IS A TRICHINOPOLY
```

"They say, Watson, that genius is an infinite capacity for taking pains. It is a bad definition, but it does apply to programming. What relief the Analytical Engine will bring us!" he remarked. "I propose to devote some years to the composition of a text which shall present the whole art of detection and the special uses of the Analytical Engine into a single volume."

"A massive undertaking," I replied. "Surely, Holmes, this will be your greatest contribution to science and humanity."

A flush of colour sprang to my companion's cheeks, and he bowed slightly, like the master dramatist who receives the homage of his audience. The same singularly proud and reserved nature that turned away with disdain from popular notoriety was capable of being moved to its depths by spontaneous wonder and praise from a friend.

Definitions:

TEXTURE	:	a texture of ash
COLOUR	:	a colour of ash
PARTICLES	:	an indication of particles
NICOTINE	:	a result of a nicotine test
STOCK	:	a class of cigar
NORMALITY	:	an indication of particles and nicotine

Algorithm:

Read TEXTURE, COLOUR, PARTICLES, NICOTINE

If TEXTURE = FLAKY or TEXTURE = CAKED then
   set STOCK to 1
else
   set STOCK to 2

If NICOTINE = ++ and PARTICLES = NO then
   set NORMALITY to NORMAL
else
   set NORMALITY to ABNORMAL

If NORMALITY = NORMAL and STOCK = 1 then
   if COLOUR = DARK and TEXTURE = FLAKY then
      write 'CIGAR IS A TRICHINOPOLY'
   else if COLOUR = DARK and TEXTURE = CAKED then
      write 'CIGAR IS AN ESPANADA'
   else if COLOUR = DARK_GREY and TEXTURE = FLAKY then
      write 'CIGAR IS A MACDUFFY'
   else if COLOUR = DARK_GREY and TEXTURE = CAKED then
      write 'CIGAR IS A TOP HAT'
   else if COLOUR = LIGHT_GREY and TEXTURE = FLAKY then
      write 'CIGAR IS A HERITAGE'
   else if COLOUR = BROWN_TINT and TEXTURE = CAKED then
      write 'CIGAR IS A LONDONER'
   else
      write '*** UNIDENTIFIED NORMAL CIGAR OF STOCK 1'

If NORMALITY = NORMAL and STOCK = 2 then
   if COLOUR = DARK_GREY and TEXTURE = GRANULAR then
      write 'CIGAR IS A LUNKAH'
   else if COLOUR = LIGHT_GREY and TEXTURE = FLUFFY then
      write 'CIGAR IS A WEST COUNTRY'
   else
      write '*** UNIDENTIFIED NORMAL CIGAR OF STOCK 2'

If NORMALITY = ABNORMAL then
   if COLOUR = BROWN_TINT and NICOTINE = +++ then
      write 'CIGAR IS AN OLD WOOD'
   else if COLOUR = DARK and NICOTINE = + and PARTICLES = YES then
      write 'CIGAR IS A LATINO'
   else
      write '*** UNIDENTIFIED ABNORMAL CIGAR'

Exhibit 5.1 *Holmes's Algorithm to Identify Cigar Ash*

As for our study of cigar ash, Holmes applied the programme shown in Exhibit 5.2 to test the Engine's performance against his own powers. I have had no keener pleasure than in following Sherlock Holmes in his professional investigations and in admiring his rapid deductions—as swift as intuitions, yet always founded on the same logical basis on which the Engine operated—with which he unravelled the many problems that were submitted to him.

```
program  IDENTIFYCIGAR (INPUT, OUTPUT);

{  -- This programme reads in four properties of cigar ash.
   -- The properties are coded as numbers.
   -- The programme attempts to identify the ash according to the
   -- properties, and prints a message giving its findings. }

   const
       DARK = 1;    DARKGREY = 2;   LIGHTGREY = 3;   BROWNTINT = 4;
       FLAKY = 1;   CAKED = 2;      GRANULAR = 3;    FLUFFY = 4;
       PLUS1 = 1;   PLUS2 = 2;      PLUS3 = 3;
       NORMAL = 1;  ABNORMAL = 2;
       NO = 1;      YES = 2;

   var
       TEXTURE, COLOUR, PARTICLES,
       NICOTINE, STOCK, NORMALITY:  INTEGER;

begin
   READ (TEXTURE, COLOUR, PARTICLES, NICOTINE);

   if (TEXTURE = FLAKY) or (TEXTURE = CAKED) then
       STOCK := 1
   else
       STOCK := 2;
```

Exhibit 5.2   *Holmes's Programme to Identify Cigar Ash*

```
    if (NICOTINE = PLUS2) and (PARTICLES = NO) then
        NORMALITY := NORMAL
    else
        NORMALITY := ABNORMAL;

    if (NORMALITY = NORMAL) and (STOCK = 1) then
        if (COLOUR = DARK) and (TEXTURE = FLAKY) then
            WRITE ('CIGAR IS A TRICHINOPOLY')
        else if (COLOUR = DARK) and (TEXTURE = CAKED) then
            WRITE ('CIGAR IS AN ESPANADA')
        else if (COLOUR = DARKGREY) and (TEXTURE = FLAKY) then
            WRITE ('CIGAR IS A MACDUFFY')
        else if (COLOUR = DARKGREY) and (TEXTURE = CAKED) then
            WRITE ('CIGAR IS A TOP HAT')
        else if (COLOUR = LIGHTGREY) and (TEXTURE = FLAKY) then
            WRITE ('CIGAR IS A HERITAGE')
        else if (COLOUR = BROWNTINT) and (TEXTURE = CAKED) then
            WRITE ('CIGAR IS A LONDONER')
        else
            WRITE ('*** UNIDENTIFIED NORMAL CIGAR OF STOCK 1');

    if (NORMALITY = NORMAL) and (STOCK = 2) then
        if (COLOUR = DARKGREY) and (TEXTURE = GRANULAR) then
            WRITE ('CIGAR IS A LUNKAH')
        else if (COLOUR = LIGHTGREY) and (TEXTURE = FLUFFY) then
            WRITE ('CIGAR IS A WEST COUNTRY')
        else
            WRITE ('*** UNIDENTIFIED NORMAL CIGAR OF STOCK 2');

    if (NORMALITY = ABNORMAL) then
        if (COLOUR = BROWNTINT) and (NICOTINE = PLUS3) then
            WRITE ('CIGAR IS AN OLD WOOD')
        else if (COLOUR = DARK) and (NICOTINE = PLUS1)
            and (PARTICLES = YES)  then
            WRITE ('CIGAR IS A LATINO')
        else
            WRITE ('*** UNIDENTIFIED ABNORMAL CIGAR')
end.
```

Exhibit 5.2 *Continued*

5.1   Compound Statements

Before moving into the area of decision making in Pascal, we pause to make note of a simple but important construct for writing programs. In previous chapters we have looked at assignment statements as well as statements to read and write data. As we have seen, these statements contain no part that is another statement.

In the discussion of decision making to follow, we will encounter new kinds of statements in which a statement may itself contain other statements. In this category we will find, for example, the *if statement*. Consider the following:

```
if (TEXTURE = FLAKY) or (TEXTURE = CAKED) then
    STOCK := 1
```

This statement, an if statement, contains another statement, an assignment statement. Both the if statement and the assignment statement are considered as a *single* statement.

Of course, there are instances where we may want to execute more than one statement after making a decision. This is achieved by means of a *compound* statement. For example, we may write:

```
if (TEXTURE = FLAKY) or (TEXTURE = CAKED) then
    begin
        STOCK := 1;
        WRITE ('STOCK 1 CIGAR')
    end
```

A compound statement has the form,

```
begin
    statement-1 ;
    statement-2 ;
      . . .
    statement-n
end
```

and is itself treated as a single statement. Each statement within the compound statement is executed in sequential order. You will have a great many uses for this simple device as we proceed.

Now let's continue with the means for making decisions in Pascal.

5.2   If Statements

The ability to make decisions is fundamental to programming. The basic mechanism for making choices in Pascal is the *if statement*. In its simplest form, there is a condition and one statement, in the following form:

```
if condition then
    statement
```

This statement means:

> If the condition is true, execute the given statement; otherwise do nothing.

Normally, an if statement will appear in a sequence of statements. As for any statement, after execution, the next statement is processed. For example,

```
statement-1;
if condition then
    statement-2;
statement-3
```

means:

1. Execute statement 1.

2. Execute the if statement; that is, if the condition is true, execute statement 2.

3. Execute statement 3.

Notice here that the if statement is itself considered a single statement. Thus, we may write something like:

```
if (NORMALITY = NORMAL) and (STOCK = 1) then
    if (COLOR = DARK) and (TEXTURE = FLAKY) then
        WRITE ('CIGAR IS A TRICHINOPOLY')
```

This should not cause any confusion, for this statement has the form,

```
if (NORMALITY = NORMAL) and (STOCK = 1) then
    statement
```

where in this case the statement following the keyword then is itself an if statement.

This ability to include one statement within another has far-reaching possibilities in Pascal. While the basic mechanism is extremely simple, we can produce rather elaborate effects, as in Holmes's program to identify cigar ash.

In the examples above, the if statements have a single condition and a single statement. An if statement may also have an *else part*, in the form:

```
if condition then
    statement-1
else
    statement-2
```

This simply means:

> If the condition is true, execute statement 1; otherwise execute statement 2.

For example, we may write:

```
if (TEXTURE = FLAKY) or (TEXTURE = CAKED) then
    STOCK := 1
else
    STOCK := 2
```

Here the value of the variable STOCK is set to 1 or 2, depending upon the truth or falsity of the condition. As always, after executing the if statement we simply proceed to the following statement.

Finally, we may generalize the ideas above to include multiple conditions. For example, consider the if statement:

```
if (COLOUR = DARK) and (TEXTURE = FLAKY) then
    WRITE ('CIGAR IS A TRICHINOPOLY')
else
    if (COLOUR = DARK) and (TEXTURE = CAKED) then
        WRITE ('CIGAR IS AN ESPANADA')
    else
        WRITE ('*** UNIDENTIFIED NORMAL CIGAR OF STOCK 1')
```

This statement has the form:

```
if condition-1 then
    statement-1
else
    if condition-2 then
        statement-2
    else
        statement-3
```

This all means the following:

> If condition 1 is true, execute statement 1;
> If condition 1 is false but condition 2 is true, execute statement 2;
> Otherwise (conditions 1 and 2 are both false), execute statement 3.

Notice here that this statement is really an if statement with an else part, with the same meaning as the if statement given before.

Each example above follows the same basic pattern: depending on one or more conditions, a given action takes place. Thus each of the examples falls into one of the following forms:

1. condition   → action A

2. condition   → action A
   else   → action B

3. condition-1   → action A
   condition-2   → action B
   else   → action C

and so on. In all cases, execution continues after the condition-action pairs.

Normally such cascades of condition-action pairs are written in the form:

```
if condition-1 then
    statement-1
else if condition-2 then
    statement-2
...
else
    statement-n
```

For example, we have:

```
if (COLOUR = DARK) and (TEXTURE = FLAKY) then
    WRITE ('CIGAR IS A TRICHINOPOLY')
else if (COLOUR = DARK) and (TEXTURE = CAKED) then
    WRITE ('CIGAR IS AN ESPANADA')
else
    WRITE ('*** UNIDENTIFIED NORMAL CIGAR OF STOCK 1')
```

This kind of scheme will be used throughout.

5.3 Conditions

Execution of an if statement depends on the truth or falsity of some given condition. We now turn to the rules for writing conditions in Pascal. These rules are analogous to the rules for writing expressions, except that in all cases, evaluation of a condition yields one of the values TRUE or FALSE.

The simplest of all conditions is the testing of values to see if they are equal. For example, we may write:

```
if STOCK = 1 then
if TEXTURE = FLAKY then
if ROOM[SUSPECT] = 14 then
if (NUMCIGARS + 1 = MAXNUMCIGARS) then
```

In each of these constructs the condition has the form:

expression-1 = expression-2

These conditions bring up two general rules in Pascal:

1. A condition always evaluates to TRUE or FALSE.

2. The type of the result, TRUE or FALSE, is said to be of type BOOLEAN.

Thus just as we may say the expression,

```
NUMCIGARS + 1
```

has a numeric value and its type is INTEGER, we say that the condition

```
TEXTURE = FLAKY
```

has a value that is either TRUE or FALSE and is of type BOOLEAN. The term BOOLEAN is named after George Boole, the English mathematician who developed symbolic logic.

Testing for the equality of two values is not the only operation we can perform in conditions. Table 5.1 lists several other operators that can be used in forming conditions. For example, to see if one value is less than or equal to another, we may write,

```
NUMCIGARS <= 10
```

which tests to see if the value of NUMCIGARS is less than or equal to 10.

TABLE 5.1 *Operators for Writing Conditions*

Relational Operators

Operator	Operation	Type of Operands	Type of Result
= <>	equality and inequality	INTEGER or REAL	BOOLEAN
< <= > >=	ordering	INTEGER or REAL	BOOLEAN
in	membership	left: INTEGER right: set of integers	BOOLEAN

Logical Operators

Operator	Operation	Type of Operands	Type of Result
and	logical and	BOOLEAN	BOOLEAN
or	logical or	BOOLEAN	BOOLEAN
not	logical negation	BOOLEAN	BOOLEAN

The operator <> appears particularly strange. This is the operator for testing for inequality. Thus, while you might be tempted to say

```
if SUSPECT ≠ COLWOODLEY then    { Illegal! }
```

which looks perfectly logical, you can't. Instead you have to write:

```
if SUSPECT <> COLWOODLEY then    { Legal }
```

The rationale here is that a < followed by a > stands for "less than or greater than" or "not equal." So much for that.

The operator in deserves a special note. This operator allows us to test whether a value is one of a range of values. For example, instead of writing,

```
if (NUMCIGARS >= 1) and (NUMCIGARS <= 10) then
```

we may write:

```
if NUMCIGARS in [1..10] then
```

The notation,

        [1..10]

stands for the range of values between one and ten. We will have more to say about this operator in later chapters when we get to other types of data.
    The condition given in,

        if (NUMCIGARS >= 1) and (NUMCIGARS <= 10) then

brings up the ability to write compound conditions. A *compound condition* consists of a sequence of relational expressions, separated by the logical operators shown in Table 5.1. For example, we may have the conditions:

        (TEXTURE = FLAKY) or (TEXTURE = CAKED)
        (STOCK = 1) and (NORMALITY = NORMAL)
        not (SUSPECT = COLWOODLEY)

This use of logical operators is quite natural and should present no problems.
    Compound conditions may involve arithmetic operators, relational operators, and logical operators. To write such conditions, the evaluation rules given in the previous chapter need expanding in order to include our new operators. In particular, operators are applied in the following order:

        1.   not
        2.   * / div mod and
        3.   + - or
        4.   = <> < > <= >= in

That is, the operator not is applied before the five operators *, /, div, mod, and and. Then come the three operators +, -, or, and so forth.
    For example, just as

        A + B * C

is equivalent to

        A + (B * C)

so too,

        A + B = C + D

is equivalent to:

        (A + B) = (C + D)

Although these examples appear innocent enough, the rules have a few anomalies that you must watch out for. For example, you *cannot* write

```
if TEXTURE = FLAKY or TEXTURE = CAKED then  { Watch Out }
```

or:

```
if A < B and C < D then   { Again, trouble }
```

The reason is that the logical operators and and or are applied *before* the relational operators. To write such expressions you have to use parentheses, as in:

```
if (TEXTURE = FLAKY) or (TEXTURE = CAKED) then
if (A < B) and (C < D) then
```

All of this means that you have to be a bit careful in writing complex conditions. One general rule should always help you.

- When in doubt, use parentheses.

If you are still unsure of the rules for writing a condition, you can always refer to the Appendix, which summarizes the grammatical rules for writing Pascal programs.

5.4 Case Statements

The if statement presented above provides a logical method for making decisions based on the truth or falsity of one or more conditions. The *case statement* provides a similar ability for making decisions, but here the action taken depends on the value of an expression.

For example, consider the case statement:

```
case DAY of
    1:  -- what to do if DAY = 1;
    2:  -- what to do if DAY = 2;
    3:  -- what to do if DAY = 3;
    4:  -- what to do if DAY = 4;
    5:  -- what to do if DAY = 5;
    6:  -- what to do if DAY = 6;
    7:  -- what to do if DAY = 7
end
```

Here we assume the integer variable DAY represents the days of the week and thus can take on one of seven values. Each alternative in the case statement determines what to do for a given value of the variable DAY. The values given before each colon (:) are called case labels, and must correspond to the possible values of the variable given after the keyword case. After each colon, you must give a statement describing the action to be taken when the value of the variable is equal to the corresponding case label.

For example, we may write:

```
case DAY of
    1:  WRITE ('TODAY IS MONDAY, START ON A NEW CASE');
    2:  WRITE ('TUESDAY, KEEP WORKING');
    3:  WRITE ('WEDNESDAY, TAKE A BREAK');
    4:  WRITE ('THURSDAY, SEE THE NEW CLIENT');
    5:  WRITE ('FRIDAY, SUMMARIZE THE FACTS');
    6:  WRITE ('SATURDAY, TRY SOMETHING NEW');
    7:  WRITE ('SUNDAY, TAKE A COMPLETE REST')
end
```

Notice here that case labels are given for every possible value of DAY. You do not always need to do this, but you will get an error if the value of DAY does not correspond to one of the case labels. Notice also that semicolons must be placed after each alternative except the last.

Now there are a few other things you should know about case statements. First, any statement, including a compound statement, can be used as an alternative. Second, several labels can prefix an alternative. Thus we could write the case alternatives

```
    1:  if DATE = HOLIDAY  then
            WRITE ('TODAY IS A HOLIDAY')
        else
            WRITE('MONDAY, START ON A NEW CASE');
```

in which the action is an if statement, or write

```
    2:  begin
            WRITE ('TUESDAY, PREPARE THE CLUES');
            WRITE ('AND INVESTIGATE ALTERNATIVES')
        end;
```

in which the action is a compound statement, or

```
    6,7:  WRITE ('TAKE A LONG BREAK')
```

in which two alternatives are combined.

One last little point. Remember the "empty" statement mentioned earlier? Yes, we can even write

```
3:  ;
```

to do nothing! This wild-looking alternative could stand a comment, so things would look better if we wrote:

```
3:  { do nothing };
```

This may look strange, but sometimes it's just what we want to do!

VI

The Adventure
of Clergyman Peter

HAT do you make of this, Watson?", asked Holmes, as he tossed a small telegram in my direction. It read :

Oxford

Must meet with you on a temporal matter of grave concern Will arrive by one o'clock today.

Peter Cowesworthy

"A temporal matter," I replied, studying the message. "I wonder what he could mean by that. I am inclined to think that the man wants your help."

"It's just after twelve now," replied Holmes. "I would say, Watson, that a matter grave enough to carry our mysterious cleric all the way from Oxford to seek my services is more of a corporeal concern than one of the spirit. I should certainly hope that my own little practice is not degenerating into an agency for clergymen to consult me concerning their next sermon. In any event, we shall soon know for certain, for I discern two gentlemen and our landlady ascending the stair."

As he spoke there came a knock on the door, after which Mrs. Hudson admitted two visitors. The elder was a man in priestly attire, a short, birdlike man with thinning white hair and nervous eyes peering from behind gold-rimmed spectacles, and obviously in considerable distress. His younger companion was a tall, lanky fellow with a bulging Adam's apple, protruding nose, and thin lips.

"Gentlemen, I am Sherlock Holmes and this is Dr. Watson, who has been my associate and helper in many matters. How may we be of service to you?"

"Oh my," replied the clergyman, somewhat startled. "This is my Deacon, Mr. Huxtable Penwether."

"Ah, yes, Mr. Penwether, I perceive that you have recently journeyed from the Midlands," observed Holmes.

"CLERGYMAN PETER COWESWORTHY."

"Oh, no, you are mistaken, sir," he said. "I have been in London this past week, on errands for the rector."

"Indeed, he has hardly been out of my sight, Mr. Holmes," observed the clergyman.

"Yes, of course," replied Holmes, as he busied himself by filling his pipe. "Well, as Watson can attest, my deductions occasionally miss their mark." With that Holmes bade our visitors over to the basket-chair and armchair beside the empty fireplace.

The clergyman had hardly settled in his chair when abruptly he sprang to his feet and exclaimed, "Mr. Holmes, if your deductions should fail in this matter we must abandon all hope! You are the only man in the whole of England who can help us. The Mazarin Bible has vanished!" With his exclamation concluded, Cowesworthy sank back into his chair.

"Yes, the Mazarin Bible," replied Holmes, "a vellum edition, is it not, a rare Schoeffer type with hand-coloured illuminations? It is a devastating loss, indeed."

Sherlock Holmes had an almost hypnotic power when he wished, and he was an accomplished master at the art of putting a humble client at his ease.

"It was taken from your rooms?" he asked.

"Often it is in my rooms, but I bring it into the church from time to time to inspire the parishioners. It was there last Sunday, but hidden carefully. No one could have known where."

"Rector, I will endeavour to assist you. Please rest assured that Watson and I will do everything within our power to recover your Mazarin Bible. Where are you staying in London, so that we may contact you and report developments as our investigation proceeds?" asked Holmes.

"We have taken two rooms at Anderson's Hotel in Fleet Street."

The next remark astonished me, for Sherlock Holmes was the least romantic of men.

"I commend a walk in Regent's Park to you. It should prove a tonic to your strain, especially on a day as fresh as this one."

When they were gone, Holmes turned to me and said, "Come quickly, Watson, we must get to Anderson's and search Penwether's room. He was surely lying. The discoloration on his boots clearly places him in Birmingham within the past few days."

We proceeded at once to Fleet Street where a sovereign for the hall porter led us quickly to Penwether's door. "I suppose that I am committing a felony," commented Holmes, as he forced the lock, "but it is just possible that I am saving a soul. There we are," he said, pushing open the door. "I don't mind confessing that I have always thought I would make a highly efficient criminal. It is certainly fortunate for society that I have chosen otherwise."

Inside the room no Bible could be found, but the missing volume did not appear to be my companion's chief concern as he occupied himself studying Penwether's soiled clothing.

Back in our rooms at Baker Street, Holmes took me deeper into his confidence.

"An excellent case for the Analytical Engine, Watson. We know that Penwether was in Birmingham and journeyed to London in a total time of four hours. Oxford is on the route, and the fastest transportation from the station there to Cowesworthy's rooms would take half an hour each way. Could Penwether have journeyed from Birmingham to London in four hours with an hour or more in Oxford?"

"But how do you know it took four hours?" I asked.

"His collar and shirt bore the grime of a long journey," said Holmes. "Allowing for an hour stop at Oxford, the amount of railway grime on his cuffs would suggest a four-hour journey. Assuming that this is the case, what do you think of our friend not taking a first-class carriage, a man of his standing?"

"Because he feared being recognised by some fellow traveller?" I suggested.

"Precisely, Watson," he replied. "Now, here I have the timetables for all of London's main-line stations, and I have arranged these in a form that the Analytical Engine can read directly."

Holmes handed me a sheet of paper to which the stations for the Birmingham-to-London timetable had been copied. As examples it had:

```
BI    0209   Birmingham
WA    2301   Warwick
OX    1524   Oxford
```

"I see that each city is given a two-letter code," I remarked. "But what are these figures?"

"Yes, Watson, each stop is coded by a two-letter abbreviation, such as BI for Birmingham; but the Engine would have difficulty interpreting these. Thus each letter of the alphabet is further coded with a number—a simple scheme in which A is represented by 01, B by 02, C by 03, and straight through the alphabet, winding up with Z as 26."

I nodded my understanding.

"Now," continued Holmes, "we enter the tables into the Engine according to this organized scheme. Look here and you will see how the stations and times are encoded. The first entry,

BI 5.10

becomes

0209 510

and thus both the city and the time may be entered as integer numbers."

I then studied Holmes's notes and the sample timetable, which are sketched in Exhibit 6.1.

"Now as you recall, our intent is to see whether it is possible to make a four-hour journey from Birmingham to London with an hour's stop in Oxford. To determine this myself, I would carefully examine the schedule for each train, searching through the timetable until I came to Oxford. I would then search for the next train to see if it makes a connection in an hour or more. And even if I found such a train, I would still have to discover how long it took to reach London and so have the length of the total journey. This is a tedious procedure involving much examination and repetitious calculation. Far better to let the Analytical Engine handle it.

"What I want as output is a table where each train is identified by a number, the length of time for a connection at Oxford to the next train, and the total journey time."

A sample sketch of Holmes's output table is given here :

DEPARTING TRAIN	OXFORD CONNECTION	TOTAL JOURNEY
---------	----------	-------
1	255	535
2	50	345
. . .	. . .	. . .

BIRMINGHAM TO LONDON TIMES, STOPPING AT OXFORD

"It has never been my habit to hide any of my methods from you, Watson," Holmes continued. "If you will permit me there are some points here that may interest you."

"Proceed, my dear Holmes."

He paused a moment. "What we need, Watson, is a way to tell the Engine to repeat the same sort of calculation over and over again. As you may remember, such repeated calculations are called *loops*. A loop must continue until the answer has been found or until some other condition has been met. Two things are needed: a means of instructing the Engine to perform a series of calculations repetitively and a means of controlling the number of repetitions."

"I say, Holmes, without the second point you would be in much the same situation as the sorcerer's apprentice who knew the magical spell to make brooms fetch pails of water, but knew not the incantation which would make them stop."

I. Sample timetable for two Birmingham-to-London trains;
    A — means no stop for the given train:

Station.	Train 1.	Train 2.
Birmingham	5.10	8.05
Warwick	5.30	8.25
Stratford	5.45	8.55
Chipping Norton.	6.15	—
Oxford	6.25	9.20
Didcot	6.40	—
Goring	6.55	—
Reading	7.15	10.05
Maidenhead	—	—
London.	7.55	10.45

II. City codes:

BI	0209	Birmingham	DI	0409	Didcot
WA	2301	Warwick	GO	0715	Goring
ST	1920	Stratford	RE	1805	Reading
CN	0314	Chipping Norton	MA	1301	Maidenhead
OX	1524	Oxford	LO	1215	London

III. Sample input, with the entries for train 1:

BI	5.10	WA	5.30	ST	5.45	CN	6.15	OX	6.25
DI	6.40	GO	6.55	RE	7.15	MA	—	LO	7.55

the input is:

0209 510	2301 530	1920 545	0314 615	1524 625
0409 640	0715 655	1805 715	1301 000	1215 755

Exhibit 6.1 *Sample Timetable and Input Representation*

"Quite so," replied Holmes. "In fact, that is just the sort of thing that often happens to beginning programmers; and, I might add, even to experienced programmers.

"There are two sorts of loops, depending on which strategy of control one employs.

"A *conditional loop* involves a set of instructions that are to be repeated until some condition is met: for example,

> As long as CITY ≠ LONDON, do the following:
>   read CITY, ARRIVAL_TIME

or

> As long as MURDERER = UNKNOWN, do the following:
>   get another clue
>   examine the clue

As you can see, Watson, when the first loop is completed, the last city read must be London. Similarly, when the second loop is completed, the identity of our murderer is no longer a mystery.

"There is also a second sort of loop called a *for loop*, involving a set of instructions that are to be repeated some fixed number of times. As an example we might say :

> For each of the next nine trains, do the following:
>   read the times of the train
>   compute the connection and journey duration

When this loop is completed, nine trains will have been processed."

I thought about this for a moment and then asked how he would keep track of how many times the loop had been repeated.

"Elementary, Watson. We have a variable that is identified with the loop and is automatically incremented each time the loop is repeated. You will see an example of this in a moment.

"Here is a sketch of my algorithm for solving our problem," he said. The sketch ran :

> Write the result table headings
> Read the times of the first train
>
> For each of the next nine trains, do the following:
>   read the times of the train
>   compute the connection and journey duration
>   print the results
>
> Write the caption for the result table

Holmes's algorithm is shown in Exhibit 6.2. I did not follow it immediately. "But Holmes," I queried, "what is the significance of the number 40?"

Definitions:

CITY   : a code for a city
TRAIN_NUM: the number of a train
CONNECTION, JOURNEY: intervals of time

START_TIME,   STOP_TIME   ARRIVAL_TIME,
NEXT_START_TIME, NEXT_STOP_TIME, NEXT_ARRIVAL_TIME: train times

Algorithm:

— Set up for first train
Write the result table headers
Read CITY, START_TIME
As long as CITY ≠ OXFORD do the following:
  read CITY, STOP_TIME
As long as CITY ≠ LONDON do the following:
  read CITY, ARRIVAL_TIME

— Handle each connecting train
Successively setting TRAIN_NUM to 2 through 10, do the following:
  read CITY, NEXT_START_TIME
  as long as CITY ≠ OXFORD do the following:
    read CITY, NEXT_STOP_TIME
  as long as CITY ≠ LONDON do the following:
    read CITY, NEXT_ARRIVAL_TIME

  set CONNECTION to NEXT_STOP_TIME - STOP_TIME
  set JOURNEY to NEXT_ARRIVAL_TIME - START_TIME

  if minutes of STOP_TIME > minutes of NEXT_STOP_TIME then
    set CONNECTION to CONNECTION - 40
  if minutes of START_TIME > minutes of NEXT_ARIVAL_TIME then
    set JOURNEY to JOURNEY - 40

  write TRAIN_NUM - 1, CONNECTION, JOURNEY

  — Prepare for handling the next train
  set START_TIME to NEXT_START_TIME
  set STOP_TIME to NEXT_STOP_TIME

Write the caption for the result table

Exhibit 6.2 *Algorithm for Calculating Train Connections*

"There are indeed some subtle points here. Our train times are expressed as decimal numbers. Thus the difference of the two train times,

935 - 625

is 310, which is correct; but

920 - 625

is 295, which is not correct for our purposes. In the second case, the answer should be 255, because there is a 2 hour and 55 minute time difference between 9.20 A.M. and 6.25 A.M. If you look at the algorithm, Watson, you will see that in these cases I have subtracted 40 minutes to correct this difficulty. It is simply a question of doing arithmetic with hours and minutes.

"A second subtlety in the algorithm involves preparing for the next train each time the loop repeats. Thus for the second train, we must subtract the time of the first. For the third train, we subtract the time of the second, and so on. Before dealing with the next train, we must save the times of the train we are presently using. Now, Watson, the algorithm should be quite clear."

It was the next day when he produced the final programme, which I offer as Exhibit 6.3.

"Holmes," I remarked. "I deduce from your algorithm and programme that this symbol mod must be Pascal's way of calculating the number of minutes in a given train time. This is hardly readable."

"My dear Watson, you are such an ideal student and helpmate, a confederate to whom each new development comes as a perpetual surprise; and your grand gift for scientific enquiry makes you an invaluable companion in these endeavours. Let us run the programme and check the output, shall we?"

I was not completely certain how I was to interpret this remark, but I interrupted him no further as he ran the data through the Engine. He sat back while the Engine worked its calculations, but suddenly sprang up in his chair, taking his pipe in his lips, and bounding like an old hound who hears the view-holloa.

"Yes, indeed," he said. "Our friend Penwether most certainly had the opportunity to betray his superior. Let us see how this evidence sits with him, shall we? For now, it remains a matter between the deacon and his creator. We shall give him a short time to decide whether he cares to discuss this with the police."

```
program TRAINTABLE (INPUT, OUTPUT);

{  -- This programme reads in a series of train times on the route
   -- from Birmingham to London.
   -- The programme calculates the total time of a journey from
   -- Birmingham to London, assuming a stop at Oxford. }

   const
      OXFORD = 1524;  { code for Oxford }
      LONDON = 1215;  { code for London }
   var
      CITY,         TRAINNUM,     CONNECTION,     JOURNEY,
      STARTTIME,    STOPTIME,     ARRIVALTIME,
      NEXTSTARTTIME, NEXTSTOPTIME, NEXTARRIVALTIME: INTEGER;

begin
   {  -- Set up for first train }
   WRITELN ('DEPARTING    OXFORD      TOTAL ');
   WRITELN ('  TRAIN     CONNECTION  JOURNEY');
   WRITELN ('---------    ----------  --------');
   WRITELN;

   READ (CITY, STARTTIME);
   while (CITY <> OXFORD) do
      READ (CITY, STOPTIME);
   while (CITY <> LONDON) do
      READ (CITY, ARRIVALTIME);

   {  -- Handle each connecting train }
   for TRAINNUM := 2 to 10 do begin
      READ (CITY, NEXTSTARTTIME);
      while (CITY <> OXFORD) do
         READ (CITY, NEXTSTOPTIME);
      while (CITY <> LONDON) do
         READ (CITY, NEXTARRIVALTIME);

      CONNECTION := NEXTSTOPTIME    - STOPTIME;
      JOURNEY    := NEXTARRIVALTIME - STARTTIME;
      if (STOPTIME mod 100) > (NEXTSTOPTIME mod 100) then
         CONNECTION := CONNECTION - 40;
      if (STARTTIME mod 100) > (NEXTARRIVALTIME mod 100) then
         JOURNEY := JOURNEY - 40;
      WRITELN ((TRAINNUM - 1):5, CONNECTION:13, JOURNEY:11);

      {  -- Prepare for handling the next train }
      STARTTIME := NEXTSTARTTIME;
      STOPTIME  := NEXTSTOPTIME
   end;

   WRITELN;
   WRITELN ('BIRMINGHAM TO LONDON TIMES, STOPPING AT OXFORD')
end.
```

Exhibit 6.3 *Programme for Calculating Train Times*

But our meeting with the deacon was not to be. Within the hour a visit from the Reverend Cowesworthy brought with it the missing Bible and news of Penwether's confession.

"When one tries to rise above Nature," Holmes commented, "one is liable to fall below it. The highest type of man may revert to criminal means if he leaves the straight road of destiny."

6.1   Looping

The concept of looping is so central to problem solving on a computer that it is hard to imagine any self-respecting computer program that does not contain at least one loop. Looping, in fact, is similar to many everyday situations, as the following informal statements illustrate:

- Duplicate the following pattern eight times.

- While the cat is asleep, let the mouse play.

- Repeat with each ingredient until the mixture thickens.

- Search through the trunk until all items are found.

- As long as a king has not been crowned, continue advancing forward.

Each of these statements implies a set of instructions to be obeyed repeatedly until a particular condition is met.

We thus see the two basic characteristics of every loop:

1.   It has a *body*: the instructions to be executed repeatedly.

2.   It has a *termination condition*: an event that must happen to signal the end of the repetition.

In Pascal there are several forms for expressing loops. The choice of a particular form depends upon the problem at hand. These forms are our next topic.

6.2   While and Repeat Loops

Perhaps the simplest form of loop in Pascal is embodied in the following example:

```
while (CITY <> LONDON) do
    READ (CITY, ARRIVALTIME)
```

The body of this loop consists of the single statement

```
READ (CITY, ARRIVALTIME)
```

which is executed repeatedly as long as the condition

```
(CITY <> LONDON)
```

remains true.

It is important to be precise here, for understanding the meaning of even this simple loop is fundamental to all that follows. The loop above is called, in Pascal jargon, a *while loop*. When this statement is executed, the following takes place:

> 1. A test is made to see if the value of the variable CITY is different from LONDON.

> 2. If the result of the test is positive, the body of the loop (in this case the READ statement) is executed and the whole process begins again from step 1.

> 3. Otherwise, the loop is terminated.

The net effect of our simple loop is that cities and arrival times at each city are read in successively until the city happens to be LONDON, at which point execution of the loop is complete.

All while loops are statements of the form:

```
while condition do
    statement
```

In particular, each while loop begins with a condition. The condition expresses some fact about our data. Each loop also contains a statement. The statement tells which actions are to be carried out repeatedly. As long as the condition remains true, the statement is executed again. Upon termination of the loop, the condition is known to be false. Notice that if the condition is initially false, the statement in the body of the loop is never executed.

The condition given at the head of the while statement has the same form as those given in an if statement. For example, we may have:

```
while (MURDERER = UNKNOWN) do
    -- what to do as long as the murderer is unknown

while (NUMCIGARS < 10) do
    -- what to do as long as there are fewer than 10 cigars
```

```
while (TIME > 1000) and (TIME < 1200) do
  -- what to do between 10 a.m. and noon
```

In all cases, the body of the loop is executed repeatedly as long as the condition remains true.

Obviously, there are many cases where we want to specify several actions in the body of a loop. For this we can use the simple device introduced earlier, the compound statement. For example, we may have:

```
while (CITY <> LONDON) do begin
  READ (CITY, ARRIVALTIME);
  WRITE ('ANOTHER CITY HAS BEEN READ IN')
end
```

Such loops have the general form:

```
while condition do begin
  statement-1;
  statement-2;
     . . .
  statement-n
end
```

Here all of the statements bracketed by begin and end are processed repeatedly as long as the condition remains true.

In Pascal, there is a very simple variant of the while loop called a *repeat loop*. This loop is a statement of the form:

```
repeat
  statement-1;
  statement-2;
     . . .
  statement-n
until condition
```

Such a loop is executed as follows:

1. The statements in the body of the loop are executed.

2. If the condition is still not satisfied, the process is repeated again from step 1.

3. Otherwise, the loop is terminated.

Notice here that the condition is tested *after* executing the body of the loop. Notice also that the condition is given the other way around; that is, the body of the loop is executed as long as the condition remains false.

For instance, consider:

```
repeat
   READ (CITY, ARRIVALTIME)
until (CITY = LONDON)
```

This loop tells us to keep reading in cities and arrival times until we find a city whose value is LONDON. This statement has exactly the same effect as:

```
READ (CITY, ARRIVALTIME);
while (CITY <> LONDON) do
   READ (CITY, ARRIVALTIME)
```

Here we can readily see that the condition used to control the repetitions of the while loop is stated in just the opposite way from that of the repeat loop.

Notice one important difference between a repeat loop and a while loop. The body of a repeat loop is always executed at least once, for the condition is tested at the end of the loop. For the while loop, since the condition is tested first, the body of the loop may not be executed even once if the condition is initially false. Thus a repeat and a while loop will have the same effect only if the condition given in the while loop is initially true.

6.3   For Loops

There is yet another form of loop that you can write in Pascal called a *for loop*. Consider the statement:

```
for TRAINNUM := 2 to 10 do begin
   READ (CITY, NEXTSTARTTIME);
   ...
   STOPTIME := NEXTSTOPTIME
end
```

which we have borrowed from Holmes's program. Here we have a series of actions that are to be executed exactly nine times. The actions are specified between the begin and end of the compound statement. Each time the actions are executed, the variable TRAINNUM takes on a new value. Its first value is 2, its second value is 3, and so forth, up to 10.

Such loops are handy in cases like this where a sequence of actions is to be executed a fixed number of times. For example, we may have:

```
for SUSPECT := COLWOODLEY to SIRRAYMOND do
   -- what to do for each of the four suspects
```

```
for MONTH := 1 to 12 do
   -- what to do for each month
for COLUMN := (FIRSTCOLUMN + 1) to (LASTCOLUMN - 1) do
   -- what to do for all medial columns
```

In general, a for loop has the form:

```
for variable := initial-value to final-value do
    statement
```

The initial and final values given in the heading of the loop determine the number of times the statement is executed. Notice that the statement can be compound, as in our train example sketched previously.

A word of caution: each for loop contains a variable given in its heading. This variable is called the *control variable*, and conceptually captures the state of the loop's execution. The initial and final values of the control variable are specified by expressions. Of course, the final value must be greater than the initial value, otherwise the loop has no effect.

The body of a for loop is executed a fixed number of times, starting with the initial value and continuing up to and including the final value. On each iteration, the value of the control variable assumes the corresponding value between the initial and final values.

Returning to our train example, the body of the loop is executed nine times; on each iteration, the value of TRAINNUM takes on one of the values from 2 through 10.

Two other small points worth remembering. First, within the body of a for loop you should never assign a new value to the control variable. This would only cause confusion—in fact, if you try to do it, you should get an error message. Second, when the entire loop is completed, the value of the control variable is undefined. This means that if you want to use the variable again, you should explicitly assign it a new value.

Summary

There is no question that, as you progress with your programming skills, loops become an important problem-solving tool. Repeated calculations are intrinsic to almost any useful computer problem.

Here's a simple strategy for deciding which kind of loop to use. Whenever you want some actions to be repeated until you arrive at some specified result, use a while or repeat loop; whenever you want certain actions to be repeated only a fixed number of times, use a for loop.

One point of caution: since the statements within a loop can include any statement, it is possible to have loops within loops, nested conditional structures within loops, and vice versa. When situations such as this arise, you have to be extremely careful to make the intent of your program clear.

We now revisit our earlier program for counting change. A revised version of this program is given in Example 6.1. Notice that this program contains a conditional statement testing whether the value of the TOTAL-CHANGE is 0. If it is, it prints a special message indicating that there are no coins. Also notice that the else part of the conditional statement is a compound statement, which in turn contains a while loop.

```
program COUNTCHANGE (INPUT, OUTPUT);

{  -- This program reads in six integer values, respectively
   -- representing the number of pennies, nickels, dimes, quarters
   -- half-dollars, and silver dollars in coinage.
   -- The program outputs the total value of the coins in dollars
   -- and cents. }
   var
       NUMPENNIES,  NUMNICKELS,  NUMDIMES,
       NUMQUARTERS, NUMHALVES,   NUMDOLLARS,
       TOTALCHANGE, DOLLARS,     CENTS:    INTEGER;

begin
   TOTALCHANGE := 0;

   READ (NUMPENNIES);
   TOTALCHANGE := TOTALCHANGE + 01*NUMPENNIES;

   READ (NUMNICKELS);
   TOTALCHANGE := TOTALCHANGE + 05*NUMNICKELS;

   READ (NUMDIMES);
   TOTALCHANGE := TOTALCHANGE + 10*NUMDIMES;

   READ (NUMQUARTERS);
   TOTALCHANGE := TOTALCHANGE + 25*NUMQUARTERS;

   READ (NUMHALVES);
   TOTALCHANGE := TOTALCHANGE + 50*NUMHALVES;

   READ (NUMDOLLARS);
   TOTALCHANGE := TOTALCHANGE + 100*NUMDOLLARS;

   if (TOTALCHANGE = 0) then
      WRITE ('NO COINS')
   else
      begin
         DOLLARS := 0;
         CENTS   := TOTALCHANGE;
         while (CENTS > 99) do begin
            CENTS   := CENTS - 100;
            DOLLARS := DOLLARS + 1
         end;
         WRITE ('CHANGE IS ', DOLLARS:2, ' DOLLARS AND ', CENTS:2, ' CENTS')
      end
end.
```

Example 6.1 *Counting Change Using Loops Instead of* div *and* mod

The while loop is used to subtract 100 from the value of CENTS and add 1 to the number of DOLLARS as long as the number of CENTS is greater than 99. This is exactly the computation provided by the arithmetic operators div and mod.

In closing, consider the great detective's observation that, "The simplest things are invariably the most important, the most powerful, and likely, the most difficult to bring home."

Like Dr. Watson, you now have at your disposal the tools for solving some very complex problems. Though simple in nature, these ideas are among the most powerful you will come across. With this behind you now, from a programmer's point of view, the game should truly be afoot.

VII

Holmes's Method Revealed

With the conclusion of the Adventure of Clergyman Peter, you, like Dr. Watson, should have a firm grasp of the elementary principles of programming. You should be able to write programs for solving a wide variety of problems.

We have been fortunate to observe Holmes in a number of programming situations; and in reviewing these, we will see that the great detective's methods are not at all mysterious. In the following pages we'll take a closer look at some of these ideas, drawing again on the reminiscences of Watson when they suit our purposes.

A word of caution is in order before continuing, however—do *not* be misled by the apparent simplicity of these ideas. True, they are, in and of themselves, very simple. But keep in mind Holmes's remark to Watson in their first case together, *A Study in Scarlet*, "To a great mind, nothing is little."

7.1 An Exception Disproves the Rule

> "*I had already perceived that Holmes had trained himself to see what others overlooked. He took great pains in preparing each problem, examining every detail of its performance, checking against all possible errors, and even drawing up an elaborate facsimile of the input and its corresponding output before approaching the Engine.*
> "*'I never make exceptions, Watson,' he once said when I remarked how tedious his precautions appeared. 'An exception disproves the rule.'*"

It is a mistake to think that as soon as you have a good general idea of the problem you may as well start developing the program; you can handle those points you initially overlooked later on. Shortcuts sometimes pay off, but for the most part they don't. Starting with an absolutely solid problem definition is the best way to get future rewards.

When starting a new problem, there are many forces at work that encourage a programmer to abandon thoughtful and effective techniques for unproven shortcuts. If you try to get speedy results, you will only have to pay the price in time and energy later on.

The place to focus your attention at the beginning, as difficult and tedious as it may seem, *must* be on the problem definition itself. If you allow some little detail to escape you, ignore some odd case, or dwell on irrelevant information, you will find yourself playing host to some larger problems down the road.

As Holmes has demonstrated, one of the best techniques is to construct a sample of the input and output for each program before attempting to solve the problem. Among the benefits of this technique are:

■ It forces you to consider the details of the problem.

■ It can help to uncover any special or annoying cases that will surely turn up later.

■ It often forces you to restructure the problem, sometimes ever so slightly, making the program easier to write.

■ Above all, it gives you a clear idea of the intent of the entire program.

This may sound too obvious; but you will find that excellent problem definitions are as rare as excellent detectives, excellent food, or excellent anything. You will recall Holmes's remark that "Excellence is an infinite capacity for taking pains. It is a bad definition, but it does apply to programming." Writing good problem definitions requires plain hard work; there's no way around it. You must take the time to specify the inputs, the outputs, and the exact task the program is to perform. What is needed is persistence and discipline; or as Edison once remarked, "one percent inspiration, ninety-nine percent perspiration."

7.2   If Matters Become Difficult

"After clearly detailing the problem comes the next step, solving the problem in the most general terms. He uses a great many psychological techniques. I have heard him think aloud, talk about similar problems, or consider the problem as if there were no Engine at all. He is certainly not reticent about discussing the problem with me. And if matters become difficult, he ignores the problem for days."

Certainly the hardest task in problem solving is developing an overall strategy. There is little sense in pretending that the methods in problem solving are very scientific; nevertheless, there are known psychological techniques to help you over these first crucial steps.

Once you have a problem firmly fixed in your mind, it is a grave mistake to believe that this is the time to start programming. What it is the time to do is to start *thinking*.

Thinking means just that—thinking. You need to think about alternative ways to solve the problem. You need to examine various approaches in enough detail to discover the possible trouble spots that may be difficult to program. You should always look for possible errors and provide against them. It is the first rule of programming just as it is the first rule of criminal investigation. You need to polish any proposed solution before attempting to carry on. Remember, it is certainly easier to discard poor thoughts than poor programs.

You may have heard it said before, and that's because it's true: it always takes longer to write a program than it first appears. On the other hand, you can safely assume that the sooner you start writing code, rather than thinking about the problem, the longer it will take to complete the task.

One of the best thinking aids is *analogy*. Presumably the problem you are about to solve is not so unfamiliar that you have not seen anything like it before, and you should recall solutions to similiar problems. You may recognize portions of the problem that have been solved in some similar fashion, or perhaps you have solved a similar problem that had nothing to do with computers. In each of these situations, the point is the same: look to previous solutions, for in them you may find the seeds to the solution of the new problem.

In attempting to solve a problem on a computer, there is a tendency to become heavily involved with the oddities of the programming language itself. Although the final solution must be programmed in some language, the best solutions are those for which there is a direct analogy to the world in which the problem is presented. To do this you should attempt to solve the problem without regard to the final computer implementation. Freed from the idiosyncrasies of a programming language, you can concentrate on the essence of the problem.

Holmes is a master of this technique. We see in his cases a tendency to think of the problem in the highest possible terms, often without any special regard to the final program. His mind remains free and uncluttered to employ techniques that he has found useful in the solution of many criminal investigations.

Recall the murder at the Metropolitan Club and the algorithm Holmes developed to solve the case. Although Holmes is well aware of the intense rigor required for programming, he concentrates on the organization of the clues, the sequence in which the clues are examined, and the construction of the tables of information. This is a powerful technique, not only for designing an original solution to a problem, but also for ensuring that the final program will reflect the real-world solution it was intended to solve in the first place.

Some problems are not at all easy to solve. It has long been an axiom among programmers that in difficult situations two heads are better than one. Working with someone else, customarily known as *brainstorming*, and simply talking about your problem has become a classic programming technique.

Holmes's conversations with Watson are more than idle chatter. In the process of discussing the problem, Holmes himself often finds inspiration. He is not afraid to expose the problem at hand and to listen to himself when he proposes a solution. It is remarkable how often the simple exposure of an idea to someone else can lead to a clearer, better formulated solution.

Of course, if your mind is already made up and your solution is well in hand, you can go right ahead. But take care—supposedly good ideas have been known to show serious flaws when put into action.

Sooner or later you will find yourself in a situation where there appears to be no reasonable solution to a particular problem. You may have tried repeatedly with a given idea, each time finding some new flaw. What should you do when all hope seems lost?

Take a break.

The technique of putting aside a problem for some period of time is generally known as *incubation*. This is a subtle but potentially powerful psychological technique. A complete distraction, a weekend away from a problem, a good night's rest, or some frivolous entertainment can often have far-reaching effects in solving difficult problems.

Our brain is supposedly at work on problems even though we are not consciously aware of it. Rest from a problem is often the predecessor of an inspiration. We have all experienced this in other areas of our lives.

In sum, there are a great many psychological techniques for solving problems. You should use these techniques to improve your problem solving skills in programming.

7.3 A Curious Language of His Own Invention

"Once Holmes had a particular solution in mind he would put to use a curious language of his own invention. His objective, apparently, was to write an algorithm at a very high level."

All solutions start from the problem and not from some programming language. Assuming that you have a solid idea of a solution, you must now take your first step towards a concrete program.

Holmes uses a simple device to sketch his ideas, writing out his solution in a very high-level language of his own. His language is a programming "interlingua," a language somewhere between English and Pascal. On the one hand, Holmes borrows extensively from English, coining phrases at will, unconstrained by a programming language.

For example, he might write:

Do the following 10 times:
    — *actions to be performed 10 times*

or:

Print the values in the table

On the other hand, the language he chooses is guided by the knowledge that the final program must be written in Pascal. He may, for example, conceptualize a variable, say NUM_SUSPECTS, and write

Set NUM_SUSPECTS to 0

or:

If NUM_SUSPECTS > 4 then
    — *what to do if more than 4 suspects*

In Pascal, the first example can be expressed by an assignment statement, the second by a conditional statement.

The point of this technique is to capture some written form of a solution. This form retains the high level of discourse of the problem domain, yet is specific enough to capture the essence of the algorithm that is being expressed.

7.4   Programs as Human Communication

"We had a pleasant dinner together, during which Holmes would talk about nothing but the use of different names he might assign to the variables in a programme. As always, he emphasized that programmes must be considered as elements of human communication, and that the choosing of names in a programme should serve its author's ends."

Assume for the moment that you were presented with two computer programs. Each performs the same, presumably very important, task for you. You will have to use one of the programs for the next several years, probably making modifications as time goes on. You are told that the programs, from a performance point of view, are absolutely identical; that is, they perform the same input and output, they run at approximately the same speed, and each has been tested thoroughly and shown to be correct.

You are not allowed to look inside and see the actual programs. The only additional information you have about the programs is that the first one required over a hundred changes in order to make it correct, while the second worked correctly the very first time it was run.

Now the obvious question. Which program would you choose?

This question leads to another: What are the characteristics of a program that would work correctly on its first test? We might conclude that the persons who wrote the program were highly skilled programmers or very lucky. But surely there is more, for there must be some element present in the second program that is lacking in the first. Our only logical conclusion is that the second program was written with such crystal clarity that it allowed its authors to comprehend it as easily as you can read these lines of text. In short, the program must be so transparent that "even a Scotland Yard official can see through it."

In all of Holmes's programs, we see an almost obsessive concern for clarity. A program is not just a set of instructions that must be understood by some computer, but a description of an algorithm that must be understood by human beings, especially the person writing and using the program.

The factors that go into making a program well suited for human comprehension are numerous. They include the design of clear algorithms, choice of control structures, the sequence in which operations are performed, and many other issues. But there is a key point mentioned in the quotation above: the choice of names used in a program.

A wise choice of names can make a great contribution to the readability of a program. Let us look at a portion of one of the programs presented earlier:

```
READ (TODAYSDATE, TIDEHR, EVENTDATE, EVENTHR);
MINSTOHIGHTIDE := (TODAYSDATE - 1) * MINSPERDAY;
MINSTOHIGHTIDE := MINSTOHIGHTIDE + HIGHTIDEHR*MINSPERHR;
```

Of course, it would be shorter to write

```
READ (DATE1, HR1, DATE2, HR2);
MINS := (DATE1 - 1) * DAYLEN;
MINS := MINS + HR1*HRLEN;
```

but then we might have to guess at the meaning of DATE1 versus DATE2 and what units DAYLEN and HRLEN stand for. The difference between the two is that the names in the first fragment have been chosen from standard *English* descriptions of the entities.

Creating good, meaningful names can be difficult, for often it is easy to pick a name with a close but dangerously incorrect connotation. As an example, suppose a programmer decided to represent a file of criminal records, and the record's three fields (the age of the criminal, the criminal's height, and the criminal's shoe size) with the respective names INPUT, FIELD1, FIELD2, and FIELD3. The name INPUT might cause a reader to associate an arbitrary file of input data with the name. A better choice would be CRIMINALFILE. Likewise, the data names FIELD1, FIELD2, and FIELD3 are far less clear than AGE, HEIGHT, and SHOESIZE. Even HEIGHT may not be so perfect, as it may be better to write HGTININCHES or HEIGHTINCM.

A name that is an abbreviation for a longer conceptual unit can also be hazardous, especially when the resulting abbreviation is an acronym that suggests another entity. For example, a programmer who desires a name for a rate of pay entry would be unwise to use the name ROPE, which does not reflect the entity's true meaning.

Names like FIELD1, FIELD2, and FIELD3 should be avoided for yet another reason. Suppose the format of the input were changed so that the age became the third field instead of the first, and the height became the first instead of the second field, etc. The name FIELD1 must be changed to FIELD3, FIELD2 to FIELD1, and so on. Needless to say, it is highly possible that some occurrence of the name FIELD3 might not be changed to FIELD1! Finding a mistake like the one just made in the last sentence is another problem with such names.

Another important aspect in choosing names is the effect of abbreviations. The first point to remember is that you should only abbreviate after you have created a full mnemonic name. Second, the chosen abreviation should not suggest a meaning different from the original name. Let us assume you created the lengthy name NUMBEROFCIGARS and that it suggests the correct meaning. Even though you surely will want to abbreviate the name, you should reject such abbreviations as NUMCIG or NOCIGAR, for they may very well be misleading. A name like NUMCIGARS would be preferable.

The choice of appropriate names is seldom an easy matter. Keeping in mind that the main reason for choosing a particular name is so that you (and others using your program) can understand it, it is well worth the effort to invest some thought in the choice of a name. You may not fully appreciate this when first designing your program; but you will, no doubt, appreciate the full value of your labors at some later date when you return to use the program.

7.5   The Seemingly Insignificant Blank Space

*"It has long been an axiom of mine," said Holmes, "that the little things
are infinitely the most important. I can never bring you to realize the
importance of every single character in a programme, and, most notably,
the seemingly insignificant blank space."*

You have probably observed in all of Holmes's programs a rather
generous use of both blank lines and blank spaces. This is no accident. Like
the choice of good mnemonic names, the use of judicious spacing rules is
primarily to assist human comprehension of a program.

Pascal, like many languages, is a "free format" language, in that there
are no column or line boundary restrictions on statements, declarations,
and comments. Such languages allow the programmer to write a program
in any way that emphasizes its logical structure. The use of spacing
conventions to illuminate structure is often called "prettyprinting."

Prettyprinting is a vital ingredient in reading programs. With good
spacing rules, typing errors are much easier to detect and the meaning of
portions easier to follow. Most importantly, the overall intent of the
program can be made more transparent to the reader. The conscious use of
good spacing conventions can even affect and improve the original code.

The development of good spacing conventions is, in large part, up to
the programmer. Only when the knowledge of the program at hand is clear
can the choice of spacing conventions be made with precision. However,
there are a number of simple conventions that can go a long way toward the
writing of clear programs. Table 7.1 lists some prettyprinting conventions
that have been followed throughout this text.

A point of caution: do not think that these conventions themselves are
enough. Like anything else in this book, the implementation of even these
simple ideas requires a great deal of thought.

This brings us full circle to our point of origin; and that is, there can
never be a substitute for thinking.

"In solving any sort of programming problem, Watson," Holmes once
remarked, "the grand thing is simple, human reasoning. It is a very useful
and easy accomplishment, though people do not practice it much. There
are fifty who can reason synthetically for one who can reason analytically. I
tell you, Watson, we have not yet grasped the results which human reason
alone can attain."

TABLE 7.1 *Some Prettyprinting Conventions*

General Considerations

1.   Each statement begins on a separate line. For example

```
X := 0;   Y := 0
```

would be better written as:

```
X := 0;
Y := 0
```

2.   No line extends beyond the standard page width of 72 characters.

3.   The keywords begin and end stand on a line by themselves (or possibly with supporting comments). For example,

```
begin READ (THIS);
    WRITE (THAT)
end
```

looks better as:

```
begin
    READ (THIS);
    WRITE (THAT)
end
```

An alternative form is used in compound while and for loops, as described below.

4.   The keywords const, type, and var stand on a line by themselves. For example, instead of

```
const MINSPERHR  = 60;
      MINSPERDAY = 1440;
var   TODAYSDATE, TIDEHR,
      EVENTDATE, EVENTHR:  INTEGER;
```

try:

```
const
    MINSPERHR  = 60;
    MINSPERDAY = 1440;
var
    TODAYSDATE, TIDEHR,
    EVENTDATE, EVENTHR:  INTEGER;
```

Table 7.1 *Continued*

Blank Lines and Blank Spaces

5.   Any comment annotating the overall purpose of a program is preceded and
followed by at least one blank line. For example,

```
program COMMENTPOORLY (INPUT, OUTPUT);
     {  This comment annotates the program, but if you notice
        it is a bit cluttered. }
     var
        SOMEVARIABLE: INTEGER;
```

looks better as:

```
program COMMENTNICELY (INPUT, OUTPUT);

{   -- Header comments can be made to stand
    -- out nicely from the program text. }

     var
        SOMEVARIABLE: INTEGER;
```

6.   At least one space appears after each comma and colon. For instance, rather
than a squeeze like

```
var
    ONEVARIABLE,ANOTHER,YETANOTHER:INTEGER;
```

use:

```
var
    ONEVARIABLE, ANOTHER, YETANOTHER:  INTEGER;
```

7.   At least one space appears before and after each = and :=. For example, instead
of

```
COUNTER:=COUNTER + 1
```

a reader will be happier with:

```
COUNTER := COUNTER + 1
```

8.   In an unparenthesized expression with several operators, spaces are used to
show the precedence of the operators. For example,

```
A + B * C - D * E
```

looks better as:

```
A + B*C - D*E
```

Table 7.1 *Continued*

Alignment and Indentation Rules

9.   Program and subprogram headings start at the left margin; the begin and end symbols for the program or subprogram also begin at the left margin. For example, rather than

```
program DOSOMETHING (INPUT, OUTPUT);
    var
        X, Y: INTEGER;
    begin
        READ (X, Y);
        WRITE (Y, X)
    end.
```

use:

```
program DOSOMETHING (INPUT, OUTPUT);
    var
        X, Y: INTEGER;
begin
    READ (X, Y);
    WRITE (Y, X)
end.
```

10. Each statement within a begin-end, while-do, for-do, or repeat-until construct is aligned. For example, you should not write:

```
repeat X := X + 1;
    Y := Y - 1
until (X > Y)
```

11. Each statement within a begin-end, while-do, for-do, or repeat-until construct is indented three or more spaces from the corresponding header keyword. For example, use

```
begin
    DOTHIS;
    DOTHAT
end
```

and:

```
DOTHIS;
for I := 1 to 10 do
    A[I] := 0;
DOTHAT;
```

Table 7.1   *Continued*

Specific Constructs

12. An if statement is formatted as

> if *condition* then
>   *statement*

or:

> if *condition* then
>   *statement*
> else
>   *statement*

13. An if statement with multiple conditions may be formatted as:

> if *condition* then
>   *statement*
> else if *condition* then
>   *statement*
> else
>   *statement*

14. Compound while and for loops, those with two or more contained statements, are formatted as

> while *condition* do begin
>   *statements*
> end

and:

> for *variable* := *initial-value* to *final-value* do begin
>   *statements*
> end

Three-pipe Problems

VIII

An Advertisement in the Times

HAD seen little of Sherlock Holmes for many months, my marriage and my return to practice in the Paddington district having caused us to drift apart. One night in early August, as my way led through Baker Street, I was seized by a keen desire to see Holmes and to know to what use he was making of his extraordinary Engine. I found him lounging upon the sofa, a pipe-rack within his reach and a pile of crumpled newspapers, apparently recent, near at hand. A lens and a number of columns that had been neatly cut from the papers were lying upon the sofa beside him, which suggested he had been in the process of examining them when I entered.

"You are engaged, I see," said I. "Perhaps I am interrupting your work."

"On the contrary, you could not have come at a better time, my dear Watson," he said cordially. "You would confer a great favour upon me should you lend me an ear, for nothing clears up a problem so much as stating it to another person. I think that your time will not be misspent," he continued as he reached for a paper. "This case has its points of interest and, especially, of instruction."

I gave the pile more careful scrutiny and realized that it was largely made up of back editions, for they were yellowed, of the *Times*.

"You are searching for something?" I asked.

"Indeed, Watson. I am searching for a series of trifles," he remarked. "You know my method. It is founded upon the premise that it is usually in unimportant matters that there is a field for observation."

He flipped rapidly through the paper, finally thrusting it under his sofa and taking up another.

"As you know, I customarily read nothing but the criminal news and the personal announcements. I have of late included the advertisements, which are proving instructive."

I waited silently, accommodating my companion's flair for the dramatic, to which I was long accustomed. He lit his pipe nonchalantly and continued.

"You may have read yourself, over the past eight months, of the series of daring burglaries that has been taking place throughout London's most fashionable districts. Scotland Yard is absolutely baffled."

"I have seen what the *Daily Telegraph* and the *Chronicle* have had to say, but not the *Times*," I replied.

"It is theorized that there are two persons involved," he continued, "and although two suspects have been under investigation, the authorities have never been able to establish their presence at the scenes of the crimes. There is nothing more stimulating than a case where everything goes against you. This particular matter is further complicated by the fact that neither suspect ever seems to communicate with the other. Now unless Scotland Yard can prove some means of communication, or better still, determine this means, intercept their messages, and catch them in the act, it is feared that these burglars will remain free. It is necessary to prove that they were indeed conspirators before they can be brought before a magistrate."

"I take it, Holmes, you have come across something in the *Times* linking these two with the crimes that the police have failed to note?"

"Yes, Watson, the *Times* is a paper that is seldom found in any hands but those of the highly educated. Crime is common but logic is rare, and I sense an extremely complex mind behind this. Therefore, it is upon the logic rather than upon the crime that one should dwell. Just when I thought that the criminal mind had lost all enterprise and originality, enter these singularly interesting specialists.

"This is one of those cases where the art of the reasoner should be used for the sifting of details rather than for the acquisition of fresh evidence. This is where Scotland Yard has wasted its energy. I, on the other hand, have considered how I might communicate with a silent partner."

Holmes rose from the sofa and walked towards the hearth rug while scanning the paper he had picked up earlier. I took this opportunity to stretch out in the comfortable armchair which I had occupied so many times before. I looked dreamily up to the mantelpiece, recollecting old adventures we had shared. I started from my reverie as Holmes abruptly pounced upon an advertisement.

"HOLMES ABRUPTLY POUNCED UPON AN ADVERTISEMENT."

"Here!" he exclaimed. "The most recent one, and at the correct time. That accounts for all seven robberies, by my calculations."

He then showed me the item which had arrested his interest.

> For Sale: Copies of the *Strand* numbering from 23 to 276 with various duplicates. Also, 3 Twybridge carriage wheels in excellent condition. Please enquire: Box 37 GPO

"I do not recognise the carriage name," I replied, "but some of those issues of the *Strand* have chronicles of your achievements."

"The magazine itself is of little import, Watson, but the numbers of these issues are. The newest volume number minus the oldest volume is a number that fits well into my theory, as is the number of carriage wheels. As for these Twybridge carriage wheels, I can safely attest that there are no such items in existence. I am familiar with forty-two impressions left by carriage wheels, having written a short monograph on the subject.

"I believe the 3 represents three o'clock in the morning, the hour the last burglary took place. Also, is it not curious, Watson, that this carriage, whose name is unfamiliar to us, should have the same name as the street on which the last victim resides?"

Holmes pulled another well-worn newspaper from the stack near him.

"Here is another from last month's paper, offering for sale 209 'Brewster' pigeons; and a robbery did occur on Sunday, July 28th."

I pondered for a moment and asked, "Holmes, I believe you may have something. But about the date, are you sure?"

"Absolutely. If we subtract the lower number from the upper number of the supposed volumes of the *Strand*, we get 253. The 253rd day of the year was September 10th, a Tuesday and the date of the last robbery. July 28th was nearly seven weeks ago. It was the 209th day of the year, a Sunday, and the date of the previous robbery. And, I might add, there are no pigeons of a type called Brewster."

"Amazing, Holmes, but how did you determine the date from just the number?"

"That is the flower that comes from this little seed, Watson. I must take care to explain it to you in detail so that you may appreciate it fully.

"Obviously, Watson, a programme on the Analytical Engine which arrives at the date from the number would be a way to achieve an efficient solution to this problem. The first of January was a Tuesday. If we enter the number

253

the programme will calculate the date

Tuesday, September 10

the date that is the 253rd day of the year. I am sure that these scoundrels just count the days off on the current calendar, but counting is tedious and prone to error. Such a solution lacks elegance and can hardly be considered of broad use."

"There are some other uses you have in mind for this programme?" I asked.

"It is what we learn from the particular construction of this programme that will be of continued use to us, Watson," said Holmes. "We are faced here with finding a means of working on a numerical device with items that have many and varying properties. We are dealing here with a theory of *types*, the representation of things from the real world.

"I have given this notion considerable thought and have taken the trouble of constructing a diagram," he said, handing me a small chart which ran this way :—

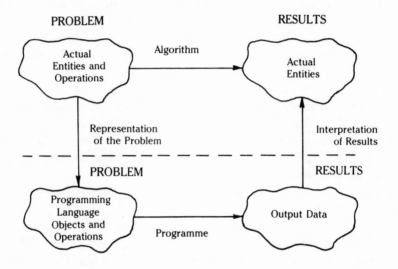

"A type, Watson, characterizes a class of objects and the operations that can be performed upon them.

"The current problem has several classes of objects with differing operations possible for them. Consider the days of the week. For us there can only be seven days of the week—Sunday, Monday, Tuesday, Wednesday, Thursday, Friday, Saturday.

"Some of the common operations that we can perform upon them are:

1. Computing the day after: Given a day of the week, we can determine the following day, for example,

DAY_AFTER(MONDAY) is TUESDAY
DAY_AFTER(FRIDAY) is SATURDAY

2. Comparison of days: In a given week we can determine if any one day precedes another, for example,

MONDAY precedes SATURDAY
MONDAY precedes WEDNESDAY

When we write programmes, we deal with many such types of objects—names, varieties of cigar ash, amounts of money, months, days, and so forth."

Holmes then displayed his algorithm for computing the date from the number of days given in the advertisements. The algorithm is reproduced here as Exhibit 8.1. I had no problem in following his simple logic.

Definitions:

DAY_OF_WEEK   : one of the days SUNDAY through SATURDAY
MONTH   : one of the months JANUARY through DECEMBER
DAY_OF_MONTH: a number from 1 to 31

CURRENT_NUM : a number from 1 to 365
NUM_OF_DAYS : a number from 1 to 365

Algorithm:

Set MONTH to JANUARY
Set DAY_OF_MONTH to 1
Set DAY_OF_WEEK to TUESDAY

Read NUM_OF_DAYS

For CURRENT_NUM set to 2 through NUM_OF_DAYS, do the following:
    Set DAY_OF_WEEK to DAY_AFTER(DAY_OF_WEEK)

        If (MONTH = JANUARY)   and (DAY_OF_MONTH = 31)
        or (MONTH = FEBRUARY)   and (DAY_OF_MONTH = 28)
        or (MONTH = MARCH)   and (DAY_OF_MONTH = 31)
        or (MONTH = APRIL)   and (DAY_OF_MONTH = 30)
        or (MONTH = MAY)   and (DAY_OF_MONTH = 31)
        or (MONTH = JUNE)   and (DAY_OF_MONTH = 30)
        or (MONTH = JULY)   and (DAY_OF_MONTH = 31)
        or (MONTH = AUGUST)   and (DAY_OF_MONTH = 31)
        or (MONTH = SEPTEMBER) and (DAY_OF_MONTH = 30)
        or (MONTH = OCTOBER)   and (DAY_OF_MONTH = 31)
        or (MONTH = NOVEMBER)   and (DAY_OF_MONTH = 30) then
            set MONTH to MONTH_AFTER(MONTH)
        set DAY_OF_MONTH to 1
        else
        set DAY_OF_MONTH to DAY_OF_MONTH + 1

Write DAY_OF_WEEK, MONTH, DAY_OF_MONTH

"Now for the representation of the problem. When we use the Engine, we have only a small number of commonly used fundamental types at our disposal, for example, integers, characters, boolean truth values, and strings. Each of these types has its own special operations defined in the programming language, so we do not have to bother ourselves constantly with defining them.

"For example, we have :

addition: We can add two numbers and get their sum.
comparison: We can compare two numbers to see which is greater.
negation: We can negate an integer or a Boolean truth value.
printing: We can print a number or a string.

"Now, Watson," he continued, "the essence of working with any actual type of data is that the objects, such as amounts of money, days of the week, and months, must be defined in terms of the programming language. We must not only choose a particular representation for an object; we must also make sure that operations upon it, as represented in the language, correctly reflect its actual properties.

"For example, we can perform all numeric operations on numeric data; but when the number represents some real entity, like the year 1889, some operations are meaningless. The difference of two years is a useful operation because it is actually sensible to consider the interval of time between two dates. On the other hand, the square root of a year has no useful meaning associated with it. To multiply two years is likewise senseless.

"Specifically, our calendar problem requires us to write an algorithm which correctly depicts the three data types:

months
days of the week
days of the month

The days of the month running from 1 to 31 can easily be represented using integers. The 'day after' DAYOFMONTH is

DAYOFMONTH + 1

Of course, when the value of DAYOFMONTH is the last day of the month, the day after is not

DAYOFMONTH + 1

but 1. This shows that, although we operate on days of the month as integers, they are not really integers; this must be kept in mind or large problems will certainly result.

"Consider also the days of the week. We could represent them as integers: Sunday with 1, Monday with 2, and so forth. Of course, days of the week are not at all numbers; and the special rule for the last day of the week is needed to represent the real world correctly. In a Pascal programme we would have:

```
if DAYOFWEEK = 7 then
  DAYOFWEEK := 1
else
  DAYOFWEEK := DAYOFWEEK + 1
```

"Simplifying the programme even further, since there are only seven days of the week, we could make each day a named constant,

```
const
  SUNDAY = 1;
  MONDAY = 2;
  . . .
```

and use the constant names instead of integers, so they would appear as the actual names of the days. Then we would have

```
if DAYOFWEEK = SATURDAY then
  DAYOFWEEK := SUNDAY
else
  DAYOFWEEK := DAYOFWEEK + 1
```

"And now, Watson, for the last step. Pascal allows us to define our own types! We can write:

```
type DAYNAME = (SUNDAY, MONDAY, TUESDAY, WEDNESDAY, THURSDAY,
                FRIDAY, SATURDAY);
```

This is a type with exactly seven values, corresponding precisely to the seven days of the week.

"Just as we can say

```
NUMITEMS: INTEGER;
```

to mean that **NUMITEMS** can take on only integer values, we could instead say

```
DAYOFWEEK: DAYNAME;
```

to mean that **DAYOFWEEK** can only take on values from **SUNDAY** through **SATURDAY**.

"To set the current day to Tuesday, we simply say,

```
DAYOFWEEK := TUESDAY
```

Once **DAYOFWEEK** has been given a value, we can obtain the day after by saying,

```
if DAYOFWEEK = SATURDAY then
   DAYOFWEEK = SUNDAY
else
   DAYOFWEEK = SUCC(DAYOFWEEK);
```

The predefined function named SUCC is Pascal's curious way of expressing the value that succeeds another value. Now it is impossible to mix an integer with a day, as one is a number and the other is a different type quite unable to take on a numerical value."

I did not know quite what to say after this great exposition on the theory of types and the days of the week. My silence made it plainly evident that I was hopelessly at sea.

"This should make things clearer, Watson," said Holmes, quickly producing the programme that I have reproduced in Exhibit 8.2. It seemed excessively elaborate to me and, after a moment of study, I enquired why Pascal did not allow him to say

```
WRITE (DAYOFWEEK)
```

"It would certainly make sense to us," he replied, "but not necessarily to the Engine. Indeed, the variable **DAYOFWEEK**, Watson, is neither a number nor a character string. The use of such data indeed has its unpleasantries.

"Well, then," I remarked after a while, "it all seems clear to me from here. You plan to anticipate the next theft, unless I am mistaken?"

"Oh, hardly my dear Watson," he replied. "You know that I look upon unnecessary bodily exertion as an extreme waste of energy. This surely is now a matter for the police. After all, Watson, I am not retained by Scotland Yard to supply their deficiencies."

```
program COMPUTEDATE (INPUT, OUTPUT);

{ -- January 1, 1889 was a Tuesday.
  -- This programme reads in a number named NUMOFDAYS,
  -- representing the number of days since January 1.
  -- The programme prints the corresponding date. }

    type
       DAYNAME    = (SUNDAY, MONDAY, TUESDAY, WEDNESDAY, THURSDAY,
                     FRIDAY, SATURDAY);
       MONTHNAME  = (JANUARY, FEBRUARY, MARCH, APRIL, MAY, JUNE, JULY,
                     AUGUST, SEPTEMBER, OCTOBER, NOVEMBER, DECEMBER);
    var
       DAYOFWEEK : DAYNAME;
       MONTH     : MONTHNAME;
       DAYOFMONTH: 1..31;
       CURRENTNUM: 1..365;
       NUMOFDAYS : 1..365;

begin
    MONTH      := JANUARY;
    DAYOFMONTH := 1;
    DAYOFWEEK  := TUESDAY;

    READ (NUMOFDAYS);

    for CURRENTNUM := 2 to NUMOFDAYS do begin
       if DAYOFWEEK = SATURDAY then
          DAYOFWEEK := SUNDAY
       else
          DAYOFWEEK := SUCC(DAYOFWEEK);

       if (MONTH = JANUARY)    and  (DAYOFMONTH = 31)
       or (MONTH = FEBRUARY)   and  (DAYOFMONTH = 28)
       or (MONTH = MARCH)      and  (DAYOFMONTH = 31)
       or (MONTH = APRIL)      and  (DAYOFMONTH = 30)
       or (MONTH = MAY)        and  (DAYOFMONTH = 31)
       or (MONTH = JUNE)       and  (DAYOFMONTH = 30)
       or (MONTH = JULY)       and  (DAYOFMONTH = 31)
       or (MONTH = AUGUST)     and  (DAYOFMONTH = 31)
       or (MONTH = SEPTEMBER)  and  (DAYOFMONTH = 30)
       or (MONTH = OCTOBER)    and  (DAYOFMONTH = 31)
       or (MONTH = NOVEMBER)   and  (DAYOFMONTH = 30) then
             begin
                MONTH      := SUCC(MONTH);
                DAYOFMONTH := 1
             end
          else
             DAYOFMONTH := DAYOFMONTH + 1
    end;
```

Exhibit 8.2   *Holmes's Programme to Compute Dates*

```
case DAYOFWEEK of
    SUNDAY    : WRITE ('SUNDAY, ');
    MONDAY    : WRITE ('MONDAY, ');
    TUESDAY   : WRITE ('TUESDAY, ');
    WEDNESDAY : WRITE ('WEDNESDAY, ');
    THURSDAY  : WRITE ('THURSDAY, ');
    FRIDAY    : WRITE ('FRIDAY, ');
    SATURDAY  : WRITE ('SATURDAY, ')
end;

case MONTH of
    JANUARY   : WRITE ('JANUARY',    DAYOFMONTH:3);
    FEBRUARY  : WRITE ('FEBRUARY',   DAYOFMONTH:3);
    MARCH     : WRITE ('MARCH',      DAYOFMONTH:3);
    APRIL     : WRITE ('APRIL',      DAYOFMONTH:3);
    MAY       : WRITE ('MAY',        DAYOFMONTH:3);
    JUNE      : WRITE ('JUNE',       DAYOFMONTH:3);
    JULY      : WRITE ('JULY',       DAYOFMONTH:3);
    AUGUST    : WRITE ('AUGUST',     DAYOFMONTH:3);
    SEPTEMBER : WRITE ('SEPTEMBER',  DAYOFMONTH:3);
    OCTOBER   : WRITE ('OCTOBER',    DAYOFMONTH:3);
    NOVEMBER  : WRITE ('NOVEMBER',   DAYOFMONTH:3);
    DECEMBER  : WRITE ('DECEMBER',   DAYOFMONTH:3)
end
end.
```

Exhibit 8.2   *Continued*

It was one of the peculiarities of his proud, self-contained nature that he was always averse to anything in the shape of public applause, and he bound me in the most stringent terms to publish no account of this matter. Nothing amused Holmes more at the conclusion of a successful problem than to hand over the actual exposure to some orthodox official.

A report in the *Times* a fortnight later described the apprehension of the criminals. Of course, there was no mention of either Holmes or the Analytical Engine. It was, I surmise, his thought that widespread dissemination in the popular press of this remarkable mechanism would naturally come to the attention of the more undesirable elements of the city. How well I recall his once commenting, "I could not rest, Watson, nor could I sit quietly in my chair, if I thought that the Analytical Engine had fallen into the hands of some diabolical mastermind, walking the streets of London unchallenged."

8.1   Types and Enumerated Types

Our latest excursion down Baker Street has introduced several new and powerful ways of describing data that are not intrinsically numeric. Further, we shall consider ways of dealing with items like train schedules and dates that, though numeric in nature, do not behave in the same way as the integers used to represent them. Problems of this sort, as Watson has learned, require careful thought in program design. They also illustrate two essential programming concerns:

■   the need to describe objects and their properties with precision and clarity.

■   the need to guarantee that the operations over objects do not violate their intrinsic properties.

This brings us to the concept of *types*.

We begin with an example from Holmes's program:

```
type
    DAYNAME = (SUNDAY, MONDAY, TUESDAY,  WEDNESDAY, THURSDAY,
              FRIDAY, SATURDAY);
```

This declaration introduces a type named DAYNAME and seven constants of that type, the names SUNDAY through SATURDAY. Just as we can say

```
COUNTER: INTEGER;
```

to declare a variable COUNTER of type INTEGER, we can say

```
TODAY: DAYNAME;
```

to declare a variable TODAY of type DAYNAME.

Similarly, just as a variable of type INTEGER can take on integer values, a variable of type DAYNAME can take on any of the seven values SUNDAY through SATURDAY. In this sense, we say that a type describes a class of values.

The type introduced above is called an *enumerated type*. For enumerated types, the type declaration explicitly enumerates the class of values. The example above illustrates the first basic idea: you introduce a type to describe a class of values needed to solve your problem.

One of the properties of every enumerated type is that the values are ordered. In particular, the values are assumed to be enumerated in increasing order. For the type DAYNAME, the first value is SUNDAY and the last is SATURDAY.

As emphasized by Holmes, a data type consists of a set of values and associated operations. The declaration of an enumerated type specifies the set of values. Just as for integers, the operations on an enumerated type are predefined in Pascal. These include the relational operators for comparing values of the type. Thus, if the variable TODAY has the value TUESDAY, we may have the following comparisons:

```
(TODAY = FRIDAY)     { Comparison is FALSE }
(TODAY = TUESDAY)    { Comparison is TRUE }
(TODAY < MONDAY)     { Comparison is FALSE }
```

Assignment is also allowed for enumerated types. For example, we may have:

```
TODAY := TUESDAY
```

The following examples are not logical, and are erroneous:

```
SUNDAY := MONDAY;    { Only variables can be assigned values }
TODAY  := 1          { 1 is not a DAYNAME }
```

In the first case, SUNDAY is not a variable. In the second case, the value assigned to a variable is not to be of the same type as that declared for the variable.

The functions SUCC and PRED are two predefined operations that apply to enumerated values. Their evaluation yields respectively the successor and the predecessor of an enumerated value. For a given enumerated type, the first value listed in the type definition has no predecessor and the last value has no successor. For example, we can have the expressions:

```
SUCC(MONDAY)         { Value is TUESDAY }
SUCC(SUCC(MONDAY))   { Value is WEDNESDAY }
SUCC(SATURDAY)       { Gives rise to an error }
```

Notice that if you try to get the successor of SATURDAY, you will get an error, and *not* the value SUNDAY as you might expect.

In Pascal, all programmer-defined types are introduced by type declarations of the form:

name = *type-definition*;

The name is a name for the type. The type definition specifies the class of values and, implicitly, the operations defining ways in which the values can be used. Except for subranges of previously-defined types (described below), every type definition introduces a distinct type.

With this discussion in mind, we recall the basic definition of a type given by Holmes:

■ A type characterizes a class of values and the set of operations that can be performed on them.

In programs, all variables have an associated type, specified when the variable is declared. The operations are defined by the language itself.

One of the key issues in programming is the security with which we can draw conclusions about a program. Consider the following declarations

```
TODAY   : DAYNAME;
NEWCOIN: COIN;
COUNTER: INTEGER;
```

where the type COIN has the definition:

```
type
    COIN = (PENNY, NICKEL, DIME, QUARTER, HALFDOLLAR, DOLLAR);
```

It would be meaningful to have the statements

```
TODAY   := TUESDAY;
NEWCOIN := NICKEL;
COUNTER := COUNTER + 1
```

but senseless and incorrect to have the statements:

```
TODAY   := NICKEL;       { NICKEL is not a DAYNAME }
NEWCOIN := TUESDAY;      { TUESDAY is not a COIN }
COUNTER := TODAY + 1     { 1 cannot be added to a DAYNAME }
```

This leads us to the two basic rules for using types:

1. A variable may only have values of its specified type.

2. The only operations allowed on a value are those associated with its type.

As a result of these two rules, we can draw a fundamental conclusion about a program: *the type properties declared by a programmer will not be violated during program execution.* This means that TODAY will always be a DAYNAME and COUNTER will always be an INTEGER. If you try to do otherwise, the computer will complain, and it should.

As mentioned earlier, an enumerated type is defined by listing its values. Such types can be used in many ways as freely as integers and often with great clarity. For example, we may have a loop iterating over the days of the week:

```
for TODAY := SUNDAY to SATURDAY do begin
  -- what to do for each value of TODAY
end
```

Notice the clarity of the loop above compared with:

```
for DAYINDEX := 1 to 7 do begin
  -- what to do for each value of DAYINDEX
end
```

Table 8.1 defines a number of enumerated types. The use of such types can add considerably to the clarity of a program.

Before going on to other basic types in Pascal, we give one word of caution. Although enumerated types can be used freely *within* a program, you cannot read or write their values directly.

TABLE 8.1   *A Sampler of Enumerated Types*

DAYNAME	=	(SUNDAY, MONDAY, TUESDAY, WEDNESDAY, THURSDAY, FRIDAY, SATURDAY);
SUSPECT	=	(COLWOODLEY, MRHOLMAN, MRPOPE, SIRRAYMOND);
CIGARTEXTURE	=	(CAKED, FLAKY, FLUFFY, GRANULAR, VARIED);
COIN	=	(PENNY, NICKEL, DIME, QUARTER, HALFDOLLAR, DOLLAR);
HALFDAY	=	(AM, PM);
ARMYRANK	=	(PRIVATE, CORPORAL, SERGEANT, LIEUTENANT, CAPTAIN, MAJOR, COLONEL, GENERAL);
MAJORCITY	=	(LONDON, OXFORD, BRISTOL, BIRMINGHAM, PLYMOUTH, LIVERPOOL, YORK, MANCHESTER);
SHAPE	=	(TRIANGLE, QUADRANGLE, PENTAGON, HEXAGON);
DIRECTION	=	(NORTH, EAST, SOUTH, WEST);
WEAPON	=	(GUN, KNIFE, CANDLESTICK, ROPE, WRENCH);
RESPONSE	=	(YES, NO, UNKNOWN);
REPORTSTATUS	=	(UNWRITTEN, DRAFTED, EDITED, COMPLETED, INPRESS, MISSING);

We see this problem in Holmes's program to compute dates. Once the final value of DAYOFWEEK is calculated, which will be one of the values SUNDAY through SATURDAY, we have to write explicit character strings to be printed for each corresponding value of the variable. Thus, for example, Holmes's program contains the statement:

```
case DAYOFWEEK of
    SUNDAY   : WRITE('SUNDAY, ');
    MONDAY   : WRITE('MONDAY, ');
    TUESDAY  : WRITE('TUESDAY, ');
    WEDNESDAY: WRITE('WEDNESDAY, ');
    THURSDAY : WRITE('THURSDAY, ');
    FRIDAY   : WRITE('FRIDAY, ');
    SATURDAY : WRITE('SATURDAY, ')
end
```

As logical as it may seem to you, you cannot simply say

```
WRITE (DAYOFWEEK, ', ');
```

which you might expect would print the value of DAYOFWEEK followed by a comma and a space. It is unfortunate that READ and WRITE cannot be applied to values of enumerated types just as they can be applied to values of integer or real types. Such is life with Pascal.

8.2 Boolean Types

In Chapter V, we discussed the writing of conditions that give values that are TRUE or FALSE. These values are said to be of type BOOLEAN, and all conditions must yield a value of type BOOLEAN. Moreover, in Pascal you can declare a variable to be of type BOOLEAN just as you can declare a variable to be of an integer type, a real type, or an enumerated type.

Suppose, for example, we wish to write a program to determine which one of a number of suspects matches a given list of characteristics. In searching the list of suspects, we may wish to keep track of whether we have found a match. To do this, we might declare a variable, say:

```
SUSPECTFOUND: BOOLEAN;
```

Such a variable can only have one of two values, TRUE or FALSE. It is analogous to having the type declaration:

```
type BOOLEAN = (FALSE, TRUE);
```

At the beginning of our program, since we clearly have not found a match, we can say:

```
SUSPECTFOUND := FALSE
```

Later in our program we will, of course, change this value to TRUE when a matching suspect is found. The status of a boolean variable may be used directly as a condition since its value is either TRUE or FALSE, for example:

```
if SUSPECTFOUND then
    -- what to do if a suspect has been found
else
    -- what to do otherwise
```

Such a statement has the same effect as writing:

```
if SUSPECTFOUND = TRUE then
    -- what to do if a suspect has been found
else
    -- what to do otherwise
```

The type BOOLEAN thus embodies a very simple but powerful idea. The type has only two values, TRUE and FALSE, and captures the essence of a condition. Furthermore, whenever we write a program and wish to keep track of a piece of information that can have only two values (for example, on or off, open or closed, known or unknown) we can represent our state of knowledge with a simple boolean-valued variable.

8.3   Character Types

It would certainly be unfortunate if the only types of data that we could read or write were numbers. Suppose we wish to read in the days of the week, a person's name, a message, or the two-letter city codes in the case of Clergyman Peter. What we would really like to do is read the characters directly into our program, rather than think up numeric codes. Fortunately we can do this in Pascal.

We use the Pascal type CHAR, which is predefined in the language, to work directly with single characters. The values of this type are all the characters you will normally find on your keyboard, and include not only letters or digits but also characters like $, <, and %.

For example, just as you can declare a variable COUNTER as having an integer type,

```
COUNTER: INTEGER;
```

you can declare a variable, say NEXTCHAR, of character type:

```
NEXTCHAR: CHAR;
```

This declaration, like all variable declarations, specifies a variable whose values will be of a certain type, in this case one of the characters on your local computer. Thus if you want to read in a character from a terminal, you can say,

```
READ (NEXTCHAR)
```

or if you wish to assign a dollar sign to this variable, you can say:

```
NEXTCHAR := '$'
```

Notice that in programs a character value must always be enclosed by single quotation marks (').

Just as for integer types or enumerated types, you can compare the character values in relational expressions, for example, as in:

```
if (NEXTCHAR = '$') then
    -- what to do if the next character is a dollar sign
else
    -- what to do otherwise
```

All of this is quite straightforward.

A few words of caution before moving on. To find out what characters you can actually use in a program, you will have to check those allowed on your implementation. Furthermore, just as for integer and enumerated types, the allowed characters have a given order. For example, the character 'A' is considered to be less than the character 'B', 'B' is less than 'C', and so forth. Similarly, the characters '0', '1', and so forth are also assumed to be in conventional order. As for any other characters, you will have to check with your manual if you want to do something fancy.

8.4 Subranges of Types

There are many cases where variables have a common type but where the values a variable can take on are known to be within certain limits. For instance, we may know that a person's age will lie between 0 and 100, or we may know a character variable can only denote certain characters. To handle this kind of situation we can use a *subrange* declaration.

For instance, consider the following variable declarations:

```
DAYOFMONTH:  1..31;
WORKDAY   :  MONDAY..FRIDAY;
NEXTCODE  :  'A'..'Z';
```

The first declaration specifies a variable DAYOFMONTH whose values lies in the range 1 through 31. The second declaration specifies a variable WORKDAY whose value is one of the weekdays MONDAY through FRIDAY. The third declaration specifies a character variable NEXTCODE, whose value is one of the letters "A" through "Z."

Subrange specifications are always given in the form

value .. value

where each of the values must be an integer, a value from some enumerated type, or a character. The type of such variables is the same as the type of the values in the subrange.

Subranges thus define a restricted sequence of values. The purpose of a subrange type is to control the range of values a variable may take during execution of your program. The bounds given in a subrange definition must belong to the same type (for example, INTEGER or the same enumerated type) and must be stated in increasing order. Thus, the following range definitions are illegal:

```
1..PENNY;        { Error, bounds not of the same type }
DOLLAR..PENNY;   { Error, bounds not in increasing order }
```

Subrange types can be declared just as for other types, by associating a name with a subrange. For example, we may have:

```
type
    DAYRANGE    =  1..31;
    WEEKDAYNAME =  MONDAY..FRIDAY;
    LETTER      =  'A'..'Z';
```

Using these explicit declarations we could alternatively declare our variables above as:

```
DAYOFMONTH: DAYRANGE;
WORKDAY   : WEEKDAYNAME;
NEXTCODE  : LETTER;
```

A subrange variable behaves much like a variable of the containing type. The only difference is that a subrange variable is constrained during execution to hold only values that belong to the declared range.

While the values of a subrange type are a subset of the containing type, the operations of a subrange type are the same as those of the containing type. Thus, the SUCC and PRED functions, comparison operators, and input-output operations apply to subrange values exactly as they apply to values of the containing type. For subrange types whose containing type is INTEGER, the arithmetic operators apply as well.

In Pascal, there is no type distinction between variables specified as a subrange and those of the containing type. The difference is simply that Pascal keeps track of your constraints on the values. For example, if you say

```
WORKDAY := SUNDAY
```

the computer will complain, since SUNDAY is not in the range given for WEEKDAYNAME. Similarly, if you say

```
DAYOFMONTH := DAYOFMONTH + 5
```

and the result is greater than 31, an error will arise.

Finally, a note on the operator in. You can use this operator to see whether a value is within some set of values. For example, you can say

```
if NEXTCODE in ['A', 'B', 'C', 'D', 'E']
```

or equivalently:

```
if NEXTCODE in ['A' .. 'E']
```

Generally speaking, the value being tested must be either an integer, a character, or an enumerated value. The set of values is specified by listing the members of the set, giving subranges, or both. Thus we may have:

```
[MONDAY..FRIDAY]
[MONDAY, WEDNESDAY, FRIDAY]
[1, 3, 5, 7, 9]
['0'..'9', '%', '$', '.']
```

8.5 String Types

Consider the statement:

```
WRITE ('MONDAY,')
```

Execution of this statement results in writing the string

```
MONDAY,
```

on your terminal or output device. In Pascal, a sequence of two or more characters enclosed by single quote marks is said to be a *character string*, and such values are said to belong to a string type.

You might think that character strings would be treated analogously to integers or enumerated values, and thus handled like our other primitive types. Unfortunately, a character string is considered to be the same as an *array* of characters; you must learn all about arrays in order to work with strings. This is unfortunate because we would like to have talked about strings here in this chapter; but for the moment, we have to pass and wait.

Summary

As Holmes points out, an important part of the programmer's task is to represent objects in terms of the constructs of a programming language. Whether these objects are varieties of cigar ash, people's names, amounts of money, or calendar dates, they all must be represented in some way in your computer program.

Any programming language comes equipped with certain basic types of data that you must use when writing your programs. In Pascal, you have several primitive types that are predefined in the language itself. These are the types:

```
INTEGER
REAL
BOOLEAN
CHAR
```

In addition to these four predefined types, Pascal allows you to define your own enumerated types. Furthermore, Pascal allows you to define subranges of integer, character, or enumerated types. For example, you may say

```
type
    INDEXVAL = 1..100;
    DAYNAME = (SUNDAY, MONDAY, TUESDAY, WEDNESDAY, THURSDAY,
               FRIDAY, SATURDAY);
    LETTER  = 'A'..'Z';
```

Thus whatever type of data your program uses, you must ultimately represent it with one of the four predefined types or one of the methods for defining your own types.

Now you certainly do have a choice in the matter. For example, you may give the days of the week as an enumerated type; you may give each day of the week a numeric value, say 1 through 7; or you may, if you wish, code each day of the week with a different single-letter character. Your choice will be guided by the problem at hand.

Once a variable in your program has been declared of a certain type, it must always have values of that type. This will give you security, for instance, that you cannot assign an integer to a character variable or an enumerated value to a real variable. Thus once you tell the computer about your types of data, it will keep things straight for you and make sure that the type properties of the data are never violated.

Table 8.2 summarizes some predefined functions and operations over these simple types. Some of these functions and operations have been mentioned earlier and others will arise later in this text.

TABLE 8.2   *Some Functions and Operations on Simple Types*

x is an expression whose value is an integer, character, or member of an enumerated type.

All such values have a given ordering. For *integers*, the values are in numerical order; for *characters*, the order is defined by the local implementation; for *enumerated* types, the values are listed in increasing order. The first value in an enumerated type is said to have the ordinal 0, the second 1, and so forth.

Functions

SUCC(x) Computes the successor of x, the value whose ordinal is one greater than x. Taking the successor of the last value is in error.

PRED(x) Computes the predecessor of x, the value whose ordinal is one less than x. Taking the predecessor of the first value is in error.

ORD(x) Computes the ordinal value of x in its given ordering. For integers, returns the integer itself; for characters, check your local implementation. Result is always an integer.

CHR(x) Yields the character whose ordinal value is x. The value of x must be an integer, and the result is a character.

Relational Operations

Operator	Operation	Type of Operands	Result Type
= <>	equality and inequality	any simple or string type	BOOLEAN
< <= > >=	ordering	any simple or string type	BOOLEAN
in	membership	Left: integer, character, or enumerated value Right: set of values	BOOLEAN

IX

The Ciphered Message

HE intimate relations that had existed between Sherlock Holmes and myself were, to an extent, modified in those years following my marriage, during which my practice increased steadily. I was occasionally able to follow my old companion's activities in the daily papers, which reported on his service to the Royal Family of Scandinavia and a matter of great importance to the French government, the details of which may never fully reach the public. While these cases brought him fame and princely rewards, they, and the one that I am about to relate, gave him the opportunity of demonstrating a fresh idea in his use of the Analytical Engine.

I called upon him late one winter's evening. As we sat on either side of the fire, Holmes was telling me once again, with great exultation, how he had purchased at a broker's in Tottenham Court Road for only fifty-five shillings a Stradivarius that was valued at over five hundred guineas. He suddenly held up his hand in a gesture of silence.

"We have a visitor," he said softly. "A gentleman of some importance, a government official perhaps."

When Mrs. Hudson showed a fellow dressed more like a gardener than a statesman into his lodgings, I must confess I had a slight feeling of amusement in my heart and hoped that this would be a lesson against the somewhat dogmatic tone he often exhibited.

"Tell me, sir," said Holmes, before any introductions had been exchanged, "do you always tend your flower beds in patent-leather boots, or is this the manner of attire appropriate to Whitehall these days?"

"Mr. Holmes," he replied solemnly, "I come on a matter of the utmost delicacy concerning the security of our nation." As he spoke he handed

Holmes his card, which identified him as an undersecretary in the Home Office.

Holmes rubbed his hands and his eyes glistened. Once our visitor was seated, Holmes leaned forward eagerly in his chair.

"State your case," he said briskly.

Uncomfortable, I rose to excuse myself.

"Please stay, Watson," asked Holmes. Then, turning to our visitor, he said, "this is Dr. Watson. You may say before this gentleman anything which you choose to say to me."

"It is known that you have assisted other heads of state on matters of the utmost confidence," said the man. "I am here, disguised so as not to draw attention to myself, on behalf of the Secretary to ask your help on a delicate matter concerning the transmission of diplomatic messages."

"Surely you are aware," answered Holmes, "that this is the special province of my brother, Mycroft. Though a government accountant, he also serves as an advisor in such matters."

"True, very true indeed, sir. However, as you yourself know very well, work of this nature neither begins nor ends in an armchair. While your brother's services remain indispensable, he lacks a certain energy."

Holmes merely nodded. "Pray continue," he said.

"Diplomatic ciphered messages are being regularly intercepted, deciphered, and acted upon. Acted upon with great damage," the Undersecretary stated in a clear and determined manner. With that, he produced a small packet of papers, unfolded them, and disclosed to us some of their contents. Holmes retrieved a small pince-nez and endeavoured to read them.

"HE ENDEAVOURED TO READ THEM."

"I thought that diplomatic ciphers were extremely difficult to break and that their keys were changed regularly. I understand also that the material they contain is often urgent, so that by the time someone could reasonably be expected to decode it, the information would no longer be important," Holmes said.

"This is true for the most part," replied the Undersecretary. "But some of our clerks are—how shall I say it—incapable of handling a cipher of great complexity or of remembering the scheme required to decipher it, and certainly incapable of relearning a new one as often as necessary. Indeed, the same code, a simple one, is used for months, so that confusion is kept to a minimum."

I am not at liberty to reveal the content of the next hour's discussion. Suffice it to say that the matters discussed were grave indeed.

As our visitor was restoring his papers to an inner pocket, Holmes said, "How may I be of assistance to you, sir?"

"Mr. Holmes, we need a more secure cipher. Will you devise one for us?"

"I shall do my best," said Holmes steadily.

"Very good," replied the Undersecretary, and he then withdrew.

"Well, Watson, what do you make of it?" asked Holmes, once we were again alone.

"A nasty business, I should say, by the sound of things. But I am afraid I cannot help you much, for I am quite unfamiliar with ciphers and codes."

"Perhaps," said Holmes. "But this cipher is one of the simplest imaginable. It is so transparent that even a Scotland Yard official could see through it. The foreign agents who intercepted the messages probably believed the cipher was so elementary that it was a blind for a deeper and more complex cipher, embedded within. Each letter of the alphabet is simply replaced by some other letter. Allow me to show you."

Holmes wrote a sequence of letters on a sheet of paper :

A B C D E F G H I J K L M N O P Q R S T U V W X Y Z

"Assume now that our cipher letters are given in the following sequence :

H I J K L M N O P Q R S T U V W X Y Z A B C D E F G

Now we write the message on top, and below it the ciphered message :

```
TWELVE SHIPS WILL LEAVE ...
ADLSCL ZOPWZ DPSS SLHCL ...
```

Thus we get a letter for each letter of the message; and as long as we have a standard table to use, enciphering the message is an easy task."

"Well, all this seems childishly simple to me," I said.

"Too simple; and therein lies our problem, Watson."

"But surely, Holmes, you must know of some other cipher the Home Office could substitute for this one."

"I am fairly familiar with all forms of secret writings; and am myself the author of a trifling monograph upon the subject, in which I analyze one hundred and sixty separate ciphers. This one, however, as I have already stated, is by far the simplest—and I need not remind you with whom we are dealing."

After a considerable pause he returned to his sample ciphering sequence. "Here again is the sequence I have just written :—

```
H I J K L M N O P Q R S T U V W X Y Z A B C D E F G
```

We can shift this sequence by one letter and get :

```
I J K L M N O P Q R S T U V W X Y Z A B C D E F G H
```

We can do likewise for a shift by two letters or three letters or even twenty-five letters. Each of these permutations is displayed in this table."

Holmes then showed me the table that I have duplicated here as Exhibit 9.1.

"Now for the key, Watson. From time to time passwords, or keywords, if you will, can be provided to the clerks. For demonstration, suppose the keyword is WATSON."

"I am flattered, Holmes," I remarked quite involuntarily.

"Now," Holmes continued, "we write the password over the message, like this :—

```
WATSON WATSO NWAT SONWA ...
TWELVE SHIPS WILL LEAVE ...
```

For the first letter (T) of the message, we look at the W row of the cipher table under the column T. We get a W. For the next message letter (W), look at the A row under column W. We get a D. Simply continuing as prescribed, the message is coded as :

```
WDEKQY VOION QLSL KZUYL ...
```

Elementary, is it not?"

"Quite," I replied. "And I suppose that you intend to hand this material over to the Analytical Engine?"

"Precisely. Think of it, Watson, a device made of wood and metal that will actually print the results of its most complicated calculations as soon as they are obtained, without any intervention of human intelligence, or lack of it, as this case would suggest. Our Engine will guarantee the mathematical accuracy of its work, so ciphering the message will be flawless."

MESSAGE LETTER

	A B C D E F G H I J K L M N O P Q R S T U V W X Y Z
A	H I J K L M N O P Q R S T U V W X Y Z A B C D E F G
B	I J K L M N O P Q R S T U V W X Y Z A B C D E F G H
C	J K L M N O P Q R S T U V W X Y Z A B C D E F G H I
D	K L M N O P Q R S T U V W X Y Z A B C D E F G H I J
E	L M N O P Q R S T U V W X Y Z A B C D E F G H I J K
F	M N O P Q R S T U V W X Y Z A B C D E F G H I J K L
G	N O P Q R S T U V W X Y Z A B C D E F G H I J K L M
H	O P Q R S T U V W X Y Z A B C D E F G H I J K L M N
I	P Q R S T U V W X Y Z A B C D E F G H I J K L M N O
J	Q R S T U V W X Y Z A B C D E F G H I J K L M N O P
K	R S T U V W X Y Z A B C D E F G H I J K L M N O P Q
L	S T U V W X Y Z A B C D E F G H I J K L M N O P Q R
M	T U V W X Y Z A B C D E F G H I J K L M N O P Q R S
N	U V W X Y Z A B C D E F G H I J K L M N O P Q R S T
O	V W X Y Z A B C D E F G H I J K L M N O P Q R S T U
P	W X Y Z A B C D E F G H I J K L M N O P Q R S T U V
Q	X Y Z A B C D E F G H I J K L M N O P Q R S T U V W
R	Y Z A B C D E F G H I J K L M N O P Q R S T U V W X
S	Z A B C D E F G H I J K L M N O P Q R S T U V W X Y
T	A B C D E F G H I J K L M N O P Q R S T U V W X Y Z
U	B C D E F G H I J K L M N O P Q R S T U V W X Y Z A
V	C D E F G H I J K L M N O P Q R S T U V W X Y Z A B
W	D E F G H I J K L M N O P Q R S T U V W X Y Z A B C
X	E F G H I J K L M N O P Q R S T U V W X Y Z A B C D
Y	F G H I J K L M N O P Q R S T U V W X Y Z A B C D E
Z	G H I J K L M N O P Q R S T U V W X Y Z A B C D E F

Exhibit 9.1   *Holmes's Cipher Table*
(Keyword letters are given on the left)

One of the most remarkable characteristics of Sherlock Holmes was his ability to put his brain out of action, switching his thoughts to lighter things whenever he had satisfied himself that he could no longer work to advantage. With a casual remark that this was indeed one of the most unimaginative tasks he had been called upon to deliver, he lapsed into our earlier discussion of violins. This led him to Paganini; and before I departed we sat for another hour over a bottle of claret, while he told me anecdote after anecdote of that extraordinary man.

I promised to return the next evening, and did so promptly at eight. Upon entering, I found Holmes peering into the internals of the device on the centre-table, which had been cleared of everything else. From where I stood I could see a very closely packed collection of meshing gears and cams. There appeared to be a cover that was swung upwards, forwards, and out of the way. Holmes studied the box for a moment and then beckoned to me.

"An amazing machine, Watson. The way Babbage uses the gears and cams to store his data is truly ingenious. We are now faced with the problem of how we are to proceed with the enciphering programme. I have been giving the matter some consideration and have written down my thoughts in the order that the machine should perform them to accomplish the task. What do you think, Watson?"

On a piece of paper Holmes had written the following :

Read in the cipher table

Repeat the following:
   read message character
   if message character is a letter then
      select cipher character using keyword and message letter
      write cipher character
   else
      write message character
until no characters are left

"Holmes, although this sketch is simple, it will actually be very cumbersome to implement, will it not?"

"How would you do it, Watson?"

I started to write almost without thinking :

If key letter is A and message letter is A then cipher is H
If key letter is A and message letter is B then cipher is I
  . . .   .
If key letter is A and message letter is Z then cipher is G

If key letter is B and message letter is A then cipher is I
If key letter is B and message letter is B then cipher is J
  . . .   .

and so on.

"My goodness, Holmes, this would take hundreds, if not thousands, of instructions. I do not see how they could possibly fit into the Engine."

"Six hundred and seventy-six, to be precise, Watson. Your method is indeed cumbersome. Perhaps a table—or as our mathematician friends call it, an *array*—would help to reduce the size of the programme. It would also eliminate the element of redundancy that your scheme requires."

"Exactly what is an array?" I enquired.

"An array is much like a chessboard," explained Holmes. "For our problem the cipher table is a 26-by-26 array, a chessboard is an 8-by-8 array.

"Each position in the cipher table or chessboard can be identified by naming the particular array and the specific element or position with which we are concerned. In the message, the first cipher letter is the letter residing at the crossing of the W row and the T column. Thus the cipher for the letter T can be obtained with the description:

CIPHER_TABLE ['W', 'T']

Equivalently, if ROW is set to 'W' and COLUMN to 'T', we can write:

CIPHER_TABLE [ROW, COLUMN]

Indeed, the description can be assumed to be the same as the actual element.

"It is a powerful concept for describing data, as it compresses the information into a form that is entirely suitable for a machine such as Babbage's, and is much more economical with the amount of space used. It also removes the need for all the words describing the choices to be made in the cipher. Rather, it uses the position in the array to convey all of this. However, I am still faced with the problem of the keyword. If it is not made to reside in the Engine, anyone could steal it and use it. The keyword will reside in the programme, so that we shall have no problems with the operator."

Holmes paced anxiously about the room for a moment and then constructed a sort of Eastern divan in one corner. He perched himself upon it, cross-legged, with a quantity of shag tobacco and a box of matches laid out before him. In the dim light of the lamp I watched him sitting there, an old briar pipe between his lips, his eyes fixed vacantly upon the corner of the ceiling, the blue smoke curling up from him, silent, motionless, with the light shining upon his strong-set aquiline features.

I knew that seclusion and solitude were necessary for Holmes in those hours of intense mental concentration, and it was noon the next day when I again found myself in his sitting room. My first impression was that a fire had broken out, for the room was thick with smoke and I could barely see Holmes in his dressing-gown, coiled up in his armchair by the fireplace.

"So you've been up all the night and all the morning poisoning yourself," I said.

"Actually, Watson, I have just returned from the Home Office," he answered.

"You have been there in spirit, perhaps?"

"Exactly. The body of Sherlock Holmes has remained here in this armchair and has, I regret to report, consumed in my absence two large pots of coffee and an incredible amount of tobacco."

"And what have you brought back with you to Baker Street?"

He then unrolled a large document upon his knee. On it were the final algorithm and the final programme, which I have duplicated here as Exhibits 9.2 and 9.3, respectively.

```
Definitions:
    ROW, COLUMN   : a letter for a row or column of the cipher table
    MESSAGE_CHAR: a character
    CIPHER_CHAR   : a character
    CIPHER_TABLE  : an array giving the cipher letter for each
                    keyword letter and message letter
    KEYWORD       : the characters used for ciphering messages
Algorithm:
    Read cipher letters for each ROW and COLUMN of CIPHER_TABLE
    Repeat the following:
        read MESSAGE_CHAR
        if MESSAGE_CHAR is a letter then
            set ROW to next letter of KEYWORD
            set COLUMN to MESSAGE_CHAR
            set CIPHER_CHAR to CIPHER_TABLE [ROW, COLUMN]
            write CIPHER_CHAR
        else
            write MESSAGE_CHAR
    until no characters are left
```

Exhibit 9.2   *Holmes's Algorithm for Enciphering a Message*

```
program ENCIPHER (INPUT, OUTPUT);

{   -- This programme reads in the characters of a message and
    -- enciphers each letter. Based on the letter and the next
    -- letter of the keyword, the enciphered letter is obtained
    -- from a cipher table initially read into the program. The
    -- message is terminated by a slash. }

    const
        NUMKEYLETTERS = 6;
        SLASH = '/';
    type
        LETTER = 'A'0..'Z';
    var
        ROW, COLUMN: LETTER;
        MESSAGECHAR,
        CIPHERCHAR : CHAR;
        CIPHERTABLE: array [LETTER, LETTER] of LETTER;
        KEYWORD    : packed array [1 .. NUMKEYLETTERS] of CHAR;
        KEYINDEX   : INTEGER;

begin
    KEYWORD := 'WATSON';
    for ROW := 'A' to 'Z' do begin
        for COLUMN := 'A' to 'Z' do
            READ (CIPHERTABLE [ROW, COLUMN]);
        READLN
    end;
    KEYINDEX := 1;
    repeat
        READ (MESSAGECHAR);
        if MESSAGECHAR in ['A'..'Z'] then
            begin
                ROW        := KEYWORD[KEYINDEX];
                COLUMN     := MESSAGECHAR;
                CIPHERCHAR := CIPHERTABLE[ROW, COLUMN];
                WRITE (CIPHERCHAR);
                if KEYINDEX = NUMKEYLETTERS then
                    KEYINDEX := 1
                else
                    KEYINDEX := KEYINDEX + 1
            end
        else
            WRITE (MESSAGECHAR)
    until MESSAGECHAR = SLASH
end.
```

Exhibit 9.3   *Holmes's Enciphering Programme*

As I examined the material he exclaimed, "Well, Watson, let us escape from this weary workaday world by the side door of music. Carina sings tonight at the Albert Hall, and we still have time to dress, drop these off at Whitehall, dine, and enjoy an evening of supreme inspiration."

9.1 Arrays

Until now we have been dealing with items like a room number, a hair color, a type of cigar, and the time of day. All of these items have a common characteristic: they denote a single piece of data in the real world. With the introduction of Holmes's enciphering table, we come to an entirely different kind of entity, that of a composite object. A composite object has components that bear some relation to one another. In Holmes's enciphering program, the cipher table is a composite object consisting of the cipher characters corresponding to each possible pair of letters.

The enciphering table raises a very general issue. In many instances we have collections of related data. To turn such data into a usable tool, we need some means of organizing the data to reflect the way they are used.

We turn here to one of the most important schemes for organizing data, the *array;* in later chapters we will examine how data may be organized into a file or a record structure. But the various methods for structuring data have the same objective: the ability to describe organized patterns of information.

You can think of an array as an ordinary table of entries. A table expresses a correspondence; that is, for each one of several items, we have a corresponding item.

For example, each of the following correspondences can be expressed in a table:

suspect	→	corresponding hair color
month	→	corresponding number of days
coin	→	corresponding value

In the first case, drawn from the murder at the Metropolitan Club, we have four suspects, each having some corresponding color of hair. In the second case, the correspondence is between the name of a month and the number of days in the month. In the third case, taken from our problem to count change, we have six coins, each with a corresponding value in cents. A simple table describing the correspondence between coins and values is shown in Figure 9.1.

	COIN	VALUE
	Penny	1
	Nickel	5
	Dime	10
	Quarter	25
	Half Dollar	50
	Dollar	100

Figure 9.1   *Table of Coin Values*

An array has two fundamental properties. The first is its set of indices, and the second is the set of components that may be stored within it. For example, the table of coin values may be described in Pascal as follows:

```
array [1..6] of INTEGER
```

This array contains six values, indexed by the numbers 1 through 6. The components of the array, the coin values, are integers. The integers give corresponding values for each of the six coins. Notice that the number of components in the array is implicitly specified when the range of index values is given in the array definition.

The indices of an array need not be limited to integer values. In Pascal, the indices of an array may be specified in the following ways:

1. by giving an explicit *range* of integer, character, or enumerated values.

2. by giving the *name* of a previously declared integer, character, or enumerated type, or the *name* of a subrange.

For instance, with the type definitions

```
type
   COINNUM = 1..6;
   COIN    = (PENNY, NICKEL, DIME, QUARTER, HALFDOLLAR, DOLLAR);
```

we can give the array definitions:

```
array [1..6]        of INTEGER
array [PENNY..DOLLAR] of INTEGER

array [COINNUM] of INTEGER
array [COIN]    of INTEGER
```

Each of these array definitions describes the simple arrangement shown in Table 9.1. In the first and third definitions, the indices are the numbers 1 through 6; in the other two definitions, the indices are the values PENNY through DOLLAR.

Naturally we want to do something with arrays, and this means we want to give them names and refer to their components. Just as we can write

```
COUNTER: INTEGER;
```

to declare a variable COUNTER of type INTEGER, we can write

```
COINVALUE: array [1..6] of INTEGER;
```

to declare a variable of an array type.

To refer to array components, we give the name of the array followed by the component index enclosed in square brackets. Accordingly, just as we can write

```
COUNTER := 1
```

to assign a value to a simple variable, we can write

```
COINVALUE[2] := 5
```

to assign a value to an array component. Similarly, just as we can refer to the value of a simple variable in an expression like

```
COUNTER + 1
```

we can also refer to the value of an array component in an expression like:

```
COINVALUE[2] * NUMCOINS
```

The general rule here is that we can treat a reference to an array component just the same as a simple variable.

Many of these ideas are illustrated in Example 9.1, yet another program for counting change. Here the values of the individual coins are stored in the array named COINVALUE. The first six assignment statements simply set the values of each coin to their respective value in pennies. In the computation of the total change, the value of each individual coin is obtained from the array COINVALUE. The rest of the program remains as it was in previous versions.

```
program COUNTCHANGE (INPUT, OUTPUT);

{  -- This program reads in six integer values, respectively
   -- representing the number of pennies, nickels, dimes, quarters,
   -- half-dollars, and silver dollars in coinage.
   -- The program outputs the total value of the coins in dollars
   -- and cents. }

   var
       NEXTCOIN, COINCOUNT, TOTALCHANGE, CENTS, DOLLARS:  INTEGER;
       COINVALUE: array [1..6] of INTEGER;

begin
    COINVALUE[1] :=   1;
    COINVALUE[2] :=   5;
    COINVALUE[3] :=  10;
    COINVALUE[4] :=  25;
    COINVALUE[5] :=  50;
    COINVALUE[6] := 100;

    TOTALCHANGE := 0;
    for NEXTCOIN := 1 to 6 do begin
       READ (COINCOUNT);
       TOTALCHANGE := TOTALCHANGE + (COINVALUE[NEXTCOIN] * COINCOUNT)
    end;

    if (TOTALCHANGE = 0) then
       WRITE ('NO COINS')
    else
       begin
          DOLLARS := TOTALCHANGE div 100;
          CENTS   := TOTALCHANGE mod 100;
          WRITE ('CHANGE IS ', DOLLARS:2, ' DOLLARS AND ', CENTS:2, ' CENTS.')
       end
end.
```

Example 9.1 *Counting Change Using an Array of Coin Values*

Next consider Example 9.2. Here we see an even greater improvement when the individual coins are represented with an enumerated type. Notice here the clarity in referring to each coin by a name rather than by a number. This clarity is especially evident in the assignments, such as

```
COINVALUE[NICKEL] := 5
```

```
program COUNTCHANGE (INPUT, OUTPUT);

{   -- This program reads in six integer values, respectively
    -- representing the number of pennies, nickels, dimes, quarters,
    -- half-dollars, and silver dollars in coinage.
    -- The program outputs the total value of the coins in dollars
    -- and cents. }

    type
        COIN = (PENNY, NICKEL, DIME, QUARTER, HALFDOLLAR, DOLLAR);
    var
        COINCOUNT, TOTALCHANGE, CENTS, DOLLARS:  INTEGER;
        NEXTCOIN : COIN;
        COINVALUE: array [PENNY..DOLLAR] of INTEGER;
begin
    COINVALUE[PENNY]        :=    1;
    COINVALUE[NICKEL]       :=    5;
    COINVALUE[DIME]         :=   10;
    COINVALUE[QUARTER]      :=   25;
    COINVALUE[HALFDOLLAR]   :=   50;
    COINVALUE[DOLLAR]       :=  100;

    TOTALCHANGE := 0;

    for NEXTCOIN := PENNY to DOLLAR do begin
        READ (COINCOUNT);
        TOTALCHANGE := TOTALCHANGE + (COINVALUE[NEXTCOIN] * COINCOUNT)
    end;

    if (TOTALCHANGE = 0) then
        WRITE ('NO COINS')
    else
        begin
            DOLLARS := TOTALCHANGE div 100;
            CENTS   := TOTALCHANGE mod 100;
            WRITE ('CHANGE IS ', DOLLARS:2, ' DOLLARS AND ', CENTS:2, ' CENTS.')
        end
end.
```

Example 9.2   *Counting Change Using the Type COIN*

or in the following loop:

```
for NEXTCOIN := PENNY to DOLLAR do begin
    READ (COINCOUNT);
    TOTALCHANGE := TOTALCHANGE + (COINVALUE[NEXTCOIN] * COINCOUNT)
end
```

Finally, notice that array types can be named in a type declaration just as for any of the other types in Pascal. For example, consider the following type declarations:

```
type
    LETTER       = 'A'..'Z';

    VECTOR       =   array [1..100] of REAL;
    GOLFSCORE    =   array [1..18]  of INTEGER;

    COINTABLE    =   array [PENNY..DOLLAR] of INTEGER;
    CIPHERTABLE  =   array [LETTER, LETTER] of LETTER;
```

These types may be used just as any other types in Pascal, for example, to name the type of variables in:

```
var
    YCOORDINATE  : VECTOR;
    PARFORCOURSE : GOLFSCORE;

    COINVALUE    : COINTABLE;
    CIPHERCODE   : CIPHERTABLE;
```

9.2   Strings as Arrays

With all of the elegance provided by the Pascal facility to describe and use arrays, we turn now to one notoriously awkward feature: character strings must be represented and used as arrays. Here goes.

Whenever we use a character string in Pascal, the computer treats it as an array of characters. The number of characters in the string specifies the indices of the array. Furthermore, the array is assumed to be "packed," which means that the computer should be very careful about economizing storage for the characters in a string. Do not worry about this "packed" business, simply use it as illustrated below.

For example, consider the string:

```
'SHERLOCK HOLMES'
```

This string has fifteen characters and is treated as a value of type:

```
packed array [1..15] of CHAR
```

Here the indices 1 through 15 correspond to the fifteen characters in the string.

Now comes the trouble. Suppose you wish to write a program to keep track of people's names. It would be nice to write something like

```
NAME := 'SHERLOCK HOLMES'
```

and then later in your program, write something like:

```
NAME := 'DR. WATSON'
```

You can't do this. Why? Because like any array, the number of components in an array is fixed, and thus there is no way to give a correct array type to the variable NAME. What you have to do first is figure out the *maximum* length that any of the strings can have, for example:

```
var
    NAME: packed array [1..20] of CHAR;
```

Here we specify that all values of type NAME have twenty characters.

To assign string values to our variable NAME, we must make sure that the character string assigned to NAME has exactly the right number of characters. Accordingly, to get the effect desired above, we have to write something like

```
NAME := 'SHERLOCK HOLMES     '
```

and later do:

```
NAME := 'DR. WATSON          '
```

Notice here that blanks have been added to the strings in order to fill the space for exactly twenty characters.

Since strings are represented as arrays, reference to the characters of a string is handled exactly as a reference to the component of an array. For example, to reference the third letter of the string NAME, we simply write:

```
NAME[3]
```

Notice, however, as for all arrays, it is impossible to say something like

```
NAME[1..8] := 'SHERLOCK'   { no luck }
```

to refer to the first eight characters of a string.

As for reading and writing strings, we are again faced with the array dilemma. The predefined procedures READ and READLN can only be used to read in integers, real numbers, or single characters. Thus to read in the value of a string variable you must read it in on a character-by-character basis. With the procedures WRITE and WRITELN we fare a bit better. These procedures can be applied to character strings, as well as character string variables. Thus, while you cannot say,

```
READ (NAME)     { error }
```

you can say:

```
WRITE (NAME)     { fine }
```

Strange.

Essentially, all you need to know about strings is that they must be defined as packed arrays of characters. You then simply apply the normal machinery of arrays to do the rest. Although conceptually it is all quite simple, you will constantly find problems when you attempt to work with strings in Pascal. It can be done, but often with a lot of work.

A string can be given a name in a constant declaration, just as a number can. Thus you can say:

```
const
    KEYWORD = 'WATSON';
    NUMKEYLETTERS = 6;
```

As for any constant, you can assign its value to a variable, but the constant itself cannot be assigned a new value. In any case, you can still refer to the characters of a named string as usual.

One last point. Your version of Pascal may have some string features that go beyond those mentioned above. If so, these features should help reduce some of the difficulties in working with strings. Check your manual.

X

A Study in Chemistry

T was a singular combination of events in the spring of '91 that found Mr. Sherlock Holmes and myself again sharing his quarters at 221B Baker Street. I need not detail the circumstances attendant upon my temporary return; suffice it to say that with the aid of a noted Harley Street specialist, I was able to persuade Holmes not to undertake a single investigation at that time. It was absolutely imperative that the great detective lay aside all his work and surrender himself to complete rest, should he wish to avoid a complete breakdown.

The morning of the present narrative began abruptly. Holmes was at my bedside, shaking me from a deep and peaceful sleep and attempting to drag me from under my sheets.

"Quick, Watson!" he exclaimed. "On your feet, man, and to the window!" His face was tinged with colour and his brows drawn into two hard black lines with the steely glitter of his eyes shining out from under them. Only in times of great crisis have I observed these battle signals flying, and I scarcely needed to rely on my companion's great muscular strength to get me standing.

I immediately became aware of a loathsome, suffocating odour as I staggered with his aid to the windows. A thick, black cloud was filtering in from the sitting room where Holmes had been experimenting with chemicals, apparently throughout the night. He tossed aside the curtains and threw open the lead-paned windows, and in a moment we were leaning out, side by side, conscious only of the glorious sunshine and the fresh, early-morning air.

Some while later we sat near my bedside wiping our clammy foreheads and surveying each other with some apprehension. "I take it there is some justifiable reason for all of this?" I queried, letting the tone of my voice carry the full weight of my irritation.

"I have, with some success," replied Holmes, his eyes twinkling, "duplicated the poisonous gas employed in the Hyde Park case."

"Indeed you have, and nearly done away with us in the bargain!"

"Well, yes, I suppose I do owe you a word of apology, as I have almost added another chapter to what the papers are calling the Hyde Park Horrors. It was, I admit, an unjustifiable experiment to carry out on oneself and doubly so considering the presence of an unsuspecting friend."

It was difficult to remain angered at Sherlock Holmes for any great length of time. His apology had been put forth with such sincerity that I was considerably touched. My anger at a rude awakening no longer seemed worth pursuing.

"The vapours have diffused by now," he said presently. "It should be safe to return."

"I am greatly disappointed with you, Holmes. You promised to engage your energies in more scholarly pursuits. The first sensational headline to come along and you've broken your word. There you are, off like a racing engine, ready to tear yourself to pieces, with a hospital bed your destination for certain!" I cried.

"On the contrary, my dear Watson," he retorted. "It was just those scholarly pursuits that have led me here, and once you have performed your morning ablutions and breakfasted I shall be pleased to elaborate on how the Analytical Engine may be most helpful in my chemical dabblings. With the Engine at my disposal our predawn discomforts could have been totally avoided. I suggest for now, however, that we take our rashers and eggs at one of London's finer eating establishments, as arsenic vapours are not pleasing to the discriminating palate."

After a pleasing breakfast in Mrs. Woolwich's Tea Rooms, we returned to Baker Street. Holmes continued his discourse at a small card table on which he had set up a makeshift laboratory.

"Do you recollect anything of my friend Dimitri Ivanovich Mendeleeff?" he asked. "A man ahead of his time in many ways."

"A chemist, as I recall."

"Quite so," he replied. "A scientific mind of the first order. Mendeleeff was the first to bring both system and structure to the family of elements: gold, most highly praised of metals, which never tarnishes or rusts; base lead, common and despised; quicksilver, a metal in liquid form; sulphur and carbon, usually powders, sometimes crystals—why, a diamond is merely carbon! Or consider the very air, a mixture of many gases. And these elements combine chemically with one another to produce the amazing variety of materials that sustain us—or that can destroy us, as was nearly the case this morning.

"It has been Mendeleeff's great insight to categorize the various elements in the form of a table for handy reference. In his table, he arranges the elements, with each assigned a specific atomic weight, vertically in groups. The elements within each group bear chemical properties similar to one another. Dimitri Ivanovich has shown that the properties of elements recur periodically, much as the sounds of musical notes recurs throughout the octaves—an idea much scorned by the Royal Society when the unfortunate Newlands first suggested it years ago."

Holmes then produced a chart from the great bundle of papers that littered his desk. It showed the elements arranged vertically in groups. Naturally I had come across this table, which I have reproduced as Exhibit 10.1, during my medical studies at the University of London.

"This is all very interesting," I said, after looking over the chart. "But of what use is it to you? Surely it is of no importance to a criminal investigator?"

"Ah, but the value of the table to me is practical. Since it lists the atomic weights of the elements, I can use the information to calculate the weight of any compound I choose. Consider, for example, the poisonous arsenic vapors

As_4O_6

Series	Group I	Group II	Group III	Group IV	Group V	Group VI	Group VII	Group VIII
1	H=1							
2	Li=7	Be=9.4	B=11	C=12	N=14	O=16	F=19	
3	Na=23	Mg=24	Al=27.3	Si=28	P=31	S=32	Cl=35.5	
4	K=39	Ca=40	—=44	Ti=48	V=51	Cr=52	Mn=55	Fe=56, Co=59, Ni=59
5	Cu=63	Zn=65	—=68	—=72	As=75	Se=78	Br=80	
6	Rb=85	Sr=87	?Yt=88	Zr=90	Nb=94	Mo=96	—=100	Ru=104, Rh=104, Pd=106
7	Ag=108	Cd=112	In=113	Sn=118	Sb=122	Te=125	I=127	
8	Cs=133	Ba=137	?Di=138	?Ce=140	—	—	—	
9	—	—	—	—	—	—	—	
10	—	—	?Er=178	?La=180	Ta=182	W=184	—	Os=195, Ir=197, Pt=198
11	Au=199	Hg=200	Tl=204	Pb=207	Bi=208	—	—	
12	—	—	—	Th=231	—	U=240	—	

Exhibit 10.1 *Mendeleeff's Periodic Table of the Chemical Elements*

that I produced this morning. According to Mendeleeff's table, arsenic weighs 75 units and oxygen weighs 16 units. The weight of a molecule of the gas is then:

$(75 * 4) + (16 * 6) = 396$

"As you can see, Watson, the calculation is trivial. But there are many elements, all of differing weights. Obtaining correct results can be tedious and subject to error when there are many such calculations to make. I would like to develop a tool for use on the Analytical Engine to assist me in calculating molecular weights. Thus I wish to enter formulae of this sort and receive as output the molecular weight."

"Yes, Holmes," I remarked. "But the problem is not so simple as you make it appear. You must instruct the Engine to make sense of the formulae, and you must store Mendeleeff's table in the Engine's memory."

"Excellent, Watson! Compound of the Busy Bee and Excelsior!" cried Holmes. "That is precisely what must be done. You see, storing Mendeleeff's table in the Engine is of great value, and having the Engine recognise the atomic abbreviations will save my brain for more important matters. This is exactly where the method of instructing the Engine is of particular interest."

In an instant Holmes was at the Engine, continuing with his lecture.

"Now, Watson, pay close attention. Here is a general algorithm that will allow the Engine to solve the problem of molecular weights."

He showed me the following :

```
Set up atomic weights table
Set TOTAL_WEIGHT to 0.0

Repeat the following:
    Obtain NEXT_ELEMENT and NUM_ATOMS
    Add ATOMIC_WEIGHT[NEXT_ELEMENT]*NUM_ATOMS
        to TOTAL_WEIGHT
until no more elements

Write TOTAL_WEIGHT
```

"As you remarked earlier, there are two interesting lines. First,

```
Set up atomic weights table
```

This requires the Engine to fill a table with Mendeleeff's atomic weights. Second,

Obtain NEXT_ELEMENT and NUM_ATOMS

This requires that the programme ask what the next element is—for example H means hydrogen and AS means arsenic—and how many atoms there are of that element.

"The point is, Watson, that by expressing the algorithm in this way, we have reduced the larger problem to two smaller subproblems, each of which is easier and simpler to develop than the original problem.

"We can now face the two subproblems precisely. Just as for any problem, there are the

input — the "givens"

output — the "finds"

For the first subproblem, there is no input; and the output is to be the completed table of atomic weights. For the second subproblem the input is the molecular formula; the output is the next element and the number of times it occurs in the molecular formula."

Holmes then produced the sketch that I have duplicated as Exhibit 10.2. His illustration shows the main algorithm, giving first the definitions of the variables used and then the algorithm itself. The main algorithm refers to the two subproblems. These are called algorithms SET_UP_TABLE and GET_ELEMENT.

Definitions:

    NEXT_ELEMENT : an element
    NUM_ATOMS   : an integer number
    TOTAL_WEIGHT : the weight of a molecule
    ATOMIC_WEIGHT : a representation of the periodic table,
                     giving the atomic weight of each element

Algorithm:

    Perform algorithm SET_UP_TABLE giving the ATOMIC_WEIGHT table
    Set TOTAL_WEIGHT to 0.0

    Repeat the following:
      perform algorithm GET_ELEMENT giving NEXT_ELEMENT, NUM_ATOMS
      add ATOMIC_WEIGHT[NEXT_ELEMENT]*NUM_ATOMS to TOTAL_WEIGHT
    until no more elements

    Write TOTAL_WEIGHT

Exhibit 10.2   *Holmes's Algorithm to Determine Molecular Weights*

Holmes noted the ease with which I could follow the algorithm, and then produced a second sketch, which I have reproduced as Exhibit 10.3. This contained the solutions to the two subproblems.

"Notice, Watson," he continued, "that the algorithm for each subproblem is separate and self-contained. Each contains, for example, definitions of data that are meaningful only within the local context of the subproblem.

"Every problem becomes elementary when once it is explained to you," said Holmes. "See how childishly simple this all is when you break the problem down into smaller components? You see, Watson, a man possessing special knowledge and powers such as my own is encouraged often to seek a simpler approach to a seemingly complex problem. Here we need only break the problem down into smaller parts and solve them separately. One might say, divide and conquer."

"Or divide and calculate!" I rejoined.

Algorithm SET_UP_TABLE—giving values for ATOMIC_WEIGHT table:

— Note: only the elements in the first five series of
— Mendeleeff's table are used

```
Set   ATOMIC_WEIGHT[HYDROGEN]   to    1
Set   ATOMIC_WEIGHT[LITHIUM]         to    7
Set   ATOMIC_WEIGHT[BERYLLIUM]  to    9.4
. . .                 . . .              . . .
Set   ATOMIC_WEIGHT[BROMINE]      to    80
```

Algorithm GET_ELEMENT—giving NEXT_ELEMENT, NUM_ATOMS:
Local definitions:
  CHAR_1, CHAR_2: characters of a formula

```
repeat the following:
    read CHAR1 of element abbreviation
    if incomplete then
        read CHAR2
    else
        set CHAR2 to blank
    get full name of NEXT_ELEMENT using CHAR1 and CHAR2
    if NEXT_ELEMENT is unknown then
        write 'ELEMENT NOT RECOGNIZED.'
    else
        obtain NUM_ATOMS
until valid entry is made
```

Exhibit 10.3 *Algorithms for the Two Sub-programmes*

"You are developing a certain vein of pawky humour, Watson, against which you must learn to guard yourself."

"So now we turn to the programme itself, I presume."

"Yes, Watson, we may nicely express this fundamental concept directly in Pascal with a 'sub-programme.' One method of writing sub-programmes is called a *procedure*. A procedure has two parts:

A *heading:* A summary of the sub-programme, giving its name, the inputs, and the outputs.

A *body:* The algorithm used, along with any local definitions.

"Consider the sub-programme to get the next element. The procedure to do this will have the form:

```
procedure GETELEMENT (parameters);
   -- local declarations
begin
   -- statements
end;
```

The parameters itemize the inputs and outputs. Each parameter must be given a name and a designation of its type.

"In addition," Holmes continued, "any output parameter must be preceded by the keyword var, which tells the Engine that the output will be assigned to a variable. So we have:

```
procedure GETELEMENT (var NEWELEMENT: ELEMENT;
                      var NUMATOMS: INTEGER);
   -- local declarations
begin
   -- statements
end;
```

The statements, of course, describe the algorithm."

It all sounded simple, but I was still a bit puzzled. I did not at all like some of the strange notation, and did not quite understand how the so-called "procedures" would be used.

"To invoke a procedure in a programme," Holmes continued, "we give the name of the procedure followed by a list of values or *arguments*, one for each parameter, as in:

```
GETELEMENT (NEXTELEMENT, NUMATOMS)
```

This is called a *procedure call*; and means, quite simply, 'do it.' That is, the Engine is commanded to perform the algorithm as spelled out in the procedure. When the procedure is completed, NEXTELEMENT will have the value computed for the first parameter, NUMATOMS for the second parameter.

"The essential idea is that the effect of solving the subproblem is summarized by values calculated for each parameter."

To appreciate this sudden bounty of instruction I found it necessary to see the actual programme. It is here duplicated as Exhibit 10.4. On some reflection, it was readily apparent that the wisest approach was breaking such complex programmes into smaller, more manageable parts.

```
program MOLECULARWEIGHT (INPUT, OUTPUT);

{  -- This programme reads in a chemical formula. Each element
   -- and its quantity are requested by the programme. Entering
   -- ZZ indicates the end of the formula.
   -- The programme determines the atomic components of the formula
   -- and prints out the total molecular weight. Only elements from
   -- the first five series of Mendeleeff's table are considered. }

const
    BLANK = ' ';

type
    ELEMENT =
        (HYDROGEN,     LITHIUM,    BERYLLIUM,    BORON,        CARBON,
         NITROGEN,     OXYGEN,     FLUORINE,     SODIUM,       MAGNESIUM,
         ALUMINIUM,    SILICON,    PHOSPHORUS,   SULPHUR,      CHLORINE,
         POTASSIUM,    CALCIUM,    TITANIUM,     VANADIUM,     CHROMIUM,
         MANGANESE,    IRON,       COBALT,       NICKEL,       COPPER,
         ZINC,         ARSENIC,    SELENIUM,     BROMINE,
         DONE,         UNKNOWN);
    PERIODICTABLE = array [ELEMENT] of REAL;

var
    NEXTELEMENT : ELEMENT;
    NUMATOMS    : INTEGER;
    TOTALWEIGHT : REAL;
    ATOMICWEIGHT: PERIODICTABLE;
```

Exhibit 10.4 *Holmes's Molecular Weight Programme*

```
procedure SETUPTABLE ({ intializing } var ATOMICWEIGHT: PERIODICTABLE);

begin
   ATOMICWEIGHT[HYDROGEN  ]  :=   1.0;
   ATOMICWEIGHT[LITHIUM   ]  :=   7.0;
   ATOMICWEIGHT[BERYLLIUM ]  :=   9.4;
   ATOMICWEIGHT[BORON     ]  :=  11.0;
   ATOMICWEIGHT[CARBON    ]  :=  12.0;

   ATOMICWEIGHT[NITROGEN  ]  :=  14.0;
   ATOMICWEIGHT[OXYGEN    ]  :=  16.0;
   ATOMICWEIGHT[FLUORINE  ]  :=  19.0;
   ATOMICWEIGHT[SODIUM    ]  :=  23.0;
   ATOMICWEIGHT[MAGNESIUM ]  :=  24.0;

   ATOMICWEIGHT[ALUMINIUM ]  :=  27.3;
   ATOMICWEIGHT[SILICON   ]  :=  28.0;
   ATOMICWEIGHT[PHOSPHORUS]  :=  31.0;
   ATOMICWEIGHT[SULPHUR   ]  :=  32.0;
   ATOMICWEIGHT[CHLORINE  ]  :=  35.5;

   ATOMICWEIGHT[POTASSIUM ]  :=  39.0;
   ATOMICWEIGHT[CALCIUM   ]  :=  40.0;
   ATOMICWEIGHT[TITANIUM  ]  :=  48.0;
   ATOMICWEIGHT[VANADIUM  ]  :=  51.0;
   ATOMICWEIGHT[CHROMIUM  ]  :=  52.0;

   ATOMICWEIGHT[MANGANESE ]  :=  55.0;
   ATOMICWEIGHT[IRON      ]  :=  56.0;
   ATOMICWEIGHT[COBALT    ]  :=  59.0;
   ATOMICWEIGHT[NICKEL    ]  :=  59.0;
   ATOMICWEIGHT[COPPER    ]  :=  63.0;

   ATOMICWEIGHT[ZINC      ]  :=  65.0;
   ATOMICWEIGHT[ARSENIC   ]  :=  75.0;
   ATOMICWEIGHT[SELENIUM  ]  :=  78.0;
   ATOMICWEIGHT[BROMINE   ]  :=  80.0
end;
```

Exhibit 10.4   *Continued*

```
procedure GETNAME ({ using } CHAR1, CHAR2: CHAR;
                   { giving } var NAME: ELEMENT);
    var
       ABBREVIATION: packed array[1..2] of CHAR;

begin
    ABBREVIATION[1]   :=   CHAR1;
    ABBREVIATION[2]   :=   CHAR2;

    if      ABBREVIATION = 'H ' then  NAME := HYDROGEN
    else if ABBREVIATION = 'LI' then  NAME := LITHIUM
    else if ABBREVIATION = 'BE' then  NAME := BERYLLIUM
    else if ABBREVIATION = 'B ' then  NAME := BORON
    else if ABBREVIATION = 'C ' then  NAME := CARBON
    else if ABBREVIATION = 'N ' then  NAME := NITROGEN
    else if ABBREVIATION = 'O ' then  NAME := OXYGEN
    else if ABBREVIATION = 'F ' then  NAME := FLUORINE
    else if ABBREVIATION = 'NA' then  NAME := SODIUM
    else if ABBREVIATION = 'MG' then  NAME := MAGNESIUM
    else if ABBREVIATION = 'AL' then  NAME := ALUMINIUM
    else if ABBREVIATION = 'SI' then  NAME := SILICON
    else if ABBREVIATION = 'P ' then  NAME := PHOSPHORUS
    else if ABBREVIATION = 'S ' then  NAME := SULPHUR
    else if ABBREVIATION = 'CL' then  NAME := CHLORINE
    else if ABBREVIATION = 'K ' then  NAME := POTASSIUM
    else if ABBREVIATION = 'CA' then  NAME := CALCIUM
    else if ABBREVIATION = 'TI' then  NAME := TITANIUM
    else if ABBREVIATION = 'V ' then  NAME := VANADIUM
    else if ABBREVIATION = 'CR' then  NAME := CHROMIUM
    else if ABBREVIATION = 'MN' then  NAME := MANGANESE
    else if ABBREVIATION = 'FE' then  NAME := IRON
    else if ABBREVIATION = 'CO' then  NAME := COBALT
    else if ABBREVIATION = 'NI' then  NAME := NICKEL
    else if ABBREVIATION = 'CU' then  NAME := COPPER
    else if ABBREVIATION = 'ZN' then  NAME := ZINC
    else if ABBREVIATION = 'AS' then  NAME := ARSENIC
    else if ABBREVIATION = 'SE' then  NAME := SELENIUM
    else if ABBREVIATION = 'BR' then  NAME := BROMINE
    else if ABBREVIATION = 'ZZ' then  NAME := DONE
    else
        NAME := UNKNOWN
end;
```

Exhibit 10.4 *Continued*

```
procedure GETELEMENT ({ giving } var NEWELEMENT: ELEMENT;
                                 var NUMATOMS: INTEGER);
    var
       CHAR1, CHAR2: CHAR;
       VALIDENTRY: BOOLEAN;
begin
   VALIDENTRY := FALSE;
   repeat
      WRITE ('ENTER ELEMENT ABBREVIATION:');
      READ (CHAR1);
      if not EOLN then
         READ (CHAR2)
      else
         CHAR2 := BLANK;
      READLN;
      GETNAME ({ using } CHAR1, CHAR2, { giving } NEWELEMENT);
      if NEWELEMENT = DONE then
         VALIDENTRY := TRUE
      else if NEWELEMENT = UNKNOWN then
         WRITELN ('ELEMENT NOT RECOGNIZED.')
      else
         begin
            WRITE ('ENTER QUANTITY OF ELEMENT:');
            READLN (NUMATOMS);
            VALIDENTRY := TRUE
         end
   until VALIDENTRY
end;


begin { -- Main algorithm }
    SETUPTABLE ({ giving } ATOMICWEIGHT);
    TOTALWEIGHT := 0.0;

    WRITELN ('ENTER EACH ELEMENT; WHEN DONE, ENTER ZZ.');
    GETELEMENT ({ giving } NEXTELEMENT, NUMATOM);
    while NEXTELEMENT <> DONE do begin
       TOTALWEIGHT := TOTALWEIGHT + ATOMICWEIGHT[NEXTELEMENT]*NUMATOMS;
       GETELEMENT ({ giving } NEXTELEMENT, NUMATOMS)
    end;

    WRITELN ('THE MOLECULAR WEIGHT IS ', TOTALWEIGHT:6:1)
end.
```

Exhibit 10.4   *Continued*

Holmes forged on. "Notice, incidentally, that in procedure GET-ELEMENT, we refer to another procedure GETNAME. This simply matches the abbreviated element name to the full element name and is an example of a sub-programme within a sub-programme."

"Enough, Holmes!" I moaned. "I can absorb no more. Are you absolutely certain that all of these complexities involve less work than simply calculating the molecular weights yourself?"

Sherlock Holmes merely smiled.

10.1 Packaging and Subprograms

With Holmes's program for calculating molecular weights, we encounter the idea of breaking a problem into parts and packaging each part as a *subprogram*. In its essence, a subprogram is a language unit that embodies the solution to a subproblem. As we attempt to scale up our programming skills to solve larger and more complex problems, the use of subprograms becomes almost indispensable. The solution to a subproblem, with all of its details and internal calculations, can be summarized into its givens and finds.

All subprograms have two general characteristics:

■ A *heading*, which summarizes the appearance of the subproblem to the rest of the program. It includes the name of the subproblem and an itemized list of its parameters.

■ A *body*, which specifies the method by which the subproblem is solved. It includes the definitions of any relevant internal data and the statements for carrying out the algorithm needed to solve the subproblem.

We now turn to the particulars for writing subprograms in Pascal.

A *procedure* is a subprogram that causes some desired effect. Consider, for instance, the simple procedure of Example 10.1. When executed, the three lines of text:

```
THE LOST PASCAL PROGRAMS
OF
SHERLOCK HOLMES
```

are printed, centered within each line. This is the so-called effect of the procedure.

The procedure in Example 10.1 has the form:

```
procedure WRITETITLE;
   -- local declarations
begin
   -- statements
end;
```

This procedure, like all procedures, has a name, in this case WRITETITLE. The procedure also contains local declarations, which specify any entities needed. The statements within the procedure specify the algorithm to be carried out.

A procedure is considered a "subprogram" because, as you will note, it has a form as well as an effect similar to that of a program. Like a program, a procedure can have both declarations and executable statements.

In order to cause the actions of a procedure to be carried out, we use a *procedure call* statement. For example, the procedure of Example 10.1 can be invoked with the call:

```
WRITETITLE
```

When this statement is executed, the algorithm specified by the procedure will be carried out.

Notice that in the procedure WRITETITLE, the body itself calls other procedures. In particular, consider:

```
for COLUMN := 1 to 35 do
   WRITE (SPACE);   { -- one procedure call }
WRITELN ('OF')      { -- another procedure call }
```

Here the called procedures, WRITE and WRITELN, are predefined in Pascal.

In Pascal, all procedures defined by the programmer must be stated in the declarative part of a program. For example, in Holmes's program we have the general structure:

```
program MOLECULARWEIGHT (INPUT, OUTPUT);
   -- constant declarations
   -- type declarations
   -- variable declarations
   -- subprogram declarations
begin
   -- statements
end.
```

```
procedure WRITETITLE;
   const
      SPACE = ' ';
   var
      COLUMN: INTEGER;
begin
   for COLUMN := 1 to 24 do
      WRITE (SPACE);
   WRITELN ('THE LOST PASCAL PROGRAMS');

   for COLUMN := 1 to 35 do
      WRITE (SPACE);
   WRITELN ('OF');

   for COLUMN := 1 to 29 do
      WRITE (SPACE);
   WRITELN ('SHERLOCK HOLMES')
end;
```

Example 10.1   *A Simple Procedure*

All procedures are declared after the constant, type, and variable declarations are given. Notice also that the statement part of the program may contain calls not only to the declared procedures but to the procedures that are predefined in Pascal.

This now allows us to state two precepts, elementary yet hard-and-fast to the fundamentals of problem solving:

■ The solution to a subproblem may be written as a procedure, which must be given in the form of a procedure declaration.

■ The actions specified by the procedure are carried out when the procedure is invoked by a procedure call statement.

10.2   Parameters

One important feature for writing subprograms is the ability to parameterize their behavior. The parameters allow you to characterize the net effect of the subprogram.

Consider Holmes's procedure to determine the element corresponding to its one- or two-character abbreviation:

```
procedure GETNAME ({ using }  CHAR1, CHAR2: CHAR;
                   { giving } var NAME: ELEMENT);
   -- local declarations
begin
   -- statements
end;
```

This procedure uses the values of CHAR1 and CHAR2 and from these two characters deduces the element corresponding to that two-letter symbol. The importance of the parameters is that we can characterize the entire effect of the procedure. That is, given input values for CHAR1 and CHAR2, we can determine the NAME of the element.

All procedures can be summarized in this simple form. A procedure takes certain inputs and produces certain outputs. We can view the procedure as a "black box" of the form:

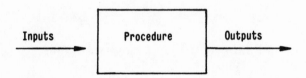

Thus we can summarize the behavior of GETNAME as:

From an outsider's point of view the parameters characterize the entire effect of the named procedure.

To invoke a procedure with parameters, we simply give the name of the procedure followed by a parenthesized list of arguments, one for each parameter. For example, in Holmes's program we may have the procedure call

```
GETNAME (CHAR1, CHAR2, NEWELEMENT)
```

or even better, using comments to indicate the role of the parameters, we may have:

```
GETNAME ({ using } CHAR1, CHAR2, { giving } NEWELEMENT)
```

Before the procedure GETNAME is called, values will have been assigned to CHAR1 and CHAR2. After the call, the name of the next element will be assigned to the variable NEWELEMENT.

Now there are several tricky points that we must take up in order to describe the use of parameters. For one, the names of the parameters given in the procedure declaration are an entirely internal matter as far as the rest of the program is concerned. These names have no significance outside the procedure.

For example, if we wanted, we could have written the procedure GETNAME as:

```
procedure GETNAME ({ using }  CH1, CH2: CHAR;
                    { giving } var RESULT: ELEMENT);
   -- local declarations
begin
   -- statements with parameter names changed
end;
```

That is, we could have changed all occurrences of the name CHAR1 to CH1, CHAR2 to CH2, and NAME to RESULT. These changes would have to be made uniformly throughout the procedure. It is in this sense that we say the names of the parameters are "dummy." We are free to choose these names as we wish without regard to any other names outside the procedure.

The ability to coin the names of parameters freely is an extremely useful feature. When you are writing a procedure to solve a subproblem, you can really think of the procedure as an entirely new program with its own inputs and outputs and its own local declarations of variables.

In describing the parameters of a procedure, you must be a bit cautious. First of all, the parameters must be given in some particular order. For the procedure GETNAME, there are three parameters given in the order CHAR1, CHAR2, and NAME. Second, a type must be specified for each parameter in the procedure header. For input parameters, the type of one or more parameters can be specified in the form:

parameter-list: *type-name*

In Holmes's case, we have:

```
CHAR1, CHAR2: CHAR
```

This specification has the same meaning as:

```
CHAR1: CHAR;   CHAR2: CHAR
```

Notice here, however, that each definition in a list of parameters must be followed by a semicolon if more parameter definitions follow.

The specification of output parameters is almost identical to that of input parameters, except that each list of parameters must be preceded by the keyword var, indicating that the corresponding argument must be a variable. In the procedure GETNAME we have one output parameter, specified by:

```
var NAME: ELEMENT
```

Thus the full list of parameters is given as

```
(CHAR1, CHAR2: CHAR;  var NAME: ELEMENT)
```

where the parentheses enclose the entire list.

Occasionally you will have a need for parameters whose values both serve as input from the caller and are updated as a result of the procedure call. Consider the procedure PLUSONE, defined as follows:

```
procedure PLUSONE (var X: INTEGER);
begin
  X := X + 1
end;
```

This somewhat trivial procedure adds one to its argument. Thus X serves as both input and output for the procedure. Such a parameter must also be specified with the keyword var, indicating that the corresponding argument must again be a variable.

From the caller's side, we also have to be concerned with a few special rules. If a procedure has one parameter, you must call it with only one argument; if the procedure has two parameters, you must call it with exactly two arguments, and so forth.

The argument corresponding to an input parameter can be any expression in Pascal as long as the type of the expression is identical to the type of the corresponding parameter. Thus, with the procedure GETNAME, we could have the call:

```
GETNAME ('N', 'A', VALUE)
```

Similarly for the predefined procedure WRITE, which takes any number of arguments of integer, real, or string type, we may have the calls:

```
WRITE (0.0)
WRITE (NUMATOMS + 1)
WRITE ('THE SQUARE ROOT OF X IS ', SQRT(X))
```

For arguments corresponding to output parameters, the case is different. Such an argument must always be the name of a variable whose type is the same as that of the corresponding parameter. Thus in the call

```
GETNAME ('N', 'A', VALUE)
```

the third argument must be the name of a variable of type ELEMENT.

10.3   Functions versus Procedures

Consider Example 10.2a. Here we see a simple procedure named GETAREA, which when given a value for a radius computes the area of a circle having that radius. If, say, the value of R is 3.0, the procedure call

```
GETAREA (R, AREA)
```

results in assigning to AREA the area of a circle of radius 3.0, or 28.2743.

Next consider the "function" of Example 10.2b. This example defines a function named AREA which has a single argument, a real value. It computes the area of a circle having this argument as a radius. Like the predefined functions in Pascal, this function can be called within an expression. If the value of R is 3.0, evaluation of the expression

```
1.0 + AREA(R)
```

yields 1 plus the area of the circle, or 29.2743.

A *function* is a subprogram that returns a value. Generally speaking, functions are used in place of *expressions* to return *values*, whereas procedures are used in place of *statements* to perform *assignments* to variables. The ability to define functions in Pascal is thus an important counterpart to the ability to define procedures.

Conceptually a function behaves just like a function in ordinary mathematics. That is, given one or more values, we can compute some result. For example, consider the following informally described functions:

- Given two numbers, the result is the greater of the two.

- Given three points, the result is the area of a triangle connecting the three points.

- Given a molecular formula, the result is the molecular weight of the formula.

- Given the initial velocity of a projectile, its angle, and a duration of time, the result is the distance traveled.

a. *A Simple Procedure*

```
procedure GETAREA ({ using } RADIUS: REAL;
                   { giving } var AREA: REAL);
   const
      PI = 3.14159;
begin
   AREA := PI * (RADIUS*RADIUS)
end;
```

b. *A Simple Function*

```
function AREA(RADIUS: REAL): REAL;
   const
      PI = 3.14159;
begin
   AREA := PI * (RADIUS*RADIUS)
end;
```

Example 10.2 *Functions Versus Procedures*

In each of these cases we have one or more givens and a single result.

The rules for declaring functions are quite similar to the rules for declaring procedures. In particular, a function declaration has the form:

```
function AREA (parameters): result-type;
   -- local declarations
begin
   -- statements
end;
```

Here we see that, like a procedure, a function may have parameters as well as local declarations describing any internal data. As with a procedure, the algorithm performed by the function is specified in the statements. Furthermore, a function returns a single result, and the type of the result must be specified in the program heading.

To establish the actual result returned by a function in Pascal, you must use an assignment statement that gives a value to the name of the function. For example, in the function of Example 10.2b we have the statement:

```
AREA := PI * (RADIUS*RADIUS)
```

This statement assigns a value to the name AREA, which is, in fact, the name of the function itself. When the statements in the body of the function are completed, whatever value has been assigned to this name will be returned as the result of the function.

The facility for defining functions in Pascal is quite general. For instance, the parameters may be of any type defined in your program. Thus you may have parameters that are arrays, strings, or values of an enumerated type. Watch out though; the result must have a simple type. Thus the result may *not* be an array or a string.

Furthermore, the statements describing the algorithm performed by the subprogram may be as complex as you like, and of course, may even contain calls to other procedures or other functions. Thus the facility for defining subprograms in Pascal is extremely powerful.

10.4   Global Information

Consider the following simple procedure:

```
procedure SKIPSPACES (NUMSPACES: INTEGER);
    const
        SPACE = ' ';
    var
        COUNT: INTEGER;
begin
    for COUNT := 1 to NUMSPACES do
        WRITE (SPACE)
end;
```

This procedure has only one parameter, an input parameter named NUMSPACES. When this procedure is executed, it prints the number of spaces given as input to NUMSPACES.

Let us next consider a revised version of the procedure WRITETITLE given earlier in Example 10.1:

```
procedure WRITETITLE;
begin
    SKIPSPACES (24);
    WRITELN ('THE LOST PASCAL PROGRAMS');
    SKIPSPACES (35);
    WRITELN ('OF');
    SKIPSPACES (29);
    WRITELN ('SHERLOCK HOLMES')
end;
```

This procedure has the same effect as Example 10.1. Here, however, the procedure WRITETITLE explicitly invokes another procedure, SKIPSPACES, defined above.

The use of the procedure SKIPSPACES within WRITETITLE demonstrates an important general point. A procedure may refer to the entities (constants, types, variables, and subprograms) declared outside the procedure in the main program. These entities are said to be *global* to the procedure.

The use of several procedures in one program is commonplace as programs solve larger and more intricate problems. Furthermore, doing this in Pascal is quite easy. You simply declare the procedures one after another.

For example, consider the general structure of Holmes's program for calculating molecular weights.

```
program MOLECULARWEIGHT (INPUT, OUTPUT);
    -- constant declarations
    -- type declarations
    -- variable declarations
    -- declaration of SETUPTABLE
    -- declaration of GETNAME
    -- declaration of GETELEMENT
begin
    -- statements
end
```

This program uses the three procedures SETUPTABLE, GETNAME, and GETELEMENT. Notice, however, in Exhibit 10.4 the procedure GETNAME is
invoked *within* the procedure GETELEMENT. This brings us to the following rule in Pascal:

■ A procedure or function must be declared before it can be called.

Thus the declaration of GETNAME must precede the declaration of GETELEMENT. Otherwise, the order of subprogram declarations is immaterial.

10.5   Danger: Side Effects

At this point we have to talk about one of the most subtle but dangerous problems in programming. In computer parlance this problem is called the use of *side effects*. A subprogram can produce a side effect in two ways: by altering its arguments or by altering a variable that is global to the procedure.

Programmers who write subprograms with side effects often get unpleasant surprises. Consider Example 10.3. These two programs are identical except for the replacement of the expression

```
F(B) + F(B)
```

in Example 10.3a by the expression

```
2 * F(B)
```

in Example 10.3b. These two programs are not equivalent because:

```
F(B) + F(B) = (11)*(3) + (12)*(3)
            = 69
2 * F(B)    = (2)*(11)*(3)
            = 66
```

Hence we lose a fundamental property of addition. The problem is caused by the side effect in the function F with the assignment

```
A := A + 1
```

where A is global to the function.

Certainly most people would be surprised to discover that evaluation of

```
F(B) + F(B)
```

is not equivalent to

```
2 * F(B)
```

despite the familiar notation for such expressions.

The difficulties with side effects become even greater when we need to change a program. Change is a daily occurrence in programming. Someone may find a more efficient algorithm, more output may be needed, a bug may be detected, or specifications may be revised.

If a piece of a program to be changed has side effects, we may need to delve deeply into the entire program for a clear understanding of any effects on other parts of the program. Adding a few extra lines of program for that desirable change may render another piece of the program incorrect. To set matters right again, another change may be needed, and so on. Even if this process succeeds, it is not likely to add to the clarity or flexibility of the program. Had the original program been written without side effects, the subprogram could be changed *without* studying the rest of the program.

a. *One Program*

```
program SIDEEFFECT (INPUT, OUTPUT);
   var
       A, B, C: INTEGER;

function F(X: INTEGER): INTEGER;
begin
   A := A + 1;
   F := A * X
end;

begin
   A := 10;
   B := 3;
   C := F(B) + F(B);  { -- Watch out }
   WRITELN (C)
end.
```

b. *An Equivalent Program?*

```
program SIDEEFFECT (INPUT, OUTPUT);
   var
       A, B, C: INTEGER;

function F(X: INTEGER): INTEGER;
begin
   A := A + 1;
   F := A * X
end;

begin
   A := 10;
   B := 3;
   C := 2 * F(B);  { -- Watch out }
   WRITELN (C)
end.
```

Example 10.3   *Side Effects in Functions*

The purpose of a procedure is to produce some effect external to itself, not to return a value. Essentially, a procedure consists of a group of statements isolated from the main algorithm for convenience or clarity. The problems encountered with side effects in procedures are quite similar to those encountered in functions. There is one important exception: when a procedure is designed to update a specific set of variables, each of the changed variables should be included in the list of parameters.

Consider Example 10.4. In this program, the procedure P causes a side effect on the global variable B. Thus the call

```
P (A)
```

gives no clue that the variable B will be changed.

There are, of course, cases where global information may indeed be useful. For example, there may be types, constants, and arrays whose (often used) values remain constant within the program. Making these quantities global to the entire program certainly causes no problems, as they do not change as the program progresses. The real culprit remains the global *variable*.

In brief, global variables and side effects can cause very serious problems. If they are used, they should be used sparingly. We close with the following rules of thumb:

1. *Functions*

Use a function only for its returned value.
Do not use a function when you need a procedure.
Do not alter the parameters.
Do not alter global variables.

2. *Procedures*

Do not use a procedure when you need a function.
Do not alter global variables.

3. *Both*

Be very, very careful when you use global variables.

```
program GLOBALS (INPUT, OUTPUT);
   var
      A, B: INTEGER;
procedure P(var X: INTEGER);
begin
   X := 2 * (X + 1);
   B := 5 * X
end;

begin
   A := 2;
   B := 3;
   WRITELN (A, B);    { Prints A as 2,  B as 3 }
   P (A);             { Changes B as well!     }
   WRITELN (A, B)     { Prints A as 6,  B as 30 }
end.
```

Example 10.4 *Side Effects in Procedures*

XI

The Coroner's Report

THE murder of the Honourable Colin Wiggs, with its curious, if not to say extraordinary circumstances, had long ceased to be a subject of interest in Fleet Street, where for months the front pages of London's many daily papers had trumpeted the disturbing details as they unfolded. Thus I was surprised to find that, more than a year after this tragedy was laid to rest, it had again become a subject of interest in Baker Street. Early one October evening I called upon my friend Sherlock Holmes, who had had a considerable share in clearing up the Wiggs case. I found him deeply engrossed in reviewing the details attendant upon the matter.

I was apprehensive of what Holmes's humour might be that evening, for his eccentricities became more pronounced when he was engaged on a case and at times his curious habit and mood, which some would call reticent, succeeded in alarming even such an old companion as myself.

To my surprise and pleasure, however, Holmes ushered me into his quarters with an exuberant gesture of welcome and propelled me into the only chair that was not cluttered with books, papers, and scientific specimens.

"You will remember, Watson," he said, "how the dreadful business in which Colin Wiggs was engaged ultimately led to his tragic end, and how the matter was first brought to my notice by a small scar on his left shoulder. A trifling point at first overlooked by the coroner."

"Indeed," said I, "and I well recall your indignation at Scotland Yard's handling of that affair. The case might have dragged on indefinitely had you not chosen to inspect the body yourself."

"Exactly, Watson, why I have now undertaken to reconstruct the material circumstances of that case. I wish to design a systematic, yet simple, means of organizing notes, documented observations, and other data that are used in compiling special presentations, such as a coroner's report."

I listened intently to this explanation, which Holmes delivered between puffs on his cigar. It was evident by a pile of manuscripts within my sight that he had contrived just such a plan for use by the Analytical Engine.

"You have devised some new programme, I take it," I ventured, "though I fear it may lie beyond my comprehension."

"I assure you, my dear Watson, that the algorithm is elementary. If you have understood our other exercises with the Engine, I believe you will find little difficulty with this one."

Holmes thereupon removed a few slips of paper from one of several notebooks that lay open nearby.

"Observe, if you will, the total disarray of these papers, which

"OBSERVE THE TOTAL DISARRAY OF THESE PAPERS."

contain crucial information pertaining to the Wiggs autopsy," he said, handing them to me. "Would it not be more practical to store this data in the Engine's memory, where it would be infinitely more secure and from which a concise report could be called upon whenever necessary?"

Holmes then displayed a summary of the data usually given in a medical examiner's report, as follows :—

General Information: 1. Coroner's name, 2. Subject's name, 3. Subject's stated age.

Data and Test Results: 4. Subject's height in inches, 5. Subject's hair colour, 6. Subject's eye colour, 7. Subject's sex, 8. Results of alcohol test, 9. Test for salicylates, 10. Bile morphine indication, 11. Gastric content, 12. Presence of bruises, 13. Presence of lacerations, 14. Presence of lesions, 15. Detected haemorrhages, 16. Fractures.

Remarks: 17. Coroner's observations.

"Now, Watson, in designing a programme to store and recall this information, I dealt with several important points. In the first place, you will observe that the data in each section of the report are of variable length and appearance. Thus when we enter the data into the machine, we do not wish to be confined to a *fixed format*, consisting of rigid columns and predetermined schemes of punctuation, letters, and numbers. Rather, we wish to use a so-called *free format*, which will allow us to separate data items as we please, with blanks and ends of lines. In fact, often a character, for instance a comma, is used to separate items. I decided to use a colon for this purpose, as commas and blanks will likely occur in the data.

"Notice also that it is always a good idea to prepare a sample of the input before coding the programme, as I have also done here. This helps clarify the task at hand. Do you follow me this far, Watson?"

Holmes's conventions are summarized in the table that I have replicated here :

FORMAT CONVENTIONS

a.   Each item is treated as a sequence of characters.

b.   Items 1 through 3 (general information) contain at most 20 characters.

c.   Items 4 through 16 (data and test results) contain at most 40 characters.

d.   Except for item 17 (coroner's observations), spaces and ends of lines preceding an item are ignored.

e.   Item 17 (coroner's observations) contains an arbitrary number of lines of characters. The first character must appear at the beginning of a line.

SAMPLE INPUT VALUES

General Information: 1. Dr. Harrison, 2. Colin Wiggs, 3. 42,

Data and Test Results: 4. 68, 5. Black, 6. Grey, 7. Male, 8. Negative, 9. Negative, 10. +, 11. Negative for organic bases, 12. Face, neck, 13. None, 14. Neck, 15. None, 16. Upper windpipe

Remarks: 17. Subject was apparently struck on the left side of the neck. Double fracture of the upper windpipe, just below the larynx, suggesting strangulation. A small scar was detected on the left shoulder.

I nodded that his explanation was extremely clear to me and begged him to continue.

"Very good," said Holmes, resuming his manner of a patient lecturer. "Now, so far as the output is concerned, our main objective is to provide a report that is at once complete, orderly, and readily intelligible to the clerks and investigators who are likely to use it. This principle is what I call the *consideration of human factors.* One must remember at all times that one is devising a programme for the benefit of other persons, not only for the Engine—though I cannot refrain from observing that our artificial brain has more aptitude for deduction than many of the natural ones employed by Scotland Yard."

Holmes paused a moment to take another cigar and then continued, as I sat attentively beside him.

"There are two simple concepts involved in the creation of output," he said as he blew a thin stream of smoke into the room.

"First, note that each item of data is viewed as a string of characters. Upon output, each is printed in a specific place.

"Second, the data are grouped into lines, and there must be some predetermined design for the appearance of the report. Thus, when the programme has printed the desired item, advancement to a new line may be called for."

"Really Holmes," I interrupted. "I fear this is all a bit much for my mind to digest at one time."

"No, no, Watson, there are unexplored possibilities about you to which you have given small attention amid your exaggerated estimates of my own performances. If you will bear with me for another moment, I am sure this will all become quite clear to you."

As he spoke he tore two more sheets from his notebook which I have reproduced as Exhibits 11.1 and 11.2.

"Here are my specimens," he remarked as I examined them, "which should shed some light on these concepts. Tell me, Watson, if they are sufficiently clear, as I intend to offer them to Scotland Yard for their own instruction."

I studied Holmes's diagrams, paying special attention to the appearance of his sample output. The specimens looked perfectly clear and readable, and once again I was astonished at the practical use that resulted from a few simple principles applied by an eminently logical mind.

"Why, Holmes," I said, "if the Engine can be programmed to fulfill a wide variety of similar purposes, the entire profession of clerking may well be undermined within a few years!"

"Nonsense, Watson!" snapped Holmes. "The Engine will surely never replace the need for human intelligence. Rather, it will free mankind from

```
                         CORONER'S REPORT
                         ---------- ------


CORONER:   ...                   SUBJECT'S NAME:  ...
                                 STATED AGE    :  ...



BASIC DATA
----- ----

          HEIGHT IN INCHES:  ...
          HAIR COLOUR    :   ...
          EYE COLOUR     :   ...
          SEX            :   ...



TOXICOLOGY DATA
---------- ----

          ALCOHOL TEST    :   ...
          SALICYLATES     :   ...
          BILE MORPHINE   :   ...
          GASTRIC CONTENT :   ...



ANATOMIC DATA
-------- ----

          BRUISES        :    ...
          LACERATIONS    :    ...
          LESIONS        :    ...
          HAEMORRHAGES   :    ...
          FRACTURES      :    ...



GENERAL REMARKS
------- -------

          ...
```

Exhibit 11.1   *Output Layout of the Coroner's Report*

```
                    CORONER'S REPORT
                    --------- ------


CORONER: Dr. Harrison              SUBJECT'S NAME: Colin Wiggs
                                   STATED AGE    : 42


BASIC DATA
----- ----

      HEIGHT IN INCHES: 68
      HAIR COLOUR    : Black
      EYE COLOUR     : Grey
      SEX            : Male


TOXICOLOGY DATA
---------- ----

      ALCOHOL TEST    : Negative
      SALICYLATES     : Negative
      BILE MORPHINE   : +
      GASTRIC CONTENT : Negative for organic bases


ANATOMIC DATA
-------- ----

      BRUISES        : Face, neck
      LACERATIONS    : None
      LESIONS        : Neck
      HAEMORRHAGES   : None
      FRACTURES      : Upper windpipe


GENERAL REMARKS
------- -------

      Subject was apparently struck on the left side of the neck.
      Double fracture of the upper windpipe, just below the larynx,
      suggesting strangulation. A small scar was detected on the left
      shoulder.
```

Exhibit 11.2   *Sample Output from the Coroner's Report Programme*

mundane tasks, those that shackle the mind and keep it from more challenging and rewarding exercises.

"Moreover," he continued, "once the Engine has been programmed correctly, it will always perform correctly, or at least with negligible chance of a random error. Time invested in programmes is cumulative, always adding to the precision of the process."

I have included Holmes's entire algorithm as Exhibit 11.3, so that the diligent reader can follow the exact steps taken by Holmes to accomplish the task described herein. You may notice that, while the algorithm is certainly straightforward, accounting for all the details is painstaking. It is especially tedious to ensure that the output is spaced properly.

Main Algorithm:
    Skip 7 lines
    Perform algorithm PRINT_TITLE
    Skip 2 lines
    Perform algorithm PRINT_GENERAL_INFO
    Skip 2 lines
    Perform algorithm PRINT_BASIC_DATA
    Skip 2 lines
    Perform algorithm PRINT_TOXICOLOGY_DATA
    Skip 2 lines
    Perform algorithm PRINT_ANATOMIC_DATA
    Skip 2 lines
    Perform algorithm PRINT_REMARKS

Algorithm PRINT_TITLE:
    Write 25 spaces, 'CORONER'S REPORT' header
    Advance to next line

Algorithm PRINT_GENERAL_INFO
    Write 'CORONER: '
    Perform algorithm PROCESS_NEXT_ITEM using 20 characters
    Write 6 spaces, 'SUBJECT'S NAME: '
    Perform algorithm PROCESS_NEXT_ITEM using 20 characters
    Advance to next line
    Write 35 spaces, 'STATED AGE   : '
    Perform algorithm PROCESS_NEXT_ITEM using 20 characters
    Advance to next line

Exhibit 11.3   *Holmes's Algorithm for the*
Coroner's Report Programme

Algorithm PRINT_BASIC_DATA:
    Write 'BASIC DATA' header
    Skip one line
    Perform algorithm PROCESS_FIELD using 'HEIGHT IN INCHES :'
    Perform algorithm PROCESS_FIELD using 'HAIR COLOUR   :'
    Perform algorithm PROCESS_FIELD using 'EYE COLOUR   :'
    Perform algorithm PROCESS_FIELD using 'SEX   :'

Algorithm PRINT_TOXICOLOGY_DATA:
    Write 'TOXICOLOGY DATA' header
    Skip 1 line
    Perform algorithm PROCESS_FIELD using 'ALCOHOL TEST   :'
    Perform algorithm PROCESS_FIELD using 'SALICYLATES   :'
    Perform algorithm PROCESS_FIELD using 'BILE MORPHINE   :'
    Perform algorithm PROCESS_FIELD using 'GASTRIC CONTENT :'

Algorithm PRINT_ANATOMIC_DATA
    Write 'ANATOMIC DATA' header
    Skip 1 line
    Perform algorithm PROCESS_FIELD using 'BRUISES   :'
    Perform algorithm PROCESS_FIELD using 'LACERATIONS   :'
    Perform algorithm PROCESS_FIELD using 'LESIONS   :'
    Perform algorithm PROCESS_FIELD using 'HAEMORRHAGES   :'
    Perform algorithm PROCESS_FIELD using 'FRACTURES   :'

Algorithm PRINT_REMARKS:
    Write 'GENERAL REMARKS'
    As long as more lines remain, do the following:
        write 5 spaces
        copy next line

Algorithm PROCESS_FIELD using HEADER
    Write 5 spaces, HEADER
    Perform algorithm PROCESS_NEXT_ITEM using 40 characters
    Advance to new line

Algorithm PROCESS_NEXT_ITEM using NUM_CHARS
    Skip leading spaces
    Read and print item
    Pad with spaces to fill the item to NUM_CHARS

Exhibit 11.3 *Continued*

Holmes's programme is given in Exhibit 11.4. It follows the stated algorithm almost exactly.

```
program CORONERSREPORT (INPUT, OUTPUT);

{ -- This programme reads in data corresponding to the items in
  -- a coroner's report. The items are separated by colons (:).
  -- The programme prints a summary report of the coroner's data. }

   const
      SPACE     = ' ';
      SEPARATOR = ':';
   type
      HEADERSTR = packed array [1..18] of CHAR;

procedure SKIPLINES (NUMLINES: INTEGER);
   var
      I: INTEGER;
begin
   for I := 1 to NUMLINES do
      WRITELN
end;


procedure PROCESSNEXTITEM ({ using } ITEMWIDTH: INTEGER);
   var
      NEXTCHAR: CHAR;
      I, NUMCHARS: INTEGER;
begin
   READ (NEXTCHAR);
   while NEXTCHAR = SPACE do
      READ (NEXTCHAR);

   NUMCHARS := 1;
   while NEXTCHAR <> SEPARATOR do begin
      WRITE (NEXTCHAR);
      READ  (NEXTCHAR);
      NUMCHARS := NUMCHARS + 1
   end;

   for I := NUMCHARS + 1 to ITEMWIDTH do
      WRITE (SPACE)
end;
```

Exhibit 11.4   *Holmes's Programme for the Coroner's Report*

```
procedure PROCESSFIELD ({ using } HEADER: HEADERSTR);
   var
     I: INTEGER;
begin
   for I := 1 to 5 do
     WRITE (SPACE);
   for I := 1 to 18 do
     WRITE (HEADER[I]);
   PROCESSNEXTITEM (40);
   WRITELN
end;


procedure PRINTTITLE;
begin
   WRITELN ('                         CORONER''S REPORT');
   WRITELN ('                         ————————— ————')
end;


procedure PRINTGENERALINFO;
begin
   WRITE ('CORONER: ');
   PROCESSNEXTITEM (20);
   WRITE ('     SUBJECT''S NAME: ');
   PROCESSNEXTITEM (20);
   WRITELN;
   WRITE ('                              STATED AGE   : ');
   PROCESSNEXTITEM (20);
   WRITELN
end;


procedure PRINTBASICDATA;
begin
   WRITELN ('BASIC DATA');
   WRITELN ('————— ————');
   SKIPLINES (1);
   PROCESSFIELD ('HEIGHT IN INCHES: ');
   PROCESSFIELD ('HAIR COLOUR   : ');
   PROCESSFIELD ('EYE COLOUR    : ');
   PROCESSFIELD ('SEX           : ')
end;
```

Exhibit 11.4   *Continued*

```
procedure PRINTTOXICOLOGYDATA;
begin
  WRITELN ('TOXICOLOGY DATA');
  WRITELN ('————————— ————');
  SKIPLINES (1);                          .
  PROCESSFIELD ('ALCOHOL TEST    : ');
  PROCESSFIELD ('SALICYLATES     : ');
  PROCESSFIELD ('BILE MORPHINE   : ');
  PROCESSFIELD ('GASTRIC CONTENT : ')
end;


procedure PRINTANATOMICDATA;
begin
  WRITELN ('ANATOMIC DATA');
  WRITELN ('———————— ————');
  SKIPLINES (1);
  PROCESSFIELD ('BRUISES         : ');
  PROCESSFIELD ('LACERATIONS     : ');
  PROCESSFIELD ('LESIONS         : ');
  PROCESSFIELD ('HAEMORRHAGES    : ');
  PROCESSFIELD ('FRACTURES       : ')
end;


procedure PRINTREMARKS;
   var
     I: INTEGER;
     NEXTCHAR: CHAR;
begin
  WRITELN ('GENERAL REMARKS');
  WRITELN ('———————— ———————');
  SKIPLINES (1);

  while (not EOF) do begin
     for I := 1 to 5 do
        WRITE (SPACE);
     while not EOLN do begin
        READ   (NEXTCHAR);
        WRITE (NEXTCHAR)
     end;
     READLN;
     WRITELN
  end
end;
```

Exhibit 11.4   *Continued*

```
begin { -- Main algorithm }
   SKIPLINES (7);
   PRINTTITLE;
   SKIPLINES (2);
   PRINTGENERALINFO;
   SKIPLINES (2);
   PRINTBASICDATA;
   SKIPLINES (2);
   PRINTTOXICOLOGYDATA;
   SKIPLINES (2);
   PRINTANATOMICDATA;
   SKIPLINES (2);
   PRINTREMARKS
end.
```

Exhibit 11.4   *Continued*

"You see, Watson," Holmes remarked, "the programme is a simple collection of procedures that extract each stored piece of information that is given to it. The important point is that the programme makes the information pleasing for the enquirer to read. If it were printed in a haphazard fashion, the Engine would not be used to its full potential to assist a human undertaking."

"A truly useful concept, Holmes, with great possibilities, assuming the Engine always works without mechanical error!"

To this he made no reply, but it was plainly evident that he was pondering the shortcomings of the Engine. Like all great artists, he was easily impressed by his surroundings; and I fear my comment had thrown him into the blackest depression. How I had learned, long ago, to dread periods of inaction for Holmes. His gaze was now fixed on the mantelpiece, where lay scattered a collection of syringes and bottles; and I knew that the sleeping friend was very near waking in times of such idleness.

11.1 Input and Output

We have been treating the reading of data and printing of results quite casually up to this point; but, as we are well aware, these matters are essential components of any computer program. Holmes's treatment of the coroner's report brings into focus some of the required fine tuning.

Your initial concern in reading data should be that the data are there and in the correct form; otherwise your program will stop and the computer will issue some strange sort of cease and desist order. What you've got to do when actually using the computer is to second-guess it and check for possible errors in input. For simplicity's sake, we've been loose about this point in the text; but in programs you'll be using routinely, you should be very careful to check for input mistakes.

As for output, your major concern should be its presentation. You and others using your program should be able to understand the results easily. Granted, producing quality output can be a tedious task, but your efforts will be amply rewarded even if you are the only person who will use the program. Keep in mind the great detective's comment in "The Adventure of the Veiled Lodger" that "the example of patient suffering is in itself the most precious of all lessons to an impatient world." If you take the occasion to suffer a little now, you will be amply rewarded later.

In Pascal, the basic how-to's of carrying this out are actually quite simple, though sometimes inconvenient.

There are two basic procedures that can accomplish most of what you need to do for reading and writing data. These are the procedures READ and WRITE, along with their variants READLN and WRITELN, as described in Table 11.1. Unless you say otherwise, these procedures operate on the standard input file named INPUT and the standard output file named OUTPUT.

For reading data, the variables that will hold the data are specified. Furthermore, the type of each input value must be compatible with the type of the corresponding variable, just as usual.

For example, if you are reading some value into an integer variable named NUMWEAPONS, the value must be an integer. Thus, if you input

6

the READ statement will assign 6 to NUMWEAPONS. On the other hand, if you input the real value

14.33

the computer will take your value as 14, and use .33 for the next value. Even worse, if you input

Q1A%

TABLE 11.1 *Basic Procedures for Reading and Writing Data*

(*Note:* v denotes a variable, e an expression.)

READ (v)	Reads the next value from the input file and assigns the value to the variable v. The variable v must be of type INTEGER, REAL, or CHAR. For integers and reals, leading spaces and line boundaries are skipped; for characters, a line boundary is treated as a blank space.
READLN	Causes a skip to the beginning of the next line, that is skips to the character after the next end of line marker.
READ (v_1, ... ,v_n)	Same as n individual calls to READ.
READLN (v_1, ... ,v_n)	Same as n individual calls to READ followed by the call READLN.
WRITE (e)	Prints the value of the expression e on the output file. The value must be an integer number, real number, boolean, character, or character string. If the printed value is too large to fit on the current output line, the value is printed on the following line.
WRITELN	Causes printing to continue on the following line, that is puts an end-of-line marker on the current line.
WRITE (e_1, ... ,e_n)	Same as n individual calls to WRITE.
WRITELN (e_1, ... ,e_n)	Same as n individual calls to WRITE followed by the call WRITELN.

then the computer will probably complain, as the whole thing doesn't make any sense. Notice that if you input the value

```
-6
```

into NUMWEAPONS, the computer will not complain, even though from a conceptual viewpoint -6 weapons just doesn't make any sense.

Something you need to understand here is that when reading numeric data, leading blanks and line boundaries are ignored. Thus, if you are reading the values of two integer variables, say NUMWEAPONS and NUMSUSPECTS, then you may input the data as

    6 8

or

    6   8

or even:

    6
    8

As far as the computer is concerned, these cases are the same and they're handled in the same manner. Leaving this then to the computer, let's move on to a somewhat more complicated issue: printing your results.

The printing of data is just like the reading of data, with one important exception: you get to tell the computer how to display the data. If you don't tell it how to display the data, the computer has its own ideas about how the data should appear and that may not be what you had in mind.

The conventions for displaying data are given in Table 11.2. Notice here that if the space provided for a value is larger than needed, the value is justified to the right: that is, the value is preceded by blanks so as to fill the given field, or the area set aside for it.

Some Examples

Recall our program for counting change, given in the previous chapters. This program contains the procedure call:

    WRITE ('CHANGE IS ', DOLLARS:2, ' DOLLARS AND ', CENTS:2, ' CENTS.')

This statement will print something like:

    CHANGE IS 3 DOLLARS AND 41 CENTS.

If we omitted the field widths for DOLLARS and CENTS and wrote

    WRITE ('CHANGE IS ', DOLLARS, ' DOLLARS AND ', CENTS, ' CENTS.')

the statement would print:

    CHANGE IS   3 DOLLARS AND   41 CENTS.

TABLE 11.2 *Controlling the Layout of the Printed Page*

Layout is controlled by giving arguments of the form

$e:w$

where e is the expression whose value is to be printed, and w specifies the minimum width of the field on the printed page.

Integer and Real Values

1. If e can be written with w or fewer characters, the value is preceded with an appropriate number of blank spaces (that is, right justified).

2. Otherwise, the number of characters needed to write the full value is used.

3. If no field width is given, a default width (for example, 10 for integers and 20 for reals) is used. For real values the number is printed with a scale factor (for example 2.100000000000E-05).

Boolean Values

1. If the value, TRUE or FALSE, can be written with w or fewer characters, the value is preceded with an appropriate number of blanks.

2. Otherwise, either TRUE or FALSE is written in full.

3. If no field width is given, either TRUE or FALSE is written in full, or a default field width (for example, 5 or 10) is used. Check your local implementation.

Character Values

1. The character is preceded by $(w - 1)$ blank spaces.

2. If no field width is given, a default width of 1 is used; thus just the character is printed.

String Values

1. If the string has w or fewer characters, the value is preceded by an appropriate number of blank spaces.

2. Otherwise, only the first w characters are printed.

3. If no field width is given, a default width equal to the length of the string is used.

Decimal Point Representation of Real Values

1. For real values, an additional field width parameter can be provided in the form $e:w:d$. The presence of this parameter causes the real value to be printed in decimal point form (for example 22.3 or 0.0002).

2. The parameter causes the value to be printed with d digits to the right of the decimal point.

186 CHAPTER XI

The output doesn't look quite right, since the length of each of the four output fields is fixed by the computer. In particular, for strings, the number of characters printed is exactly the number of characters in the string; but for integers, a default width, such as 10, is assumed.

Now for the step up. Suppose we wish to get a bit fancy and print something like:

```
CHANGE IS $3.41
```

A good and seemingly logical approach would be something like:

```
WRITE ('CHANGE IS $', DOLLARS:2, '.', CENTS:2)
```

This will result in printing the following:

```
CHANGE IS $ 3.41
```

Notice here that a space appears after the dollar sign. This is because the printed number of dollars only needs to occupy one digit. If the number of dollars were 13, we would get

```
CHANGE IS $13.41
```

and if the number of dollars were 113, we would then get:

```
CHANGE IS $113.41
```

Notice in this last case that, although the field width of DOLLARS is given as 2, an additional digit is used, since the number 113 requires more than two digits to be printed. This is typical of the kind of detail that you need to be concerned about when you want to produce readable output.

But wait a minute. Suppose the change were $3.05, that is, the value of DOLLARS would be 3 and CENTS would be 5. The above WRITE statement would give:

```
CHANGE IS $ 3. 5
```

This odd result occurs because the number of cents is printed as 5 not 05. The remedy here is an explicit test for this case, as in:

```
if CENTS < 10 then
   WRITE ('CHANGE IS $', DOLLARS:1, '.', '.0', CENTS:1)
else
   WRITE ('CHANGE IS $', DOLLARS:1, '.', CENTS:2)
```

Here the 1 in

```
DOLLARS:1
```

will even eliminate the space after the dollar sign.

Enumerated Types

As we mentioned earlier, one of the painful realities of discovering Pascal is the input and output of strings and enumerated types. READ is defined only for numbers and characters; WRITE for numbers, booleans, characters, and character strings — hardly symmetrical.

Consider the following definitions:

```
type
    DAYNAME = (SUNDAY, MONDAY, TUESDAY, WEDNESDAY, THURSDAY,
              FRIDAY, SATURDAY);
var
    DAYOFCRIME: DAYNAME;
```

In this case DAYOFCRIME has an enumerated type, and you would think that you could read a value into it just as you could for NUMWEAPONS. However if you say

```
READ (DAYOFCRIME)
```

or

```
WRITE (DAYOFCRIME)
```

you will find you are in error.

So what's the big mystery? Well, on input you could read in integers corresponding to the seven days of the week and manually assign corresponding values to DAYOFCRIME. This would look something like:

```
READ (DAYNUM);
if DAYNUM = 1 then
   DAYOFCRIME := SUNDAY
else if DAYNUM = 2 then
   DAYOFCRIME := MONDAY
...
```

On output, you then have to write strings corresponding to each day name, for example, by writing

```
if DAYOFCRIME = SUNDAY then
   WRITE ('SUNDAY')
else if DAYOFCRIME = MONDAY then
   WRITE ('MONDAY')
...
```

or by writing an equivalent case statement. As for reading in strings, you just have to read them in a character at a time.

In brief, then:

- You can read in values of type INTEGER, REAL, or CHAR.

- You can print values of type INTEGER, REAL, BOOLEAN, or CHAR, as well as those with a string type.

Granted, all of this can be quite annoying, but all languages have their little idiosyncrasies; some are just easier to live with than others.

11.2   Files

The data on the standard input and output files INPUT and OUTPUT are recorded as a sequence of characters. Of course, when you read in an integer it is expected that the characters will form a meaningful number, but the basic READ and WRITE operations are performed over characters. This sequence of characters is said to form a *text file.*"

In Pascal, a file of data can be explicitly declared in a program. For example, we may have:

```
type
    SUSPECTNAME = packed array[1..20] of CHAR;
    SUSPECTDATA = file of SUSPECTNAME;
var
    SUSPECTFILE: SUSPECTDATA;
```

Here the type SUSPECTDATA represents a file of the names of possible suspects.

All files have certain properties. For one, a file may have an arbitrary number of items. In the above case, SUSPECTFILE may contain two, ten, or even 500 suspect names. Second, the last item in the file is always followed by a special marker called an "end-of-file." Obviously this marker is put there so your program can know when it has read all of the data.

Third, recall the program parameters INPUT and OUTPUT that are required in the program header. These are, in fact, the names of two predefined files whose declarations would be

```
var
    INPUT, OUTPUT:  TEXT;
```

where TEXT is a predefined type given as:

```
type TEXT = file of CHAR;
```

That is, INPUT and OUTPUT are the names of text files through which your program can read and transmit information.

All of this leads us to two general rules about Pascal.

1.   All reading and writing of data is conceptually performed through a file.

2.   All external files that your program uses (that is, files used for input or output) must be named in the program header.

These two rules hold whether you are using the standard text files INPUT and OUTPUT or files whose type is declared within your program, as for SUSPECTFILE.

Now let us revisit the basic procedures READ and WRITE. When we use these procedures, input and output take place on a file. The relevant file may be explicitly named in the procedure call by giving the name of the file as the first argument. For example, if we have

```
var
    YARDFILE,
    MASTERFILE: SUSPECTDATA;
    NEWNAME    : SUSPECTNAME;
```

we may have the procedure call

```
READ (YARDFILE, NEWNAME)
```

which reads a suspect name from YARDFILE and assigns it to NEWNAME, or

```
WRITE (MASTERFILE, NEWNAME)
```

which appends the value assigned to NEWNAME to the file MASTERFILE. Notice that for files other than INPUT or OUTPUT, arbitrary types of data may be stored and read in.

And now for the final blessing. If it happens, as has been the case throughout this text, that no file name is given with a READ or WRITE statement, the standard files INPUT and OUTPUT are assumed. So when you say

```
READ  (NUMWEAPONS);
WRITE (NUMWEAPONS + 1)
```

this really means:

```
READ  (INPUT,  NUMWEAPONS);
WRITE (OUTPUT, NUMWEAPONS + 1)
```

Elementary, my dear reader, is it not?

11.3   Some Details

As mentioned above, a file can have an unspecified number of items. However, at some point you will have finished reading all of the data and there will be nothing else left in the file. You can test for this condition with the boolean-valued end of file function EOF. You can apply this function to any file, for example, you may write:

```
if EOF(SUSPECTFILE) then
    -- what to do if no more suspects on file
else
    -- what to do otherwise
```

The function EOF will return the value TRUE if there are no more data items in the file, and FALSE otherwise. As indicated by our example, this function is useful whenever you want to test if you are at the end of your data. Just as for the basic procedure READ, you may omit the name of a file to be tested. In this case, the standard text file INPUT will be used, as in:

```
if EOF then
    -- what to do if no more INPUT data
```

Thus the function call EOF is the same as EOF(INPUT).

Similarly, when you are reading data from INPUT, you may test for an end-of-line by saying

```
if EOLN(INPUT) then
    -- what to do if at the end of a line
```

or equivalently:

```
if EOLN then
    -- what to do if at the end of a line
```

Watch out, though, for one tiny detail: the ends of lines are considered as blanks, so normally when you're reading data you can pass right over them. If you need to be careful about what's on a line, you must call EOLN.

The function EOLN raises another point for consideration. The function EOLN may be applied to any file declared with type:

```
file of CHAR
```

In fact, *all* of the procedures and formatting conventions mentioned in Table 11.1 and Table 11.2 apply to any file of this type.

Every once in a while you may want to "peek" at a file, for example, to see if some item you are looking for is there before you actually read it. To do this you simply place the symbol ˆ immediately after the name of the input file. For example, you may wish to say something like:

```
if SUSPECTFILEˆ = KNOWNCRIMINAL then
   -- what to do if the next suspect is a known criminal
```

You must be a bit careful here. Assuming that the value of KNOWNCRIMINAL is the 20-character name of some suspect, the boolean test compares the next name in the SUSPECTFILE with the value of KNOWNCRIMINAL. Importantly, the name given on the SUSPECTFILE is not read in during this comparison but is used only for the comparison.

If you work with external files (other than INPUT or OUTPUT), there are two predefined procedures that you must know about. The first, RESET, positions a file of data at the beginning for reading. Thus you must write

```
RESET (SUSPECTFILE)
```

to set up the file SUSPECTFILE in order to read in the first value. Similarly, you must use the procedure REWRITE to erase the contents of a file in order to store new data in it. Thus

```
REWRITE (RESULTFILE)
```

will erase the previous contents of RESULTFILE.

XII

The Adventure of the Gold Chip

T is really very good of you to come along, Watson," said Sherlock Holmes, as he rummaged through a litter of newspapers. We had the carriage to ourselves and were sitting in the two corner seats opposite each other as our train moved rapidly along to Reading. We were responding to a summons from Lestrade which arrived as we were breakfasting.

"It does make a considerable difference, having someone with me on whom I can thoroughly rely. I am sure the aid we will find in Reading will be so terribly biased as to render it worthless. You are familiar with the particulars of this ghastly murder?"

"Not at all," I replied. "My practice has kept me quite busy and I have not seen a newspaper in days."

"The press have not had very full accounts," he replied. "But it has been reported that our unfortunate victim was something of a recluse and a miser, with over three thousand pounds to his name at the time of his death. It was also widely known that he had numerous acquaintances in the London blackmail industry, hence the interest of Scotland Yard in the affair. He was last seen walking away from the village of Eyford late yesterday morning with a man who witnesses say had a bald patch crowning his matted hair. While there is no strong evidence that this stranger was the murderer, the police are left with no other suspects."

It was fairly late in the afternoon when we arrived to find Inspector Lestrade of Scotland Yard waiting for us upon the platform.

"I have ordered a carriage," said Lestrade, as we desembarked. "I know your energetic nature and that you would not be happy until you had been on the scene of the crime.

"We certainly appreciate your help, Mr. Holmes," added the Inspector. "But let me forewarn you that I myself and my best men could find no clue out here. As you will soon see, there is nothing but a jumble of footprints where the final confrontation apparently took place."

"Judge not too hastily, Lestrade," Holmes replied nonchalantly. "If I had a shilling for every clue your best men have overlooked in the last ten years, I would retire at once to the country and never want for the rest of my days. Surely you know, Lestrade, that there is no branch of detective science so important and so much neglected as the art of tracing footsteps."

A short while later we arrived at the scene. Holmes sprang down from our carriage, his face flushed and dark; once on a hot scent like this, he was transformed.

Like a foxhound, with gleaming eyes and straining muscles, Holmes was down on his knees, and at one point lay flat on the ground. For a long time he remained there, carefully surveying the earth with his pocket lens. Eventually, he scooped something up into a small envelope, which he returned to his pocket.

"Are there any points to which you would draw my attention?" asked Lestrade, as Holmes returned to us.

"Beyond the obvious facts that there were three men present here at the time of the incident, that the man who led our victim down this path wears a size-nine boot and is in good standing with the London financial community, and that the killer himself is a highly underpaid labourer and former officer in the Royal Marine Light Infantry, I can deduce nothing else. After all, Lestrade, one cannot make bricks without clay."

"FOR A LONG TIME HE REMAINED THERE."

The Inspector opened his mouth to speak, but Holmes quickly added, "And do take the trouble of extinguishing your pipe before examining evidence. That left foot of yours with its inward twist and the ash from your Arcadia mixture are all over the place. A mole could trace your movements. Oh, how much simpler it would be if I could only get a look at things before you and your men come in here like a herd of buffalos, trampling over everything!"

Convinced that there was no further need for his services, Holmes called for the carriage, and we were soon heading for Baker Street again. In the privacy of our carriage he shed some light on our abrupt departure.

"As a rule, when I have observed some slight indication of the course of events, I am able to guide myself by the thousands of other similar cases which occur to my memory," he began. "As you are aware, over the course of my career I have amassed data on well over a thousand criminals. In recent years I have stored these data in files suitable for the memory of the Analytical Engine. Furthermore, I have designed a programme that will read the description of each criminal and then print out the names of all those fitting a given description."

I have reproduced here a small section of my companion's curious assortment of criminal data, which he showed me upon our return to Baker Street.

Name	:	The name of a person
Height	:	Height in inches, ranging from 48 to 84
Hair colour	:	One of the colours brown, black, red, or grey
Eye colour	:	One of the colours brown, blue, or hazel
Hat size	:	A number from 4 to 10
Shoe size	:	A number from 5 to 15
Teeth marks:		One of the characteristics normal, crooked, gold-filled, partially missing, or (totally) missing
Cigar type	:	One of the cigar types Lunkah, Trichinopoly, Espanada, Heritage, Londoner, MacDuffy, Top Hat, or West Country
Facial scar	:	Yes or no
Hand scar	:	Yes or no
Eye patch	:	Yes or no
Bald patch	:	Yes or no
Leg limp	:	Yes or no
Tattoo	:	Yes or no

"I must confess Watson, as I look over these possibilities, that this case does have its points of interest. We know that the suspect has a slight bald patch and wears a size-nine boot. The most singular clue in this mystery, however, is this gold chip I found in amongst the gravel." He showed me the object. "It is a gold dental filling and surely narrows down our list of candidates. Just as you can tell an old master by the sweep of his brush, I can tell a Moriarty when I see one."

"A Moriarty?" I queried.

"The power behind half that is evil and nearly all that is undetected in this great city, Watson. I have been at great pains to work out all my programmes for the Analytical Engine before he becomes aware of its utility, for Moriarty is a mathematical mind of the highest order; and I shudder to think what he could carry out with the Engine at his command."

"What are the ingredients of this particular programme?" I asked, after a considerable pause.

"The most important feature of this programme is, aptly enough, called a *record*," replied Holmes. "A record is a collection of data on some item of interest. In this instance, of course, the record is a collection of facts about a known criminal. Each record consists of one or more *components*, with each component bearing a *name* and a *value*. Here is a sample of my record structures," he continued, handing me a sheet from his portfolio.

What he showed me is duplicated here :—

Name	:	a 30-character string
Height	:	0 if unknown; 48 to 84 if known
Hair colour	:	0 if unknown; 1 if brown; 2 if black; 3 if red; 4 if grey
Eye colour	:	0 if unknown; 1 if brown; 2 if blue; 3 if hazel
Hat size	:	0 if unknown; 4 to 10 if known
Shoe size	:	0 if unknown; 5 to 15 if known
Teeth marks	:	0 if unknown; 1 if normal; 2 if crooked; 3 if gold-filled; 4 if partial; 5 if missing
Cigar type	:	0 if unknown; 1 if Lunkah; 2 if Trichinopoly; 3 if Espanada; 4 if Heritage; 5 if Londoner; 6 if MacDuffy; 7 if Top Hat; 8 if West Country
Facial scar	:	0 if unknown; 1 if yes; 2 if no
Hand scar	:	0 if unknown; 1 if yes; 2 if no
Eye patch	:	0 if unknown; 1 if yes; 2 if no
Bald patch	:	0 if unknown; 1 if yes; 2 if no
Leg limp	:	0 if unknown; 1 if yes; 2 if no
Tattoo	:	0 if unknown; 1 if yes; 2 if no

"For simplicity, such data as colour values and shoe sizes are entered as integers," said Holmes, jotting illustrations of his ideas on a scrap of paper, as follows:

Hair colour: 1 brown   2 black   3 red   4 grey

Moreover, truth values are also stored as integer numbers, as follows:

1 for yes, 2 for no

In all cases, if a value is unknown, its place is held by the number 0."

"How can you possibly use these records to find the name of a suspect?" I asked, for I still had no idea how he could use such data to advantage.

"Easily," remarked Holmes. "In Pascal, variables that stand for records can be declared as such, just like variables that stand for arrays or integers. Here is an example :—

```
var
   CRIMINAL: record
                NAME    :  packed array[1..30] of CHAR:
                SHOESIZE:  0..15
             end;
```

"An even better method of describing this information would be as follows:

```
type
   NAMESTRING = packed array[1..30] of CHAR;
   DATARECORD =
      record
         NAME    :  NAMESTRING;
         SHOESIZE:  0..15
      end;
var
   CRIMINAL: DATARECORD;
```

"Moreover," continued Holmes, "one can refer to a component of a record by specifying the name of the record variable and the name of the component, as follows:

```
CRIMINAL.SHOESIZE
```

This reference can be used in Pascal statements like any other variable, such as

```
if CRIMINAL.SHOESIZE = 9 then
   -- print criminal's name
```

or:

```
CRIMINAL.SHOESIZE := 9
```

"What our programme will do, Watson, is read in the characteristics of a suspect, such as a bald patch or a size-nine boot, and then print out the names of all those criminals in its files that fit the description. Let us give it a try, shall we? I can tell you well in advance, however, whose signature we shall find on this latest criminal masterpiece."

Holmes then carefully entered the data according to the programme, which I have duplicated here as Exhibit 12.1, paying special attention to enter the codes for a size-nine boot, gold-filled teeth, and the presence of a bald patch. We watched for several minutes before the names of three criminals within the file had been printed.

```
program SEARCH (INPUT, OUTPUT, MASTERFILE);
{  -- This programme reads in values corresponding to data saved
   -- in a file of records kept on known criminals.  For
   -- each item, a prompt indicates which item is to be input.
   -- A value of 0 indicates that the item is unknown.
   -- The programme outputs the name of each criminal for which
   -- the input values match those on the criminal's record. }
   const
      UNKNOWN = 0;
   type
      YESNOCODE  = 0..2;
      NAMESTRING = packed array[1..30] of CHAR;
      DATARECORD =
         record
            NAME      : NAMESTRING;
            HEIGHT    : 0..84;
            HAIRCOLOUR: 0..4;
            EYECOLOUR : 0..3;
            HATSIZE   : 0..10;
            SHOESIZE  : 0..15;
            TEETHMARKS: 0..5;
            CIGARTYPE : 0..8;
            FACIALSCAR: YESNOCODE;
            HANDSCAR  : YESNOCODE;
            EYEPATCH  : YESNOCODE;
            BALDPATCH : YESNOCODE;
            LEGLIMP   : YESNOCODE;
            TATTOO    : YESNOCODE
         end;
   var
      SUSPECT, CRIMINAL: DATARECORD;
      MASTERFILE       : file of DATARECORD;
```

Exhibit 12.1 *Holmes's Programme for the Criminal Search*

```
procedure GETSUSPECTINFO (var SUSPECT: DATARECORD);
begin
   WRITELN ('IN ENTERING DATA, USE 0 IF ITEM IS UNKNOWN.');

   WRITELN ('ENTER HEIGHT IN INCHES:');
   READLN  (SUSPECT.HEIGHT);

   WRITELN ('ENTER HAIR COLOUR CODE:');
   WRITELN ('1 BROWN,  2 BLACK,  3 RED,  4 GREY');
   READLN  (SUSPECT.HAIRCOLOUR);

   WRITELN ('ENTER EYE COLOUR CODE:');
   WRITELN ('1 BROWN,  2 BLUE,  3 HAZEL');
   READLN  (SUSPECT.EYECOLOUR);

   WRITELN ('ENTER HAT SIZE:');
   READLN  (SUSPECT.HATSIZE);

   WRITELN ('ENTER SHOE SIZE:');
   READLN  (SUSPECT.SHOESIZE);

   WRITELN ('ENTER TEETH MARKS CODE:');
   WRITELN ('1 NORMAL,  2 CROOKED,  3 GOLD FILLED,');
   WRITELN ('4 PARTIAL, 5 MISSING');
   READLN  (SUSPECT.TEETHMARKS);

   WRITELN ('ENTER CIGAR TYPE CODE:');
   WRITELN ('1 LUNKAH,   2 TRICHINOPOLY, 3 ESPANADA,');
   WRITELN ('4 HERITAGE, 5 LONDONER,    6 MACDUFFY,');
   WRITELN ('7 TOP HAT,  8 WEST COUNTRY');
   READLN  (SUSPECT.CIGARTYPE);

   WRITELN ('NOW USE 1 FOR YES, 2 FOR NO:');
   WRITELN ('FACIAL SCAR? HAND SCAR? EYEPATCH?');
   WRITELN ('BALD PATCH?  LEG LIMP?   TATTOO?');
   READLN  (SUSPECT.FACIALSCAR,  SUSPECT.HANDSCAR,  SUSPECT.EYEPATCH,
            SUSPECT.BALDPATCH,   SUSPECT.LEGLIMP,   SUSPECT.TATTOO)
end;
```

Exhibit 12.1   *Continued*

```
function ITEMMATCH (ITEM1, ITEM2:  INTEGER):  BOOLEAN;
begin
   if (ITEM1 = UNKNOWN) or (ITEM2 = UNKNOWN) or (ITEM1 = ITEM2) then
      ITEMMATCH := TRUE
   else
      ITEMMATCH := FALSE
end;


function MATCH ({ between } SUSPECT, CRIMINAL: DATARECORD): BOOLEAN;
begin
   if  ITEMMATCH (SUSPECT.HEIGHT,      CRIMINAL.HEIGHT)
   and ITEMMATCH (SUSPECT.HAIRCOLOUR, CRIMINAL.HAIRCOLOUR)
   and ITEMMATCH (SUSPECT.EYECOLOUR,  CRIMINAL.EYECOLOUR)
   and ITEMMATCH (SUSPECT.HATSIZE,     CRIMINAL.HATSIZE)
   and ITEMMATCH (SUSPECT.SHOESIZE,    CRIMINAL.SHOESIZE)
   and ITEMMATCH (SUSPECT.TEETHMARKS, CRIMINAL.TEETHMARKS)
   and ITEMMATCH (SUSPECT.CIGARTYPE,  CRIMINAL.CIGARTYPE)
   and ITEMMATCH (SUSPECT.FACIALSCAR, CRIMINAL.FACIALSCAR)
   and ITEMMATCH (SUSPECT.HANDSCAR,    CRIMINAL.HANDSCAR)
   and ITEMMATCH (SUSPECT.EYEPATCH,    CRIMINAL.EYEPATCH)
   and ITEMMATCH (SUSPECT.BALDPATCH,   CRIMINAL.BALDPATCH)
   and ITEMMATCH (SUSPECT.LEGLIMP,     CRIMINAL.LEGLIMP)
   and ITEMMATCH (SUSPECT.TATTOO,      CRIMINAL.TATTOO)    then
      MATCH := TRUE
   else
      MATCH := FALSE
end;


begin  { -- Main Algorithm }
   GETSUSPECTINFO (SUSPECT);
   RESET (MASTERFILE);

   while not EOF(MASTERFILE) do begin
      READ (MASTERFILE, { giving } CRIMINAL);
      if MATCH (SUSPECT, CRIMINAL)  then
         WRITELN ('POSSIBLE SUSPECT ', CRIMINAL.NAME)
   end;
   WRITELN ('ALL ENTRIES HAVE BEEN CHECKED')
end.
```

Exhibit 12.1 *Continued*

"Moriarty," Holmes whispered. "These other two, Watson, are certainly capable of carrying out such a crime. However, I happen to know one of them is in Newgate; and if I am not mistaken, this other is awaiting trial here in London."

"Surely you haven't enough evidence to convict Moriarty," I protested.

"Oh, hardly, Watson," replied Holmes. "But count on it, this crime fits into something much larger which we fail to see presently, for there are certain subtleties that even our Engine cannot detect. True, it has removed a lot of the painstaking drudgery from our work; but it is up to us to find where and how this piece fits into the larger scheme of things.

"For now, Watson, there is a cold partridge on the sideboard and a bottle of Montrachet here. Let us renew our energies before we make fresh calls upon them."

12.1 Record Structures

Certainly one of the most useful features of Pascal is its capability for defining record structures. A *record* is a collection of information pertaining to some real-world entity.

Consider the following declarations:

```
SUSPECT:
   record
      HEIGHT  : 0..84;
      HATSIZE : 0..10;
      SHOESIZE: 0..15
   end;

CIGAR:
   record
      BRAND    : (TRICHINOPOLY, LUNKAH, OLDWOOD, LONDONER);
      TEXTURE  : (FLAKY, CAKED, GRANULAR, FLUFFY);
      NICOTINE : (PLUS1, PLUS2, PLUS3);
      PARTICLES: BOOLEAN;
      DATA     : record
                    UNITVOLUME: REAL;
                    UNITWEIGHT: REAL;
                    DENSITY   : REAL
                 end
   end;
```

The first declaration defines a variable named SUSPECT, whose type is a record. The record has three components, HEIGHT, HATSIZE, and SHOESIZE. Each component is a subrange of integers.

The components of a record can be of any type, even other records. This is shown in the second declaration, which defines a record variable named CIGAR. Here the component BRAND has a value that is from an enumerated type. The component DATA is itself a record structure defining the physical characteristics of the cigar's ash.

Record structures can be defined in a type declaration, just as for any other type. Thus we may **rewrite** the above definition of cigar properties as

```
type
   CIGARBRAND  = (TRICHINOPOLY, LUNKAH, OLDWOOD, LONDONER);
   ASHTEXTURE  = (FLAKY, CAKED, GRANULAR, FLUFFY);
  ·TESTRESULT  = (PLUS1, PLUS2, PLUS3);
   DENSITYDATA =
      record
         UNITVOLUME: REAL;
         UNITWEIGHT: REAL;
         DENSITY   : REAL
      end;

   CIGARINFO  =
      record
         BRAND    : CIGARBRAND;
         TEXTURE  : ASHTEXTURE;
         NICOTINE : TESTRESULT;
         PARTICLES: BOOLEAN;
         DATA     : DENSITYDATA
      end;
```

and then simply say

```
CIGAR: CIGARINFO;
```

to declare the variable CIGAR.

Just as for components of arrays, we can refer to the components of a record. For example, we may say

```
SUSPECT.HEIGHT   := 71;
SUSPECT.HATSIZE  := 7;
SUSPECT.SHOESIZE := 9;
```

to establish values for each of the properties of SUSPECT. The general rule here is simple. If R is the name of a record variable and C is the name of one of its components, then

```
    R.C
```

is the name of the record component.
    Notice in our cigar example that

```
    CIGAR.DATA
```

is also a record. Thus it makes sense to say

```
    CIGAR.DATA.DENSITY
```

to refer to the density of the cigar ash. For example, we may have:

```
    CIGAR.DATA.DENSITY := CIGAR.DATA.UNITWEIGHT / CIGAR.DATA.UNITVOLUME
```

Again, just what you would expect.
    There is one little anomaly we must watch out for here. In Pascal, you
can assign one record to another, provided they have the same type. Thus
with

```
    MYCIGAR, YOURCIGAR: CIGARINFO;
```

you can say:

```
    MYCIGAR := YOURCIGAR    { Ok }
```

But watch out. You cannot say something like:

```
    if MYCIGAR = YOURCIGAR then     { Trouble }
```

To get the same effect, you must write

```
    if  (MYCIGAR.BRAND            = YOURCIGAR.BRAND)
    and (MYCIGAR.TEXTURE          = YOURCIGAR.TEXTURE)
    and (MYCIGAR.NICOTINE         = YOURCIGAR.NICOTINE)
    and (MYCIGAR.PARTICLES        = YOURCIGAR.PARTICLES)
    and (MYCIGAR.DATA.UNITVOLUME  = YOURCIGAR.DATA.UNITVOLUME)
    and (MYCIGAR.DATA.UNITWEIGHT  = YOURCIGAR.DATA.UNITWEIGHT)
    and (MYCIGAR.DATA.DENSITY     = YOURCIGAR.DATA.DENISTY)  then
```

which certainly is tedious. In practice, you will probably not need to
compare all the components. For example, in the above case

```
    if (MYCIGAR.BRAND = YOURCIGAR.BRAND) then
```

may suffice.

12.2   Storing Records

Recall the first line of Holmes's program:

```
program SEARCH (INPUT, OUTPUT, MASTERFILE);
```

Here the program parameter MASTERFILE is declared as

```
MASTERFILE: file of DATARECORD;
```

where DATARECORD is the type:

```
record
   NAME  : NAMESTRING;
   HEIGHT: 0..84;
   ...
   TATTOO: YESORNOCODE
end
```

Thus the external file is a file of records.

Such a use of record structures is common in many applications. Typically, whenever we have a large collection of data, the data are stored in a file that is external to the program. Often the data are collected into records, and the purpose of the program is to analyze the records in some way.

Now this would suggest that there are, in essence, two kinds of data. On one hand there are data that are designed for human consumption, such as when we read and write numbers and characters during input and output. On the other hand, there are data, such as files and records, that are designed entirely for use by the machine. The computer's ability to maintain huge amounts of data is greatly enhanced by Pascal's ambidextrous talents for working with external files as well as its record structure mechanism.

That's really all there is to know about records in Pascal, though you might want to check on Pascal's facility for variant records.

But remember, as the great detective remarked in "The Adventure of the Dancing Men," involving a complex code, "Every problem becomes very childish when once it is explained to you."

The Last Bow

XIII

Holmes Delivers
A Lecture

N O record of the doings of Mr. Sherlock Holmes and his contributions to the development and understanding of the Analytical Engine would be complete without a report on his brilliant address to the Royal Society in the late autumn of 1895. Shortly after the conclusion of the case involving Arthur H. Staunton, the rising young forger, came the publication of the great detective's much celebrated monograph, "Upon the Use of the Analytical Engine in the Work of the Criminal Investigator," which earned him an invitation to speak before the annual meeting of the Royal Society.

It may be remembered that I had sold my Kensington practice a year earlier and that I was again sharing lodgings with my old companion at 221B Baker Street. He insisted that I accompany him to the assembly, and it was my great privilege to do so. I offer here an account of his address, which I have reconstructed from my notes.

A special carriage was sent for us bearing two emissaries of the Royal Society. These gentlemen escorted us to a stately house situated off Pall Mall, to the rooms that were home to the learned group, where a reception was already in progress. Here Holmes and I had the opportunity to mingle with some of Britain's most renowned scientific figures.

At a certain point, Holmes was escorted to a podium and, following a brief introduction, commenced his lecture.

"Gentlemen and fellow scientific investigators," Holmes began. "It is without doubt an honour to appear before this assembly tonight in order to share a few of my ideas on the use of the Analytical Engine.

"A SPECIAL CARRIAGE WAS SENT FOR US."

"Though all of you are doubtless already aware of the advantages that the Engine promises to bestow upon science, and although many of you may be considering applying this new device to your own areas of investigation, it is likely that you have as yet had little experience in designing programmes for the Engine. It is my hope that my lecture will furnish you with a general, logical method for organizing programming tasks and attacking scientific problems with the Analytical Engine. This method I have called "programming from the top-down," although elementary in its fundamental concepts, it is invaluable as a technique for constructing all types of programmes, including the most complex ones you are likely to encounter.

"In my engagements as a criminal investigator I have always been careful to arrange all clues systematically and devise a complete hypothetical approach to a case before taking a single step out of my rooms in pursuit of a solution. This principle applies equally well to the use of the Analytical Engine. No matter how simple the task, it is necessary at the outset to formulate a *clear* and *complete* statement of the problem at hand, as well as a basic plan for solving it. The programmer should prepare sample input and output formats and design a general algorithm before writing any programme. This precaution ensures that a minimal amount of confusion and lost time will result during interactions with the Engine.

"Let me now enumerate the characteristics of the top-down approach.

"The first concept essential for a grasp of programming top-down is the idea of *design in levels*. The programmer should construct his programme according to a conceptual hierarchy. The upper levels of his hierarchy should indicate the more general features of the problem, with details and elaborations introduced at the lower levels.

"The highest level is thus the initial conception of the solution. The individual paths from each level represent the possible solutions at each conceptual stage. Each lower level thus elaborates the preceding level. Here is a chart," said Holmes, "that illustrates this idea."

I have reproduced this graphic representation as Exhibit 13.1.

"Secondly, the language used to formulate this preliminary model need not be the special language of the Engine, and for this reason the top-down method is described as being *language independent*. At this early stage of programming, ordinary English will generally be sufficient. Later, of course, it should be possible to encode the programme in a form intelligible to the Engine.

"Thirdly, as in all forms of scientific reasoning, it is advisable to attain a firm grasp of the broad aspects of a problem before proceeding to the minute details of analysis. Accordingly, in the top-down approach, *details should be deferred* to lower levels. Typical of such detail is the internal representation of data.

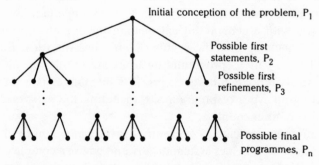

Exhibit 13.1   *The Top-Down Approach*

"Fourthly, before advancing to a lower level, the programmer must ascertain that the solution is stated in *precise* terms. By this I mean that instead of using a very vague statement that has no immediate consequences, the programmer should seek a more meaningful statement that entails one or more submodules.

"Fifthly, as a new level unfolds in the programme's development, the programmer must take pains to *verify the solution*. You will conserve appreciable amounts of time and energy by detecting errors in style or content as early as possible, rather than after numerous subprogrammes have already been generated and the errors must be traced to their sources further up in the hierarchy.

"And finally, each step of the programme must be elaborated, improved, and meticulously examined until it is ready to be transformed into the Engine's special language.

"Although this lengthy process of refinement may seem tedious to the lofty theorists among you, I assure you that there is no other way to use the computing machine efficaciously. In fact, as you become more adept at designing programmes, this stage of the task will become less and less burdensome; and you may well discover that you enjoy the intellectual exercise it affords.

"I myself found no difficulty in adapting to the requirements of programme design, for my career as a detective has sharpened my faculties to such a degree that I routinely dissect cumbersome problems into manageable components with little effort.

"Now, gentlemen, if my explication is clear to you thus far, I should like to offer some observations concerning the art, or science, as you would perhaps prefer to designate it, of programming from the top-down. I cannot emphasize too strongly that you must thoroughly understand the given task and its solution before attempting to write a programme.

"Therefore, you should initially be far less concerned with your notation—for example, ordinary English would suffice—than with your overall comprehension of the problem. This is especially important at the top levels of the hierarchy. Eventually, sub-programmes must be explicitly stated; and in particular all input and output arguments must be described.

"Again, allow me to emphasise the importance of scrupulous examination and refinement of each stage of a top-down model. One should always look for possible errors and provide against them.

"Here is an example at an intermediate level of refinement," continued Holmes, gesturing towards another illustration that I have duplicated as follows :

```
case DAY_OF_THE_WEEK of
    MONDAY:     -- generate last week's criminal summary
    TUESDAY:    -- do nothing
    WEDNESDAY:  -- update criminal records
    THURSDAY:   -- process new reports
    FRIDAY:     -- generate lab item reports
    SATURDAY:   -- generate weekly statistics
    SUNDAY:     -- do nothing
end
```

"The language in this illustration is obviously informal, yet each statement can be transformed into instructions as required for the Engine. Of course, the programme must ultimately provide explicit instructions for performing each operation, such as the updating of criminal records, but this occurs at a later stage of the refinement process.

"Once again, gentlemen, may I direct your attention to our first illustration (Exhibit 13.1). As I remarked previously, this is a graphic representation of the top-down concept. The highest level, P_1, constitutes the most general description of the problem; and the downward branchings represent the alternative methods of programme design available to the programmer at each step. As the programmer reaches each successive level, he must choose the branches that best fit the stated purposes. If all the branches at a certain level seem unsuitable, it may be necessary to return upward in the tree and select a different solution at a higher level. In advancing from P_1 to the bottom of the tree, the programmer thus moves from a general statement of the problem, through a series of decisions about the design, and finally to a working programme.

"Let us turn our attention to this illustration of the top-down structure of a particular programme containing five levels."

Holmes directed their attention to the chart I have included here as Exhibit 13.2.

"Observe how individual paths from P_1, as they were designated in our first illustration (Exhibit 13.1), are elaborated to produce the individual parts charted in this illustration (Exhibit 13.2).

"I imagine that by this time my learned listeners have conceived some applications of the top-down method to their own investigations in various scientific disciplines. As a man acquainted with several branches of natural science, and especially chemistry, I am confident that the principles outlined in this lecture can be of service to investigators in all fields, mundane as well as academic."

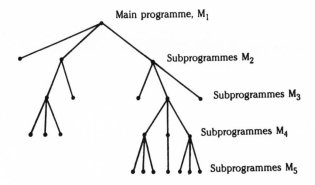

Exhibit 13.2 *Top-Down Structure of a Programme*

As could only be expected, the members of the Royal Society greeted Holmes's lecture with considerable applause and afterwards detained him for nearly an hour with their questions concerning the details of the top-down method. Many of them were delighted to meet the famous detective, whose adventures they confessed to having followed in my modest chronicles; and they pressed Holmes to discuss his latest endeavours in criminal investigation.

Once we were back at our comfortable lodgings in Baker Street, sitting on either side of the fire, Holmes, who was always amenable to flattery, allowed his more sombre and cynical spirit to comment on the evening's course of events.

"Do you realize, Watson, that none of our distinguished company this evening enquired as to my plans for applying the Analytical Engine in my future criminal investigations? If these are the greatest minds our generation can offer, I fear that the world may not yet be ready or deserving of this magnificent Engine. It was indeed a disappointment, for I would surely like to contemplate tomorrow's challenges as well as yesterday's laurels."

"I fear, Holmes, that I am entirely to blame for this," I remarked. "My highly exaggerated accounts of your doings, as you yourself have called them, have given the public a distorted view of the seriousness with which you go about your business."

"On the contrary, Watson. You have given prominence not so much to the many sensational causes in our cases together, but rather to those seemingly trivial incidents that have given room for those faculties of deduction that I have made my special province. For this, I am eternally grateful. As for the Analytical Engine, I offer my work to the next generation of scientific investigators—to those young boys still in boarding school, capsules they are, hundreds of bright little seeds from which will doubtless spring a wiser, and indeed better, England."

13.1   Revisiting the Top-Down Approach

There are many different approaches to a programming problem. Holmes's use of the top-down approach is in marked contrast to other methods. Consider the following list:

1.   Linear approach
2.   Bottom-up approach
3.   Inside-out or forest approach
4.   Imitation approach

The first method is the "linear" approach. Here you immediately start writing code as it will appear when executed, first line first, second line second, and so forth. The drawback with this approach is the need to make specific, detailed decisions with very little assurance that they will be appropriate to the problem at hand.

It is a capital mistake to theorize before one has data, as Holmes has remarked on a number of occasions, because one begins to twist facts to suit theories, instead of theories to suit facts. It is just so with programming; if one begins to construct a program without sufficient data one must be prepared to accept the consequences. The linear technique may seem obviously poor, but the temptation to use it can be very strong, especially on those problems that appear "easy." But beware of this temptation—the little, easy problems have a way of ending up much more complicated than they first appear.

In the "bottom-up" approach, the programmer designs and writes the lower components first, and the upper levels later. The bottom-up approach is in a sense the inversion of the top-down approach. It suffers severely by requiring the programmer to make specific decisions about the program before the overall problem and algorithm are understood.

In between the top-down and bottom-up approaches, we have the "inside-out" or "forest" approach, which consists of starting in the middle of the program and working down and up at the same time. Roughly speaking, it goes as follows:

1. *General idea.* First we decide upon the general idea for programming the problem.

2. *A rough sketch of the program.* Next we write any "important" sections of the program, assuming initialization in some form. In some sections we write portions of the actual program. In doing this, we hope that the actual intent of each piece of program will not change several times, necessitating rewriting parts of our sketch.

3. *Programming the first version.* After Step 2, we write the entire program. We start with the lowest level module. After an individual component has been programmed, we debug it and immediately prepare a description of what it does.

4. *Rethinking and revising.* As a result of Step 3, we should be close to a working program, but it may be possible to improve on it. So we continue by making improvements until we obtain a complete working program.

It is probably fair to say that many programmers, even experienced ones, often work inside out, starting neither very close to the top or to the bottom level. Instead they start in the middle and work outward until a program finally appears on the horizon. The approach is a poor one, for the program may undergo many changes and patches and thus seldom achieves a clear logical structure.

As another method, consider the "imitation" approach, a method superficially resembling the top-down approach. This approach is discussed in detail because many programmers *think* that the top-down approach is really the way they have always programmed. There are, however, subtle but important differences. The imitation approach is described as follows:

1. *Thinking about the program.* Having been given a programming task, take the time to examine the problem thoroughly before starting to program. Think about the details of the program for a while, and then decide on a general approach.

2. *Deciding on subprograms.* After having thought about the problem in detail, decide on what sections will be sufficiently important to merit being made into subprograms.

3.   *Writing of subprograms.* At this point write each subprograms. After each is completed, write down what it expects as input, what it returns as output, and what it does. The subprograms should be written in a hierarchical manner: the most primitive first, calling routines second, and so forth. Doing this will ensure that the subprograms are fully written before the upper-level program structures are finalized.

4.   *Writing the main program.* After all subprograms have been written, write the main program. The purpose of the main program is to sequence and interface the subprograms.

The imitation approach has some important similarities to the top-down approach:

■   The problem must be understand thoroughly before writing the program.

■   The actual writing of the program is postponed until after certain decisions have been made.

■   The problem is broken up into clear, logical units.

However, there are important differences between the two approaches:

■   In the top-down approach, a *specific* plan of attack is developed in stages. Only the issues relevant to a given level are considered, and these issues are formalized completely.

■   Furthermore, whenever the programmer decides to use a subprogram, the interfaces (arguments, returned values, and effects) are decided *first*. The inputs and outputs are formalized before developing the subprograms; that is, the subprograms are made to fit the calling routine instead of the other way around.

■   Most important, at *every step* in the top-down approach, the programmer must have a complete, correct "program."

The disadvantages of the imitation approach are that it is more likely to produce errors, to require extensive program modifications, or to result in a somewhat ill-conceived program. Choosing a partially specified attack may require serious changes to the program. Writing subprograms first may result in confusing program logic if the subprograms do not integrate easily into the upper-level code designed later.

In summary, think carefully about programming technique. The top-down approach, as described by Holmes, may provide the best alternative.

XIV

The Final Programme

ITH Mr. Sherlock Holmes at Baker Street, one's morning paper presented infinite possibilities. The air of London remains all the sweeter for his absence but the days of the great cases are past following his retirement to the Sussex Downs.

During this period of my life, Holmes passed almost entirely beyond my ken, save for an occasional weekend pilgrimage I might make to his little villa at Fulworth. I was surprised and delighted, therefore, when one morning in June the maid brought in a small package and a note from my old companion. Removing the wrappings I found a slim volume entitled, *Practical Handbook of Bee Culture, with Some Observations upon the Segregation of the Queen.* The accompanying note read :—

> *Watson,*
>
> *As you can see, I have been considering some of the problems furnished by Nature, rather than those of a more superficial character for which our artificial state of society is wholly responsible. Of late, however, I have been tempted to direct my thoughts towards the Analytical Engine. Can you spare me a few days? Air and scenery are perfect.*
>
> *Holmes*

Owing to my experience in the rough-and-tumble camps of Afghanistan, I was quite a ready traveller. My bag was packed and I was rattling out of Victoria station within the hour.

Mrs. Hudson, his old housekeeper, showed me into Holmes's sitting room where I found him engaged in conversation with a distinguished gentleman, vaguely familiar to me.

"Surely you remember Major General Henry Prevost Babbage?" said Holmes.

"Of course," I replied. "We met at the annual meeting of the Royal Society. I am delighted to meet you again, sir."

"The pleasure is mine, Dr. Watson," he answered, extending his hand. We sat for a while and, naturally enough, the conversation turned to the Analytical Engine.

"NATURALLY THE CONVERSATION TURNED TO THE ANALYTICAL ENGINE."

"As you know, Watson, I am now preparing the *magnum opus* of my career, a comprehensive treatise of my methods entitled *The Whole Art of Detection*, with illustrations from my most noteworthy cases. As you may imagine, this is the longest and most difficult work I have ever attempted, over five hundred pages in its entirety. I have spent countless hours and many sleepless nights verifying minute points and making hundreds of emendations.

"The content and style of this manuscript have so engrossed my attention that I simply have no patience left for the more mundane aspects of its creation, such as typing and proofreading. Yet I dare not entrust the copying and editing of such an important work to just anyone. Do you understand, Watson?"

"Yes, quite, Holmes," I replied, with some apprehension lest he ask me to serve as his scribe. A sudden thought came to me. "Perhaps the Engine can be put to good use here?"

"Precisely what I had in mind, Watson. Now, you may well wonder how the Engine is equipped to serve in this capacity. Imagine, if you will that I have scribbled out a paragraph of my manuscript without observing the conventions of margins, indentation, *et cetera*, as in this fragment.

He placed before Babbage and myself a card with the following inscription :—

> While the   criminal investigator
> typically does
> not consider himself a   disciple
> of empirical science,
> his work, like the chemist's,
> consists in a logical and systematic
> quest   for Truth.

"Obviously I could not submit a collection of such fragments to a publisher. I am trying to design a programme that will, among other things, arrange such fragments of text correctly, as follows."

He thereupon handed us another card on which was written an emendation of the first :

> While the criminal investigator typically does
> not consider himself a disciple of empirical science,
> his work, like the chemist's, consists in a logical
> and systematic quest for Truth.

"Notice here that the words are arranged to fill the line properly," Holmes continued. "You see, the typing and editing process can be made considerably simpler. I can enter the text at leisure; and if a mistake is encountered or a change is deemed necessary, I can simply correct the original version. The Engine can then be commanded to print a perfect, corrected copy. Here I have made an outline of the desired format for my entire manuscript."

I inspected the proffered conventions, which are reproduced here :

1. Page Size (standard 8 1/2-by-11 page)
   85 characters per line
   66 lines per page

2. Margins
   Left: 15 characters in from left edge of page
   Right: 10 characters in from right edge of page

> Top: 6 lines down from top of page
> Bottom: 6 lines up from bottom of page

3. Printing Area (standard 10 point spacing)
    60 characters per line
    54 lines per page

4. Page Numbers
    3 lines down from bottom margin, centered between the left and right
    margin, and enclosed by hyphens, for example:

    –14–

I immediately thought of my own writings and the great amount of time
that could be saved with the implementation of such a scheme. It would
sometimes take up to a year for my manuscripts to be edited by my literary
agent, Dr. Arthur Conan Doyle, again by *his* editors, and finally appear in
their printed form. I noted that in addition to spacing each line of text
properly, the Engine would ensure that the margins were observed and that
page numbers were correctly incremented.

"Well, Holmes," I said after a time, "this idea of yours will undoubtedly
spare you much of the tedium authors ordinarily suffer."

"True, Watson," he replied, "but this is only the beginning of my work.
Remember that before approaching the Engine it is imperative to define
the problem completely and exactly, using the top-down approach. In
particular, one must enumerate every possible detail of the input and
output. On these pages I have described the commands for formatting text
and worked out a hypothetical input with its corresponding output."

Holmes then showed us the commands as well as samples of the input
and output to his programme. I have replicated them here as Exhibits 14.1
and 14.2, respectively.

"The Engine would also be employed to control the general scheme of
the printed page, that is to say, it would handle the paragraphing and
indentation patterns. Thus a command such as

```
:INDENT 10
```

would cause following lines of text to be indented ten spaces. Then if one
wished to return to the left margin, the command

```
:INDENT 0
```

would suffice."

"I beg your pardon, Mr. Holmes," Babbage interjected at this point.
"But what exactly do you have in mind when you speak of enumerating
every possible detail of the input and output?"

Commands	Meaning
:PARAGRAPH	Marks the beginning of a paragraph. All following lines of text up to the next command line are treated as a sequence of words without line boundaries. The words are printed with end-of-line markers inserted so that each line (except the last) will be filled with one space between each pair of words. The first line of each paragraph is indented 5 spaces. The right margin is ragged.
	If the paragraph is followed by a blank line or one or more commands (excluding the **VERBATIM** command), then the next line of text will be considered the beginning of a new paragraph.
:VERBATIM	Marks the beginning of a series of lines that are to be output exactly as given, except for possible indentation. All lines (excluding command lines) between the **VERBATIM** command line and the next **PARAGRAPH** command line (or the end of the input) are to be printed verbatim.
:INDENT n	Causes all following lines of text to be indented n spaces from the left margin (n from 0 through 60).
:CENTER n	Causes the following n lines of text ($n > 0$) to be centered between the left and right margins. If n is omitted, then only the next line will be centered.
:SPACE n	Causes n blank lines ($n > 0$) to be printed. If n is omitted, then one blank line is printed. Note that a blank line of text in the input is treated exactly as a ":SPACE 1" command line.
:PAGE	Causes the next line to be printed at the top of a new page. This is also done automatically whenever a page is filled.

Exhibit 14.1   *Text Formatting Commands*

Sample Input

```
:CENTER 2
THIS IS A TITLE
____ __ _ ____


:PARAGRAPH
The text of a paragraph is adjusted
on a line to fit on
a line with at most 60 characters.

:INDENT 10
One or more lines can be indented from the left margin
with an INDENT command.

:INDENT 0
One can also specify that lines are to be printed
verbatim, as in the following short table:

:VERBATIM
    ITEM       AMOUNT
      1          18
      2           6
      3          11
```

Corresponding Output

```
                THIS IS A TITLE
                ____ __ _ ____


     The text of a paragraph is adjusted on a line to fit on
a line with at most 60 characters.

               One or more lines can be indented from the
          left margin with an INDENT command.

     One can also specify that lines are to be printed
verbatim, as in the following short table:

    ITEM       AMOUNT
      1          18
      2           6
      3          11
```

Exhibit 14.2   *Sample Input and Output*

"I am delighted that you asked, Mr. Babbage," said Holmes, "for that is the most difficult aspect of this programme's design. When creating a programme intended for intimate use by a person such as this, we must always ask ourselves such questions as: What sorts of command are useful? What precisely are the actions these perform? What sorts of error might one make while using the programme? What would happen if one incorrectly entered some input to the Engine? And what are all the possible ways of entering input incorrectly?"

"But Mr. Holmes," interrupted Babbage. "With all due respect, my first impression is that all this detail and fussing only complicates the problem before one even begins to solve it. My research has trained me to find the shortest possible route to a problem's solution and then take that route without a glance at the more convoluted byways. Does this top-down approach not result in considerable wasted time?"

"On the contrary, my dear Babbage," Holmes replied, as he reclined in his sofa and reached for a cigarette case on a table near at hand. He lit one end of a cigarette and blew a thin cloud of smoke into the room before he continued. "You must know the value of taking pains in any scientific endeavour. It has long been an axiom of mine that the little things are infinitely the most important, and that one must realize the need for analyzing a situation thoroughly before making a single attempt to call upon the Engine.

"You will recall my address to the Royal Society, when we had occasion to meet for the first time, and your own brilliant paper in the Proceedings of the British Association. Keep in mind that we are not merely seeking a single answer to a perfectly defined problem, as an engineer does many times in his daily work. Rather, we must instruct the Engine to deal with an entire host of problems. Our first and foremost task is to define these problems, as it remains impossible to solve them without first grasping an understanding of the general situation and all its ramifications. This procedure may appear very time-consuming at the outset. However, it usually results in an accurate programme requiring few emendations; thus our method will actually save us time."

Holmes then produced yet another chart, given here as Exhibit 14.3. I now began to see that his problem was not a simple one at all. The Engine would have to keep track of many details and even be tolerant to the errors of its employer. He had obviously spent a considerable amount of time thinking about the design of the programme.

"I have asked you out for the weekend, Watson," said Holmes, turning his attention to me, "to call upon your remarkable powers of stimulating genius, which I have, of late, found in short supply. I have been lost without my Boswell. I would appreciate your company also, Mr. Babbage; and, at any rate, there is no return train to London tonight and I have unwittingly condemned you to the horrors of my hospitalities. I have oysters and a brace of grouse, with something a little choice in red wines."

1.   An input line beginning with a colon is not followed by a legitimate command.

   Response: The line is output verbatim with five asterisks in the left margin to call attention to the problem.

2.   The argument given for an **INDENT** command is not numeric or too large (> 60); the argument given for a **CENTER** or **SPACE** command is not numeric or too large (> 99).

   Response: As above.

3.   One of the lines to be centered with a **CENTER** command is a command line.

   Response: The line is output centered with five asterisks in the left margin to call attention to the problem.

4.   A line to be output extends beyond the right margin. This can be a verbatim line that is too long or a word in a paragraph line that is too long (for example, if the indent happens to be 50 characters and a word will not fit in the remaining ten spaces).

   Response: Allow the line to be output up to, but not beyond, the edge of the page. Place five asterisks in the left margin to call attention to the problem.

5.   A text line is seen before either a **PARAGRAPH** or **VERBATIM** command is seen.

   Response: Assume that a **PARAGRAPH** command has been seen at the very beginning.

Exhibit 14.3   *Holmes's List of Exceptional Conditions*

We enjoyed a pleasant meal together and continued our discussion of the Analytical Engine well into the evening, with a bottle of claret among us. When the conversation again turned to the design of a top-down outline of a programme for formatting Holmes's manuscripts, Babbage tried his hand at sketching a preliminary design.

"I am not wholly certain how far to delve into your list of exceptions and details, or where to draw the line," said Babbage. "Perhaps something like this would suffice." He then scribbled on a sheet of paper and handed it to Holmes. It read :

Initialize programme variables

As long as INPUT_FILE is not empty, do the following:
    read NEXT_CHARACTER
    process NEXT_CHARACTER

Print last PAGE_NUM

"Very good," said Holmes. "But there remain some points in need of clarification. In the first place, what programme variables are to be initialized? And the specification for reading characters is not explicit enough. The characters, you see, may be either part of the text or part of a command; and these two categories must of course be treated differently.

"A line of input falls into the command category if it begins with a colon. Otherwise, it is a line of text. Notice that in practice, lines will tend to occur in groups belonging to one category or the other. Thus we may view the input as groups of one or more lines of a given category.

"Notice also that command lines are treated uniformly, regardless of their context, whereas this is not true of text lines. The treatment of a text line depends upon whether the line is part of a paragraph or is to be printed verbatim. Moreover, this distinction depends on the context. When a PARAGRAPH or VERBATIM command is entered, the Engine must 'remember' the command so that all following groups of text lines can be treated accordingly. The input mode is initially assumed to be paragraph mode in order to accept input text directly, and is altered when a VERBATIM command is entered."

We then waited in silence while Holmes's mind worked uninterrupted. Finally he continued.

"I'm glad you wrote this out, Mr. Babbage, as it has forced me to consider several alternatives. I would now formulate my approach to this problem as follows."

Holmes began to outline a format programme and wrote the following sketch :

Assume TEXT_MODE is paragraph mode
As long as INPUT_FILE is not empty, do the following:
  if next input character is ':' then
    process one or more command lines
  else — next line is a text line
    if TEXT_MODE is paragraph mode then
      process one or more paragraph lines
    else
      process one or more verbatim lines
Print last page number

"Yes, now I see," said Babbage. "Your method is becoming clearer to me. In the first draft of a top-down analysis you want to be very general, yet also account for all the various possibilities as they might logically arise."

"Quite so," replied Holmes. "But I should like to make this analysis even more precise, for no surprises should arise later as a result of initial misjudgment. There are some details this first top-down sketch does not include—for example, the line number on the output page, the page number if a page becomes full, or the possibility of an input line resulting in a change to the indentation."

"Well, Mr. Holmes," said Babbage after some length, "I fear that Dr. Watson and I have been of very little help to you this evening. Perhaps tomorrow will bring more profitable results."

"Nonsense," snapped Holmes. "I cannot agree with those who rank modesty among the virtues. To a logician all things should be seen exactly as they are, and to underestimate oneself is as much a departure from truth as to exaggerate one's own powers. You have both paid me a great service this evening and I am most appreciative."

Here was a different Holmes at work, for historically it had been one of the peculiarities of his proud, self-contained nature that, though he docketed any fresh information very quickly and accurately in his brain, he seldom made any acknowledgment to the provider.

I rose the next morning earlier than usual to find Sherlock Holmes pacing back and forth in his sitting room. He was in excellent spirits. I could see that he had been up the whole night working on his programme and, furthermore, that he had good news to report.

"You have met with success, Holmes," I stated confidently.

"Indeed, Watson, I have," he replied, looking me over curiously. "The top level of the design is completed and sketched in Pascal, but the papers are stored away in my desk. How is it that you knew?"

"Obvious, my dear Holmes. What else am I to assume when I see your right cuff so very shiny and spotted with ink for nearly four or five inches, and the left one with the smooth patch at the elbow where it has rested for some length of time upon your desk?"

"I must say, Watson, the faculty of deduction is certainly contagious."

And so I close this account of Mr. Sherlock Holmes and his contributions to the development of the Analytical Engine. A detailed sketch of his final top-down design is reproduced here as Exhibit 14.4, and a top-level sketch of the design as written in Pascal is here shown as Exhibit 14.5.

Definitions:

```
TEXT_MODE    : paragraph or verbatim
INDENTATION  : the current indentation
LINE_NUM     : the current line for output
PAGE_NUM     : the current page being printed
```

Algorithm:

```
Set TEXT_MODE to PARAGRAPH_MODE
Set INDENTATION to 0
Set LINE_NUM to 1
Set PAGE_NUM to 1

As long as INPUT_FILE is not empty, do the following:
   if next input character = ":" then
      process commands, possibly updating TEXT_MODE, INDENTATION,
                                 LINE_NUM, PAGE_NUM
   else
      if TEXT_MODE = PARAGRAPH_MODE then
         process paragraph lines, using INDENTATION,
                    possibly updating LINE_NUM, PAGE_NUM
      else
         process verbatim lines, using INDENTATION,
                    possibly updating LINE_NUM, PAGE_NUM

Print last PAGE_NUM
```

Exhibit 14.4   *Second Version of Holmes's Top-level Design*

```
program FORMAT (INPUT, OUTPUT);
    const
        PAGESIZE    = 66;  { Number of lines from top edge of page to
                              bottom edge of page. }
        TEXTWIDTH   = 60;  { Number of columns from left margin to right
                              margin. }
        COMMANDCHAR = ':';
        -- remaining constant declarations

    type
        MODE        = (PARGRAPHMODE, VERBATMODE);
        COMMANDNAME = (PARAGRAPH,  VERBATIM,  INDENT,
                        CENTER,    SPACE,    PAGE,   ILLEGAL);
        INDENTRANGE = 0..RIGHTMARGIN;
        -- remaining type declarations

    var
        TEXTMODE   : MODE;
        INDENTATION: INDENTRANGE;
        LINENUM    : 1..PAGESIZE;
        PAGENUM    : INTEGER;

    -- Procedures and functions, for example procedures DOCOMMANDS,
    -- DOPARAGRAPH, DOVERBATIM, and the function NEXTINPUTCHAR


begin { -- Main algorithm }

    TEXTMODE    := PARGRAPHMODE;
    INDENTATION := 0;
    LINENUM     := 1;
    PAGENUM     := 1;

    while not EOF do begin
        if NEXTINPUTCHAR = COMMANDCHAR then
            DOCOMMANDS ({ updating } TEXTMODE, INDENTATION)
        else
            case TEXTMODE of
                PARGRAPHMODE: DOPARAGRAPH ({ using } INDENTATION);
                VERBATMODE  : DOVERBATIM  ({ using } INDENTATION);
            end
    end;
    FINISHPAGE
end.
```

Exhibit 14.5 *Top-level Sketch of Text Formatting Programme*

I have also included, under the heading of Exhibit 14.6, the complete programme that Holmes worked out a few weeks later. It was my first experience with a programme of this scale, and Holmes's meticulous initial design proved highly useful throughout the project.

```
{  --   ** Programme Title: FORMAT
   --
   --
   --   ** Programme Intent:
   --      This programme reads a text file and formats it according to
   --      conventions given below. The text file contains lines of text
   --      and command lines. Each command line begins with a colon
   --      and must be followed by a legal command name.
   --
   --
   --   ** Input and Output Files:
   --      INPUT: A file containing text lines and command lines.
   --      OUTPUT: The formatted text.
   --
   --
   --   ** General Layout Conventions:
   --      Page Size: Standard 8 1/2 by 11 page, 85 characters per
   --      line, 66 lines per page.
   --
   --      Margins:
   --          Left  : 15 characters in from left edge of page
   --          Right : 10 characters in from right edge of page
   --          Top   : 6 lines down from top of page
   --          Bottom: 6 lines up from bottom of page
   --
   --      Printing Area: Standard 10 pitch spacing, 60 characters per
   --      line, 54 lines per page
   --
   --      Page Numbers: 3 lines down from bottom margin, centered
   --      between the left and right margin, and enclosed by hyphens,
   --      For example
   --
   --                              - 14 -
```

Exhibit 14.6 *Holmes's Text Formatting Programme*

```
--   ** Commands:
--      :PARAGRAPH  Marks the beginning of a paragraph. All
--                  following lines of text up to the next command line
--                  are treated as a sequence of words without line
--                  boundaries. The words are printed with
--                  ends-of-lines inserted so that each line (except the
--                  last) will be filled with one space between each pair
--                  of words. The first line of each paragraph is indented
--                  5 spaces. The right margin is ragged edged.
--
--                  If the paragraph is followed by a blank line or one
--                  or more commands (excluding the VERBATIM command),
--                  then the next line of text will be considered
--                  the beginning of a new paragraph.
--
--      :VERBATIM   Marks the beginning of a series of lines that are
--                  to be output exactly as they are given, except for
--                  possible indentation. All lines (excluding command
--                  lines) between the VERBATIM command line and the next
--                  PARAGRAPH command line (or the end of the input) are
--                  treated as text to be printed verbatim.
--
--      :INDENT n   Causes all following lines to be indented n
--                  spaces from the left margin (n from 0 through 60).
--
--      :CENTER n   Causes the following n lines of input text (n > 0)
--                  to be centered between the left and right margins.
--                  If n is omitted, then only the next line
--                  will be centered.
--
--      :SPACE n    Causes n blank lines (n > 0) to be printed. If n is
--                  omitted, then only one blank line is printed. Note
--                  that a blank line of text in the input is treated
--                  exactly as a ":SPACE 1" command line.
--
--      :PAGE       Causes the next line to be printed at the top of a
--                  new page. This is also done automatically whenever
--                  a page is filled.
```

Exhibit 14.6   *Continued*

```
--   ** Sample Input:
--
--   :CENTER 2
--   THIS IS A TITLE
--   ---- -- - -----
--
--   :PARAGRAPH
--   The text of a paragraph is  adjusted
--   on a line to fit on
--   a line with at most 60 characters.
--
--   :INDENT 10
--   One or more lines can be indented from the left margin
--   with an INDENT command.
--
--   :INDENT 0
--   One can also specify that lines are to be printed
--   verbatim, as in the following short table:
--
--   :VERBATIM
--        ITEM        AMOUNT
--         1           18
--         2            6
--         3           11
--
--
--
--   ** Corresponding Output:
--
--                    THIS IS A TITLE
--                    ---- -- - -----
--
--        The text of a paragraph is adjusted on a line to fit on
--   a line with at most 60 characters.
--
--             One or more lines can be indented from the
--           left margin with an INDENT command.
--
--        One can also specify that lines are to be printed
--   verbatim as in the following short table:
--
--        ITEM        AMOUNT
--         1           18
--         2            6
--         3           11
```

Exhibit 14.6   *Continued*

```
--   ** Error Conditions:
--
--
--      1. An input line beginning with a colon is not followed by a
--      legitimate command.
--
--         Response:  The line is output verbatim with five asterisks
--         in the left margin to call attention to the problem.
--
--
--      2. The argument given for an INDENT command is not numeric or
--      too large (> 60); the argument given for a CENTER or SPACE
--      command is not numeric or too large (> 99).
--
--         Response:  As above.
--
--
--      3. One of the lines to be centered with a CENTER command is a
--      command line.
--
--         Response:  The line is output centered, but five asterisks
--         are placed in the left margin to call attention to the
--         problem.
--
--
--      4. A line to be output extends beyond the right margin. This
--      can be a verbatim line that is too long or a word in a
--      paragraph line that is too long (for example, if the indent
--      happens to be 50 characters, and a word will not fit in the
--      remaining 10 spaces).
--
--         Response:  Allow the line to be output up to, but not
--         beyond, the edge of the page.  Place five asterisks in the
--         left margin to call attention to the problem.
--
--
--   ** Global Variables:
--      There are two global variables, LINENUM and PAGENUM, which
--      are manipulated solely by the two procedures, NEWLINE
--      and NEWPAGE. They are used to paginate the formatted text
--      and print page numbers.
```

Exhibit 14.6   *Continued*

```
program FORMAT (INPUT, OUTPUT);
    const
        PAGESIZE      = 66;  { Number of lines from top edge of page to
                                bottom edge of page. }
        LINESPERPAGE  = 54;  { Number of lines from top margin to bottom
                                margin. }
        LEFTMARGIN    = 15;  { Number of columns from left edge of page
                                to left margin. }
        TEXTWIDTH     = 60;  { Number of columns from left margin to
                                right margin. }
        MAXLINELENGTH = 70;  { Number of columns from left margin to
                                right edge of page. }

        COMMANDCHAR   = ':';
        BLANK         = ' ';
        NORMALMARGIN  = '                   ';
        ERRORMARGIN   = '*****              ';

    type
        MODE          = (PARGRAPHMODE, VERBATMODE);
        COMMANDNAME   = (PARAGRAPH,  VERBATIM,  INDENT,
                         CENTER,     SPACE,     PAGE,    ILLEGAL);

        INDENTRANGE   = 0..TEXTWIDTH;
        ARGRANGE      = 0..99;
        COLUMNNUM     = 0..MAXLINELENGTH;

        LINEINFO      = record
                            LENGTH: 0..MAXLINELENGTH;
                            IMAGE : array [1..MAXLINELENGTH] of CHAR
                        end;
        COMMANDINFO   = record
                            NAME    : COMMANDNAME;
                            ARGUMENT: ARGRANGE;
                            LINE    : LINEINFO
                        end;

    var
        TEXTMODE   : MODE;
        INDENTATION: INDENTRANGE;
        LINENUM    : 1..PAGESIZE;
        PAGENUM    : INTEGER;
```

Exhibit 14.6   *Continued*

```
{ -- Utility Routines  NEXTINPUTCHAR, DIGITVALUE, PRINTTEXT, SPACEOVER }


function NEXTINPUTCHAR: { returns } CHAR;
   { -- This function returns the look ahead character on input. }
begin
   NEXTINPUTCHAR := INPUT^
end;




function DIGITVALUE(C: CHAR): { returns } INTEGER;
   { -- This function returns the numeric value of a digit character. }
begin
   DIGITVALUE := ORD(C) - ORD('0')
end;




procedure PRINTTEXT ({ using } LINE: LINEINFO);
   { -- This procedure prints the text of a line. }
   var
      COLUMN: COLUMNNUM;
begin
   for COLUMN := 1 to LINE.LENGTH do
      WRITE (LINE.IMAGE[COLUMN])
end;




procedure SPACEOVER ({ by } NUMSPACES: INDENTRANGE);
   { -- This procedure advances over a given number of spaces. }
   var
      COLUMN: COLUMNNUM;
begin
   for COLUMN := 1 to NUMSPACES do
      WRITE (BLANK)
end;
```

Exhibit 14.6 *Continued*

```
{ -- Utility Routines  FINISHPAGE, NEWPAGE, NEWLINE }

procedure FINISHPAGE;
   { -- This procedure completes a printed page. }
   const
      PAGENUMCOLUMN = 27;
      PAGENUMLINE   = 57;
   var
      LINECOUNT: 1..PAGESIZE;
begin
   for LINECOUNT := LINENUM + 1 to PAGENUMLINE do
      WRITELN;

   WRITE (NORMALMARGIN);
   SPACEOVER (PAGENUMCOLUMN);
   WRITE ('-', PAGENUM:1, '-');

   for LINECOUNT := PAGENUMLINE to PAGESIZE do
      WRITELN
end;




procedure NEWPAGE;
   { -- This procedure advances to a new page. }
begin
   FINISHPAGE;
   LINENUM := 1;
   PAGENUM := PAGENUM + 1
end;




procedure NEWLINE;
   { -- This procedure advances to the next line on a page. }
begin
   if LINENUM = LINESPERPAGE then
      NEWPAGE
   else
      begin
         WRITELN;
         LINENUM := LINENUM + 1
      end
end;
```

Exhibit 14.6   *Continued*

```
procedure GETWORD ({ returning } var WORD: LINEINFO);

    { -- This procedure gets the next full word on the input file. }

    var
        BLANKCHAR: CHAR;
begin
    while (NEXTINPUTCHAR = BLANK) and not EOLN do
        READ (BLANKCHAR);

    WORD.LENGTH := 0;
    if not EOLN then
        repeat
            if WORD.LENGTH < MAXLINELENGTH then
                begin
                    WORD.LENGTH := WORD.LENGTH + 1;
                    READ ( WORD.IMAGE[WORD.LENGTH] )
                end
            else
                GET (INPUT)
        until (NEXTINPUTCHAR = BLANK) or EOLN

end;
```

Exhibit 14.6   *Continued*

```
procedure GETCOMMAND ({ from }              LINE        : LINEINFO;
                      { returning } var NAME            : COMMANDNAME;
                                    var ENDOFCOMMAND: COLUMNNUM   );
```

```
    { -- This procedure scans a command line to determine the name of the
      -- command given. It also determines the column position of the
      -- character after the command name. }
    const
        MAXCOMMANDLENGTH = 10;
    var
        COMMANDSTRING: packed array [1..MAXCOMMANDLENGTH] of CHAR;
        COLUMN       : COLUMNNUM;
        BREAKFOUND   : BOOLEAN;

begin
    BREAKFOUND   := FALSE;
    ENDOFCOMMAND := 0;

    for COLUMN := 1 to 10 do begin
        if (COLUMN > LINE.LENGTH) or BREAKFOUND then
            COMMANDSTRING[COLUMN] := BLANK
        else if LINE.IMAGE[COLUMN] = BLANK then
            begin
                COMMANDSTRING[COLUMN] := BLANK;
                BREAKFOUND            := TRUE
            end
        else
            begin
                COMMANDSTRING[COLUMN]  := LINE.IMAGE[COLUMN];
                ENDOFCOMMAND := ENDOFCOMMAND + 1
            end
    end;

    if      COMMANDSTRING = ':PARAGRAPH' then
        NAME := PARAGRAPH
    else if COMMANDSTRING = ':VERBATIM ' then
        NAME := VERBATIM
    else if COMMANDSTRING = ':INDENT   ' then
        NAME := INDENT
    else if COMMANDSTRING = ':CENTER   ' then
        NAME := CENTER
    else if COMMANDSTRING = ':SPACE    ' then
        NAME := SPACE
    else if COMMANDSTRING = ':PAGE     ' then
        NAME := PAGE
    else
        NAME := ILLEGAL
end;
```

Exhibit 14.6   *Continued*

```
procedure GETARGUMENT ({ from }              LINE         : LINEINFO;
                       { starting at }       ENDOFCOMMAND: COLUMNNUM;
                       { updating }    var NAME           : COMMANDNAME;
                       { returning }   var ARGUMENT       : ARGRANGE);

   { -- This procedure determines the argument (if any) of a CENTER,
     -- SPACE, or INDENT command. Conversion of numeric characters
     -- to numeric values is performed. }

   var
      COLUMN  : COLUMNNUM;
      NEXTCHAR: CHAR;

begin
   if ENDOFCOMMAND = LINE.LENGTH then
      if NAME in [CENTER, SPACE] then
         ARGUMENT := 1
      else
         NAME := ILLEGAL
   else
      begin
         COLUMN := ENDOFCOMMAND + 1;
         while LINE.IMAGE[COLUMN] = BLANK do
            COLUMN := COLUMN + 1;
         NEXTCHAR := LINE.IMAGE[COLUMN];

         if not(NEXTCHAR in ['0'..'9']) then
            NAME := ILLEGAL
         else
            begin
               ARGUMENT := DIGITVALUE(NEXTCHAR);
               if COLUMN <> LINE.LENGTH then
                  begin
                     COLUMN := COLUMN + 1;
                     NEXTCHAR := LINE.IMAGE[COLUMN];

                     if (COLUMN <> LINE.LENGTH)
                     or not(NEXTCHAR in ['0'..'9']) then
                        NAME := ILLEGAL
                     else
                        ARGUMENT := ARGUMENT*10 + DIGITVALUE(NEXTCHAR)
                  end
            end
      end
end;
```

Exhibit 14.6 *Continued*

```
procedure GETLINE ({ returning } var LINE: LINEINFO);

   { -- This procedure reads in a line from the input file,
     -- deleting any trailing blanks. }
   var
      TRAILINGBLANKS: BOOLEAN;

begin
   LINE.LENGTH := 0;

   while (LINE.LENGTH < MAXLINELENGTH) and not EOLN do begin
      LINE.LENGTH := LINE.LENGTH + 1;
      READ (LINE.IMAGE[LINE.LENGTH])
   end;

   READLN;

   TRAILINGBLANKS := TRUE;
   while TRAILINGBLANKS and (LINE.LENGTH <> 0) do begin
      if LINE.IMAGE[LINE.LENGTH] <> BLANK then
         TRAILINGBLANKS := FALSE
      else
         LINE.LENGTH := LINE.LENGTH - 1
   end
end;
```

Exhibit 14.6   *Continued*

```
procedure PARSELINE ({ returning } var COMMAND: COMMANDINFO);

   { -- This procedure determines the name and argument (if any)
     -- of a command line. Erroneous combinations or lines with
     -- extra characters are reported as illegal commands. }

   var
      ENDOFCOMMAND: COLUMNNUM;
      BADARGUMENT : BOOLEAN;

begin
   GETLINE ({ returning } COMMAND.LINE);

   GETCOMMAND ({ from }      COMMAND.LINE,
               { returning } COMMAND.NAME,
                             ENDOFCOMMAND);

   if (COMMAND.NAME in [PARAGRAPH, VERBATIM, PAGE])
   and (COMMAND.LINE.LENGTH <> ENDOFCOMMAND) then
       COMMAND.NAME := ILLEGAL;
   if COMMAND.NAME in [INDENT, CENTER, SPACE] then
      begin
         GETARGUMENT ({ from }       COMMAND.LINE,
                      { starting at } ENDOFCOMMAND,
                      { updating }    COMMAND.NAME,
                      { returning }   COMMAND.ARGUMENT);
         if (COMMAND.NAME = INDENT)
         and (COMMAND.ARGUMENT > TEXTWIDTH) then
            COMMAND.NAME := ILLEGAL
      end
end;
```

Exhibit 14.6   *Continued*

```
procedure CENTERLINE;

    { -- This procedure reads and prints lines that are to
      -- be centered. Command lines or lines that are too long
      -- are treated as erroneous. }

    var
        LINE          : LINEINFO;
        LEADINGBLANKS: INTEGER;
        NEXTCHAR      : CHAR;
        ISCOMMANDLINE: BOOLEAN;
        COLUMN        : COLUMNNUM;

begin
    if not EOF then
        begin
            ISCOMMANDLINE := (not EOLN) and (NEXTINPUTCHAR = COMMANDCHAR);
            while (NEXTINPUTCHAR = BLANK) and not EOLN do
                READ (NEXTCHAR);
            GETLINE({ returning } LINE);

            if LINE.LENGTH > 0 then
                begin
                    if LINE.LENGTH < TEXTWIDTH then
                        LEADINGBLANKS := (TEXTWIDTH - LINE.LENGTH) div 2
                    else
                        LEADINGBLANKS := 0;

                    if ISCOMMANDLINE or (LINE.LENGTH > TEXTWIDTH) then
                        WRITE (ERRORMARGIN)
                    else
                        WRITE (NORMALMARGIN);

                    SPACEOVER (LEADINGBLANKS);
                    PRINTTEXT (LINE)
                end;

            NEWLINE
        end
end;
```

Exhibit 14.6   *Continued*

```
procedure DOCOMMANDS ({ updating } var TEXTMODE    : MODE;
                                    var INDENTATION: INDENTRANGE);


   { -- This procedure handles one or more command lines.
     -- It terminates when a text line or end of file is found. }


   var
      COMMAND  : COMMANDINFO;
      LINECOUNT: ARGRANGE;

begin
   repeat
      PARSELINE ({ returning } COMMAND);

      case COMMAND.NAME of
         PARAGRAPH: TEXTMODE := PARGRAPHMODE;
         VERBATIM : TEXTMODE := VERBATMODE;
         INDENT   : INDENTATION := COMMAND.ARGUMENT;
         CENTER   : for LINECOUNT := 1 to COMMAND.ARGUMENT do
                       CENTERLINE;
         SPACE    : for LINECOUNT := 1 to COMMAND.ARGUMENT do
                       NEWLINE;
         PAGE     : NEWPAGE;
         ILLEGAL  : begin
                       WRITE (ERRORMARGIN);
                       PRINTTEXT (COMMAND.LINE);
                       NEWLINE
                    end
      end { case }

   until (NEXTINPUTCHAR <> COMMANDCHAR) or EOF
end;
```

Exhibit 14.6   *Continued*

```
procedure PRINTWORD ({ using } WORD: LINEINFO; INDENTATION: INDENTRANGE;
                     { updating } var COLUMN:  COLUMNNUM );

   { -- This procedure prints the next word in a paragraph.
     -- It updates the column position for the following word. }

   var
      FIRSTWORDONLINE: BOOLEAN;
      ENDOFWORD      : INTEGER;
begin
   if COLUMN = INDENTATION then
      begin
         FIRSTWORDONLINE := TRUE;
         ENDOFWORD       := COLUMN + WORD.LENGTH
      end
   else
      begin
         FIRSTWORDONLINE := FALSE;
         ENDOFWORD       := COLUMN + WORD.LENGTH + 1
      end;
   if not FIRSTWORDONLINE and (ENDOFWORD > TEXTWIDTH) then
      begin { won't fit on current line }
         NEWLINE;
         COLUMN := INDENTATION;
         FIRSTWORDONLINE := TRUE;
         ENDOFWORD := INDENTATION + WORD.LENGTH
      end;
   if ENDOFWORD > TEXTWIDTH then
      begin { is first word on line and still won't fit }
         WORD.LENGTH := WORD.LENGTH - (ENDOFWORD - MAXLINELENGTH);
         WRITE (ERRORMARGIN);
         SPACEOVER (INDENTATION);
         PRINTTEXT (WORD);
         NEWLINE
      end
   else
      begin
         if FIRSTWORDONLINE then
            begin
               WRITE (NORMALMARGIN);
               SPACEOVER (INDENTATION)
            end
         else
            WRITE (BLANK);
         PRINTTEXT (WORD);
         COLUMN := ENDOFWORD
      end
end;
```

Exhibit 14.6 *Continued*

```
procedure DOPARAGRAPH ({ using } INDENTATION: INDENTRANGE);

   { -- This procedure processes text lines in paragraph mode.
     -- It terminates when a command line or end of file is found. }

   const
      EXTRAINDENT = 5;
   var
      WORD        : LINEINFO;
      COLUMN      : COLUMNNUM;
      NEWPARAGRAPH: BOOLEAN;

begin
   COLUMN := INDENTATION;
   NEWPARAGRAPH := TRUE;

   repeat
      GETWORD ({ returning } WORD);
      if WORD.LENGTH = 0 then
         begin { blank line found }
            if COLUMN <> INDENTATION then
               begin { close off last line }
                  NEWLINE;
                  COLUMN := INDENTATION
               end;
            NEWPARAGRAPH := TRUE;
            NEWLINE
         end
      else
         repeat
            if NEWPARAGRAPH then
               begin
                  COLUMN := COLUMN + EXTRAINDENT;
                  PRINTWORD ({ using } WORD, INDENTATION + EXTRAINDENT,
                                 { updating } COLUMN);
                  NEWPARAGRAPH := FALSE
               end
            else
               PRINTWORD ({ using }    WORD, INDENTATION,
                              { updating } COLUMN);
            GETWORD ({ returning } WORD)
         until WORD.LENGTH = 0;
      READLN
   until (NEXTINPUTCHAR = COMMANDCHAR) or EOF;

   if COLUMN <> INDENTATION then
      NEWLINE
end;
```

Exhibit 14.6   *Continued*

```
procedure DOVERBATIM ({ using } INDENTATION: INDENTRANGE);

   { -- This procedure handles text lines in verbatim mode.
     -- It terminates when a command line or end of file is found. }
   var
      LINE     : LINEINFO;
      NEWLENGTH: INTEGER;

begin
   repeat
      GETLINE ({ returning } LINE);

      if LINE.LENGTH > 0 then
         begin
            NEWLENGTH := LINE.LENGTH + INDENTATION;

            if NEWLENGTH > TEXTWIDTH then
               WRITE (ERRORMARGIN)
            else
               WRITE (NORMALMARGIN);

            SPACEOVER (INDENTATION);
            if NEWLENGTH > MAXLINELENGTH then
               LINE.LENGTH := LINE.LENGTH - (NEWLENGTH - MAXLINELENGTH);
            PRINTTEXT (LINE)
         end;

      NEWLINE
   until (NEXTINPUTCHAR = COMMANDCHAR) or EOF
end;
```

Exhibit 14.6   *Continued*

```
begin { -- Main algorithm }

   TEXTMODE    := PARGRAPHMODE;
   INDENTATION := 0;
   LINENUM     := 1;
   PAGENUM     := 1;

   while not EOF do begin
      if NEXTINPUTCHAR = COMMANDCHAR then
         DOCOMMANDS ({ updating } TEXTMODE, INDENTATION)
      else
         case TEXTMODE of
            PARGRAPHMODE: DOPARAGRAPH ({ using } INDENTATION);
            VERBATMODE  : DOVERBATIM  ({ using } INDENTATION)
         end
   end;
   FINISHPAGE

end.
```

Exhibit 14.6   *Continued*

His decision to test out the programme on a complete chapter from his forthcoming work, *The Whole Art of Detection*, brought to mind my first encounter with Sherlock Holmes in January of 1881. A chance reunion with young Stamford, a dresser at St. Bartholomew's, brought Holmes and me together. How well I recall Stamford, standing there at the Criterion Bar, saying of Holmes, "I could imagine his giving a friend a little pinch of the latest vegetable alkaloid, not out of malevolence, you understand, but simply out of a spirit of inquiry in order to have an accurate idea of the effects. To do him justice, I think that he would take it himself with the same readiness."

14.1   The Remaining Subprograms

It is with a heavy heart that we sit down to our word processor to write these, the last words in which we record the singular gifts by which Mr. Sherlock Holmes distinguished himself as a pioneer in the field of computer programming. His "final programme" is a full scale application of computers that we may employ in many circumstances and with a variety of computers.

Let us begin with the structure of the entire program. It has the form of a tree, much like that in Exhibit 11.2 mentioned by Holmes in his lecture on top-down programming. The tree for Holmes's formatting program is given in Figure 14.1. The root point of the tree is the main program. Each successive point at a level of the tree is a subprogram. The branches emanating from a subprogram point are the subprograms that, in turn, are called from the subprogram.

The individual subprograms are quite straightforward, and we will not elaborate on each. We will describe one subprogram to get a feel for the entire program.

As the sample subprogram, let us look at DOPARAGRAPH. The procedure performs the actions required for adding input lines to a paragraph. The procedure has one parameter named INDENTATION, giving the current indentation from the left margin. The body of the procedure begins with:

```
COLUMN := INDENTATION;
NEWPARAGRAPH := TRUE;
```

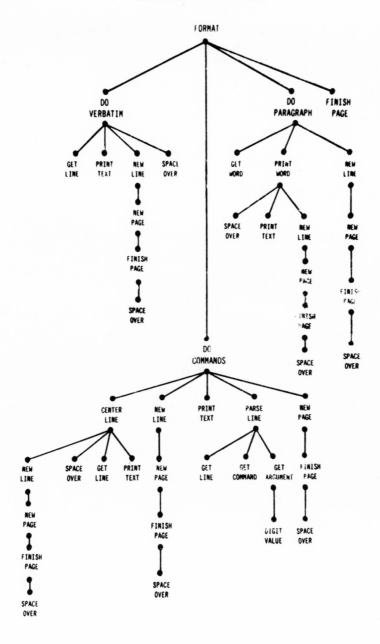

Figure 14.1 *Structure of Holmes's Formatting Program*

These statements set the column position of the next printed word to the indentation, and a new paragraph flag to true.

The major work in the procedure is accomplished next in the loop:

```
repeat
  GETWORD ({ returning } WORD);
  if WORD.LENGTH = 0 then
    -- what to do if the next line is blank
  else
    -- what to do for a nonblank line;
  READLN
until (NEXTINPUTCHAR = COMMANDCHAR) or EOF
```

This loop keeps reading and processing lines until a new command is encountered or the end of the text is reached. The call to READLN simply reads the end-of-line marker.

Finally we have

```
if COLUMN <> INDENTATION then
  NEWLINE
```

which closes the last line of the paragraph.

Elementary, but keep in mind that when using the top-down approach the main program should be so carefully defined and mapped out that each procedure can be written *independently*. Thus any subprograms that are true to the behavior expected by the main program will suffice.

As always, the complete, final program comprises the main program and the declarations of all the subprograms, as shown in Exhibit 14.6. You may wish to read over the main program and all its subprograms until you are satisfied that they work correctly. While doing this you may note several ways of "speeding up" the program. The fact is, we confess, that efficiency was not a significant design criterion during development, though it could have been.

The Real Story

The development of the text-formatting program, with a suitable change of names and places, is, by and large, accurate. We have, in fact, attempted to adhere to the top-down approach in composing this chapter. In fairness to the reader, we would like to summarize what actually transpired.

First of all, a program similar to this had been written some months before, which naturally led to a deeper insight into the problem. Second, the inputs and outputs underwent a number of minor revisions as a result of writing the actual program. This, of course, is to be expected. Third, two global variables were introduced, one to keep track of the line number and the other for the page number. Debate continues, we might add, over the wisdom of this choice.

Finally, there was much discussion over the style of the program and the actual error-checking mechanism carried out by the program. These are sticky areas and the influence of Pascal had some effect on our final decisions.

In parting, we would like to underline a few points:

■ Like Holmes, we strongly advocate the top-down approach.

■ Regardless of the approach a programmer settles upon, we cannot over-emphasize the importance of *thinking*. Recall the great detective's thoughts on human reasoning in earlier chapters, especially *before* attempting to write any code.

■ Finally, we should not forget that ultimately computer programs are designed to do useful things, for *human* users.

Sadly, our narrative is all but done. "What is the use of having powers, Doctor, when one has no field upon which to exert them?" inquired Holmes in "The Sign of Four." Indeed. Surely, dear reader, you have some field of your own to address?

Notes on the Programs

The programs presented by Holmes were written with two major objectives: brevity and simplicity. It was more important to us to illustrate the concept being presented than write, for example, an efficient program or one that would respond to erroneous input. Such programs would be longer and more complicated. We comment on these program issues here.

The program of Exhibit 3.1 does not completely reflect the algorithm from which it was drawn, Exhibit 2.1. In the program, the initial value for the suspect is set before the loop, and updated after each iteration. A more faithful rendition of the program, although longer, would test an individual clue against all four suspects.

Holmes's program of Exhibit 4.2 could stand a major improvement. This would allow the user to enter the hour *and* minutes of high tide. Moreover, it would be nicer here to print the output with only one or two digits after the decimal point.

In Holmes's program to classify cigar ash of Exhibit 5.2, there is a small anomaly. Suppose some different, probably less well known, cigar were found whose texture was granular, color was dark gray, and strength was normal. In this case, the cigar characteristics would not be sufficient to identify the cigar uniquely, and Holmes would have to resolve the matter himself.

The program to compute dates of Exhibit 8.2 is quite straightforward, but it can be made to run faster. The problem arises in counting the days by ones. It's faster, for instance, to count a month at a time until the correct month is found, and then count by ones.

The ciphered message program, Exhibit 9.3, brings up another issue— whether the cipher table should be resident in the program or defined externally to the program. This issue, we believe, depends on the application.

The program for "A Study in Chemistry" really brings out the issue of checking the user's input for errors. The program makes a small attempt to do this, but not enough for an actual application. For example, the number of atoms may not be an integer, or extra spaces may be typed by the user. On a separate matter, the program does not handle "radicals." For example, calcium hydroxide, $CA(OH)_2$ must be entered as 1 calcium, 2 oxygens, and 2 hydrogens.

Exhibit 12.1, the program to search files, could be improved in various ways. Certainly the program should be more tolerant of input errors. A particularly sticky problem is checking for compatibility of input values. A suspect of 6 feet in height would hardly wear a size 2 shoe, although the program will certainly accept these values. Such issues take us far beyond our intent.

As for the final program, Exhibit 14.6, we have not too much too add. Any program of this scale is open to debate, and there are numerous ways to extend it.

Appendix

Pascal at a Glance

The following table summarizes the rules for writing the Pascal programs given in this text. These rules define much, but not all, of the Pascal language in standard use. In the table describing our subset of Pascal, the following conventions have been used.

1. Italicized names appearing in the left column, for example,

    variable-declaration

give the names of constructs in Pascal.

2. The symbol → separates the name of a construct from the form for writing the construct in Pascal. The symbol → may be read "is written as" or "is defined as."

3. If a construct has two or more alternative forms, the symbol |
is used to separate each alternative. The symbol | may thus be as read "or."

4. Braces, for example, the braces in

    { *parameter-part* }

enclose optional items.

5. An ellipsis symbol (...) following a name or an item in braces, for example, the ellipses in

    digit...
    { *adding-operator term* }...

specifies that the preceding name or item can be repeated one or more times.

Programs

program   →   program *identifier* (*file-list*);
                                            declaration-part
                                        begin
                                            statement-part
                                        end.

declaration-part   →   { const *constant-declaration*... }
                                        { type *type-declaration*... }
                                        { var   *variable-declaration*... }
                                        { *subprogram-declaration*... }

statement-part   →   *statement* { ; *statement*} ...

Declarations

constant-declaration   →   *identifier* = *constant*;

type-declaration   →   *identifier* = *type*;

variable-declaration   →   *identifier-list*: *type*;

subprogram-declaration   →   *procedure* | *function*

procedure   →   procedure *identifier* { *parameter-part* };
                                            declaration-part
                                        begin
                                            statement-part
                                        end;

function   →   function *identifier*{*parameter-part*}: *result-type*;
                                            declaration-part
                                        begin
                                            statement-part
                                        end;

parameter-part   →   (*parameter-definition*{ ;*parameter-definition*} ...)

parameter-definition   →   {var} *identifier-list* : *type-identifier*

result-type   →   *type-identifier*

Statements

statement	→	*assignment-statement* | *if-statement*
	|	*case-statement* | *while-statement*
	|	*repeat-statement* | *for-statement*
	|	*procedure-statement* | *compound-statement*

assignment-statement → *variable* := *expression*
\| *function-identifier* := *expression*

if-statement → if *condition* then
  statement
{else
  statement}

case-statement → case *expression* of
  constant : *statement* {;
  constant : *statement* }...
  end

while-statement → while *condition* do
  statement

repeat-statement → repeat
  statement {;
  statement }...
  until *condition*

for-statement → for *variable* := *expression* to *expression* do
  statement

procedure-statement → *procedure-identifier*
\| *procedure-identifier* (*expression-list*)

compound-statement → begin
  statement {;
  statement }...
  end

condition → *expression*

Types

type	→	*type-identifier* | *enumerated-type* | *subrange* | *array-type* | *record-type* | *file-type*
enumerated-type	→	(*identifier-list*)
subrange	→	*constant..constant*
array-type	→	{packed} array [*index-list*] of *type*
index-list	→	*index-type* { , *index-type* }...
index-type	→	*type-identifier* | *subrange*

record-type	→	record
		   identifier : *type* { ;
		   identifier : *type* }...
		end

file-type	→	file of *type*

Variables and Expressions

variable	→	*identifier* | *array-component* | *record-component* | *file-component*
array-component	→	*variable* [*expression-list*]
record-component	→	*variable . identifier*
file-component	→	*variable^*
expression-list	→	*expression* { , *expression* }...
expression	→	*simple-expression* | *simple-expression relational-operator* *simple-expression* | *simple-expression* in *set*
simple-expression	→	{*sign*} *term* { *adding-operator term* }...
term	→	not *operand* | *operand* { *multiplying-operator operand* }...
operand	→	*unsigned-constant* | *variable* | (*expression*) | *function-identifier* {(*expression-list*)}
set	→	[*element* { , *element*}...]
element	→	*expression* | *expression..expression*

sign	→	+ | –
relational-operator	→	= | <> | < | <= | >= | >
adding-operator	→	+ | – | or
multiplying-operator	→	* | / | div | mod | and

Identifiers, Numbers, and Strings

type-identifier	→	*identifier*
procedure-identifier	→	*identifier*
function-identifier	→	*identifier*
file-list	→	*identifier-list*
identifier-list	→	*identifier* { , *identifier* } ...
identifier	→	*letter* { *letter-or-digit* } ...
constant	→	{*sign*} *unsigned-constant*
unsigned-constant	→	*number* | *identifier* | *string*
number	→	*integer* | *real-number*
integer	→	*digit* ...
real-number	→	*integer.integer*
	|	*integer.integer* E *scale-factor*
scale-factor	→	{*sign*} *integer*
string	→	'*character* ...'
letter-or-digit	→	*letter* | *digit*
character	→	*letter* | *digit* | *special-character*
digit	→	0 | 1 | 2 | 3 | 4 | 5 | 6 | 7 | 8 | 9
letter	→	A | B | C | D | E | F | G | H | I | J
	|	K | L | M | N | O | P | Q | R | S | T
	|	U | V | W | X | Y | Z
special-character	→	+ | – | * | / | = | < | > | [|] |)
	|	) | . | : | ; | # | % | $ | ! | ? | "
	|	_ | &

Postscript

This book is the outgrowth of an idea proposed by Andrew Singer during a discussion at Versailles, France, in December 1978. Since that time, the project has served as an extension of our general work in human factors and as a focus for several objectives.

First, we believe that it is possible to capture the fundamental ideas of programming in a simple way. We know that programming is difficult for almost everyone, and often very confusing. Yet, the motivation for much of the basis of in programming stems from a few elementary ideas. The design of the Watson-Holmes dialogue and the technical points raised by the detective are a deliberate attempt to convey these underlying ideas in a way that is at once easy to follow and enjoyable.

Second, we believe that the best method to teach programming is through problems. The traditional approach has been to convey the programming language first and then try to use it to solve problems. We have taken the road less travelled. In each chapter here, the detective solves a problem — a "real" problem and at the same time a problem in program design. Then the language ideas needed to support the solution are presented by the narrator.

In writing this, we asked ourselves if the world really needed yet another text on programming. If the question were as simple as that, so too would be the answer. We wanted to write a very serious text on programming, covering not all but most of Pascal in a complete manner. In limiting ourselves this way, we believe that what we present here leaves no loose ends.

Last and most obvious, we believe that engaging the learner's interest is fundamental to effective teaching. At the root of this approach is our reader for the student as a human being. This theme is central to the entire text.

The version of Pascal presented here follows the draft standard definition for Pascal. This document is known formally as X3J9/81-003 (draft proposal IS0/DP7185). The final document should be available from the American National Standards Institute, 1430 Broadway, New

York, NY 10018. A close-to-final draft version appears in Pascal News, published by the Pascal User's Group (care of Rick Shaw, Box 888524, Atlanta, Georgia 30338). The Pascal User's Group is a friendly, informal group of people interested in almost every aspect of Pascal.

This text was designed as a series. Other members of this series are expected to follow, first on the programming language Basic. Versions tailored to specific language implementations using particular computers are also planned.

Three previous works had a strong influence on parts of this work. One of the earlier texts on Basic, *Fundamental Programming Concepts* (Harper and Row, New York, 1972) by Jonathan Gross and Walter Brainerd, set a gently spirited tone for presenting programming, along with excellent exercises. A book by William Lewis, *Problem Solving for Programmers* (Hayden Book Company, Rochelle Park, New Jersey, 1980), sharpened our attention to the real problem-solving issues in programming. *The Fortran Coloring Book* by Roger Kaufman (MIT Press, Cambridge, Massachusetts, 1978), set an example for a radically different style of presentation.

This text was under development for approximately three years; and during this time, many persons contributed their work and wisdom. A special bow goes to E. Patrick McQuaid, who possesses extraordinary knowledge of Sherlock Holmes, and who rewrote and edited this text from top to bottom. Much of its creativity is due to him.

Jon Hueras contributed to the technical content of the book, including a working draft of the "Final Programme," a complete check of the technical aspects of Pascal, and the idea for the Ciphered Message example.

Karen Herman provided excellent drafts of many of the Holmes stories, integrating the technical content in an easily readable way. John Whiteside was the man behind the scenes for "The Adventure of the Bathing Machine" and "A Study in Chemistry." Ed Judge was the source of the text for "The Ciphered Message" and "The Advertisement in The Times." He also kindly provided on-the-spot ideas at various times.

We are grateful to Michael Marcotty and to Edwin Carter for providing their knowledge of England and many particulars of Victorian language. Edwin Carter also provided the pen of Sherlock Holmes. His daughter, Edwina Carter, kept a vigilant eye on each of the Holmes stories, editing them with a flair for proper British terminology. She has supported the entire effort in many ways since its inception.

Dede Ely-Singer contributed to many of the ideas in this book and was a collaborator in the design of the typography. Ron Lewton, Michael Samuels, Erik Sandberg Diment, and Lillian Singer all contributed in various ways to the development of the project.

Special thanks go to Murray Gallant and E & L Instruments, Inc. for permitting one of the authors (A. Singer) to take vacation time at the oddest moments.

Stephen Chernicoff provided a superlative review of the entire manuscript; his suggestions on grammar, style, programming, and Sherlock Holmes were used throughout.

We are grateful to Louis Chmura for his thoughtful questions on the matter of teaching programming. To Robbie Moll we owe the idea of having a 20th-century narrator follow each of Dr. Watson's accounts. Many other people, including Cookie Daniels, Rich Scire, and Richard Tenney, offered their assistance. To each we are grateful.

Permission for the photographs of the Analytical Engine, Charles Babbage, and Ada Lovelace was obtained from the British Science Museum, London. Portions of this text contain excerpts from *Pascal With Style* by Henry Ledgard, Paul Nagin, and Jon Hueras, copyright 1979, reprinted with permission of Hayden Book Company.

Holly Whiteside drew the picture of the bathing machine. Gordon Daniels took the photographs of the original Sidney Paget pictures. Jack Tracey, author of *The Encyclopedia Sherlockiana* (Avon Books, New York, 1979), kindly provided key information at various times. Peggy Farrell provided excellent assistance on delicate matters of state.

A very special word of thanks to Linda Strzegowski, a person with many talents. Besides humoring us at critical times, she creatively managed the entry, composition, and production of this text from its first day to its last.

Finally, we are grateful to Sir Arthur Conan Doyle, creator of the true Sherlock Holmes.

HENRY LEDGARD
Number Six Road
Leverett, MA

ANDREW SINGER
P.O. Box 734
Woodbury, CT

Index

About the Authors

Henry Ledgard received his B.A. from Tufts University and his Ph.D from the Massachusetts Institute of Technology in 1969. After a year teaching and doing research at the University of Oxford, he joined the faculty of Johns Hopkins University and later the faculty of the University of Massachusetts. In 1977 he joined the Honeywell design team on the Department of Defense program to develop a new computer language (Ada). In 1979 he started his own consulting and writing practice, Human Factors Limited. He is the author of a series of friendly books on programming style, known as *The Programming Proverbs*. One of these, *Pascal with Style* has had its effect on this work. He is also the author of *Ada: An Introduction* and co-author of a textbook, *A Programming Language Landscape*. His view on his primary research area, making computers more fit for human users, are expressed in a monograph with the stuffy title, *Directions on Human Factors for Interactive Systems*. He lives in Leverett, Massachusets.

As a computer scientist, Andrew Singer has long been fascinated by the problems people have with computers. He is the co-author of a recent research monograph in this area, and his lighter comments on the subject have appeared in the personal computing magazine, *ROM*, for which he was a contributing editor. Mr. Singer is a well-known seminar leader and consultant and has been a member of the research staffs at New York University Medical Center, Haskins Laboratories, and the Department of Social Psychology at Harvard. Since 1979 he has been Vice President for Research and Engineering at E&L Instruments, a manufacturer of products for education in electronics and computing. Mr. Singer holds a Ph.D. and M.S. degrees in Computer Science from the University of Massachusetts. He lives in Woodbury, Connecticut.